A MAP HISTORY OF
MODERN CHINA

Brian Catchpole

Maps and diagrams by
Regmarad

HEINEMANN EDUCATIONAL BOOKS LTD
LONDON

Heinemann Educational Books Ltd
LONDON EDINBURGH MELBOURNE AUCKLAND TORONTO
HONG KONG SINGAPORE KUALA LUMPUR
IBADAN NAIROBI JOHANNESBURG
LUSAKA NEW DELHI
KINGSTON

ISBN 0 435 31095 X

Published by
Heinemann Educational Books Ltd
48 Charles Street, London W1X 8AH

Printed in Great Britain by
Butler & Tanner Ltd
Frome and London

CONTENTS

ACKNOWLEDGEMENTS

The author and publishers wish to thank the following
for permission to reproduce photographs on the pages indicated:

Camera Press, 49, 57, 77, 101, 112, 120
Eastfoto, New York, 95, 97(a)
Richard and Sally Greenhill, 97(b)
Robert Harding Associates, 6
John Hillelson Agency, 82

Hong Kong Government Information Services, 135
Keystone Press Agency, 51
Times Newspapers Ltd., 124
Underwood and Underwood, New York, 58
U.S. Army, 71

The sketches on pp. 9, 11, 15, 35, 36 and 38 were drawn by an unknown Chinese artist for the Rev.
Cobbold when he was a missionary in North China (about 1855).

PREFACE

For most of their history the Chinese have believed that their country was the centre of the world. They labelled everyone who lived beyond the frontiers of the *Middle Kingdom* as barbarians and made them anything but welcome. Consequently, the Western world remained largely ignorant of the achievements of Imperial China. So, when the Western merchants eventually forced themselves upon the unwilling Chinese they brought with them very little respect for the past. They saw that China was the 'first for greatness, riches, and grandeur, of any country ever known' and promptly began relieving her of all three qualities in exchange for chests of opium. Hard on the heels of the traders came the Christian missionaries who never really understood why the Chinese preferred religions which might improve their quality of life on earth rather than one which offered a chance of salvation after death.

This contact between the Middle Kingdom and the West heralds the beginning of *modern* Chinese history. It was a violent affair. Western weapons and Western fighting methods played a crucial rôle and military matters increasingly dominated the lives of the people. Opium wars, the Taiping Rebellion, the war with Japan, the Boxer Revolt and the 1911 Revolution made peace a luxury. Civil war then merged with the events of the Second World War and it was not until 1949 that the Communists emerged triumphant.

Their victory lead to the remodelling of Chinese society, now numbering over 750 million people, according to the thought of Mao Tse-tung. He was the first Chinese ruler who deliberately set out to care for the needs of his people and twenty-five years later the Communists could claim, while agreeing that living standards were 'rather low', that they had abolished unemployment and assured to every person sufficient work, food and clothing. At the same time the *People's Republic of China* had become a major force in international affairs and a champion of the Third World. No longer confined to her frontiers, the new China carried her revolutionary message to all parts of the world and notably to Africa where, after Chinese engineers had built the *Uhuru* railway, it could be fairly said that 'the locomotive of revolution travels on two rails'.

The aim of this history is to tell these and other stories by means of maps and illustrations directly related to the text.

THEME 1

The Ancient Empire

Over a period of some 3,200 years nine major dynasties created the Ancient Empire, a civilization which in many respects still endures today.

Dynasty	Dates	
Shang	*c.* **1600–1100** B.C.	Created the nucleus of empire in the valley of the Hwang-ho, the Yellow River.
Chou	**1100–256** B.C.	The 'Classical Age' of imperial China in which the pattern of life in the Empire emerged. The Chou began building defence systems in the north.
Ch'in	**221–206** B.C.	United some of the Chou defence systems to begin the Great Wall of China.
Han	**206** B.C.**–220** A.D.	Created a huge empire which sprawled across East Asia and even made a few tentative contacts with Imperial Rome.
Sui	**589–618**	Built the Grand Canal.
T'ang	**618–907**	Began the expansion of empire westwards but checked by the advancing Arabs.
Sung	**960–1279**	Forced south by Mongol invaders and built a new imperial capital at Hangchow.
Mongol	**1279–1368**	Captured Hangchow and used it as a base to defeat the Sung.
Ming	**1368–1644**	The last native dynasty, it pushed the Mongols out of China and rebuilt Peking as the imperial capital. Among its many remarkable achievements was the despatch of fleets of junks to Arabia and East Africa. China had undoubtedly the most advanced maritime technology in the world and her sailors, had they so wished, could have rounded the Cape of Good Hope a hundred years ahead of Vasco da Gama.

1 Starting points: the land and its legends

The cradle of Chinese civilization

From the towering mountain ranges of Asia two vast streams flow eastwards towards the China Seas. The longer of the two, the Yangtze-kiang (3,430 miles), springs from the plateau of Tibet, carves its way through the rocks of Szechwan and wanders across a land dotted with lakes and water-courses. Further north, the Hwang-ho (the Yellow River—2,900 miles), carries in its waters the yellow Mongolian silt that forms the huge alluvial deposits around Shantung. Between them, these two great rivers have helped to create the fertile North China Plain—the cradle of Chinese civilization.

Legendary origins

The Chinese have lots of legends to explain their origins. One of the best known is the story of Pan Ku who emerged from a giant egg—half of which became the earth and half the sky. Pan Ku survived for 18,000 years and when he died his limbs became China's mountains while his blood fed the great rivers. His breath became the wind and his voice the thunder; his eyes turned into the Sun and the Moon. All the parasites living on his body then crawled off—and became the Chinese people. 'These people of ancient times', wrote the philosopher Mo-ti, 'lived on high ground and dwelt in caves ... Their garments were the skins of animals and their belts long grass. They ate simply and lived in segregation.'*

Archaeological evidence

Mo-ti was close to the truth. Human beings of a kind (*homo erectus*) were living on the hilly fringes of the North China Plain 500,000 years ago. Lantien Man had his home in Shensi while Peking Man lived in the caves of Choukoutien. Peking Man was about five feet tall and an expert hunter. He could fashion stone tools and knew how to make fire. He was also a cannibal; archaeological evidence revealed that Peking Man's diet included the bone marrow and brain of his fellow men. But of Peking Man's descendants very little is known for literally hundreds of thousands of years.

Neolithic farmers

About 6,000 years ago the first farmers began to cultivate the river terraces north and south of the Hwang-ho. Inside their circular village sites at Yang Shao, Pan Po and Pan Shan they built thatched huts, installed cupboards, chairs and grain-pits and created superb, hand-made pottery. A little later some farmers at Lung Shan enclosed their settlements with earthen walls and made fine black pottery on the potter's wheel. By about 2000 B.C. thousands of thriving agricultural communities existed in and around the North China Plain. Some were on low-lying hills; others chose the more fertile soils near the river and therefore built their villages on knolls for protection against the unpredictable flood waters of the Hwang-ho. Most grew millet and raised herds of cattle. Already their society had produced specialist potters, carpenters and weavers and it was not long before it laid the foundation of the most important and unifying feature of Chinese civilization: a written language. The first hint comes in the oracle bones used by the villagers of Lung Shan. They would ask a question of the oracle—and a bone would be thrust into the fire. A wise man would interpret the cracks and scorch marks left by the heat and would then give his answer. It was a natural step to *write* the question and the answer on the bones—and such bones were found in the 1927–34 Anyang excavations. There, in one startling discovery, evidence of a supposedly legendary dynasty *and* a written language came to light.

*Mo-ti was himself writing in the fifth century B.C.

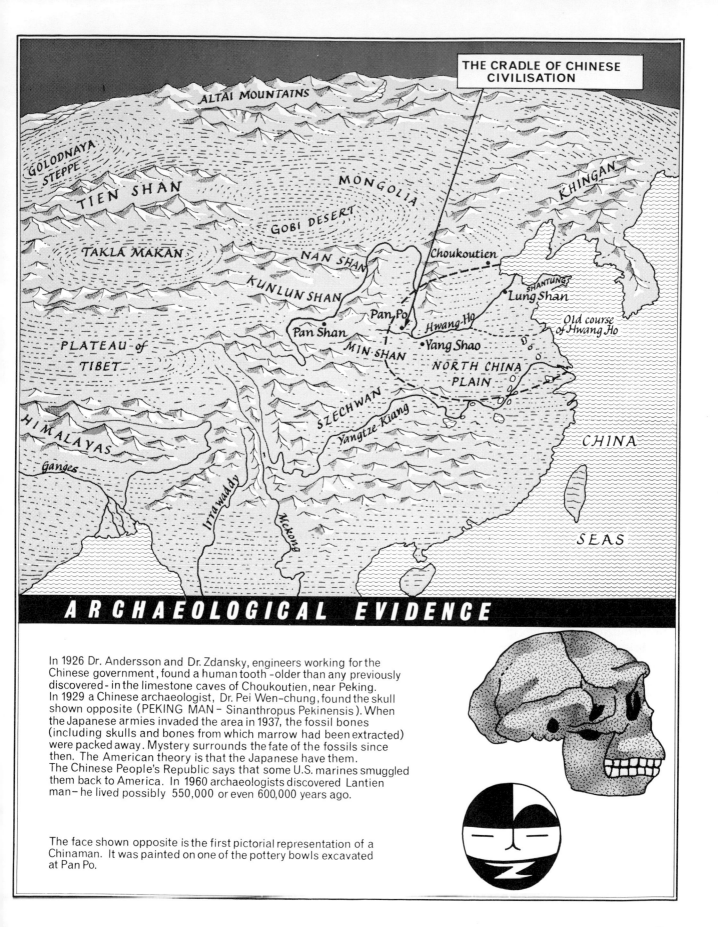

THE CRADLE OF CHINESE CIVILISATION

ALTAI MOUNTAINS

GOLODNAYA STEPPE

TIEN SHAN

MONGOLIA

KHINGAN

GOBI DESERT

TAKLA MAKAN

NAN SHAN

Choukoutien

KUNLUN SHAN

SHANTUNG
Lung Shan

Pan Po

PLATEAU of TIBET

Pan Shan

Hwang Ho

Old course of Hwang Ho

MIN SHAN

Yang Shao

NORTH CHINA PLAIN

HIMALAYAS

SZECHWAN

Ganges

Yangtze Kiang

CHINA

Irrawaddy

Mekong

SEAS

ARCHAEOLOGICAL EVIDENCE

In 1926 Dr. Andersson and Dr. Zdansky, engineers working for the Chinese government, found a human tooth -older than any previously discovered- in the limestone caves of Choukoutien, near Peking.
In 1929 a Chinese archaeologist, Dr. Pei Wen-chung, found the skull shown opposite (PEKING MAN – Sinanthropus Pekinensis). When the Japanese armies invaded the area in 1937, the fossil bones (including skulls and bones from which marrow had been extracted) were packed away. Mystery surrounds the fate of the fossils since then. The American theory is that the Japanese have them. The Chinese People's Republic says that some U.S. marines smuggled them back to America. In 1960 archaeologists discovered Lantien man– he lived possibly 550,000 or even 600,000 years ago.

The face shown opposite is the first pictorial representation of a Chinaman. It was painted on one of the pottery bowls excavated at Pan Po.

2 Shang and Chou: the first Chinese dynasties

The Shang

By 1600 B.C. the more sophisticated farming communities had formed themselves into clans. Armed with war chariots and bronze weapons, their soldiers gradually won control of the fertile lands west of Shantung. Known as the Shang, these clans were the creators of China's Bronze Age civilization.

City dwellers

The Shang kings located their palaces inside well-defended cities such as Chengchou and Anyang. They based their power on a standing army and a highly literate priesthood. Governing a city such as Anyang as well as its agricultural hinterland became increasingly complex and whenever a Shang king needed to make a policy decision he consulted the oracle. It was the priest's job to interpret the oracle bone, record the answer on it and then store the bone in the Shang archives.* The presence of large numbers of priests and soldiers in the city provided plenty of work for the bronzesmiths, whose workshops turned out thousands of spears, arrowheads, halberds and chariot fittings. The most highly skilled bronzesmiths had the task of casting the beautiful *ritual vessels* for use in the many religious ceremonies and state occasions that characterized the Shang dynasty.

The peasants

Nobody applied the technical skills of the bronzesmiths to agriculture. The peasants still had to make do with their digging sticks and stone sickles. Nevertheless, they were content to keep the city supplied with food so long as the king would defend them from enemy clans and protect their fields from the floodwaters of the river. These were the two worlds of China during the Shang dynasty: the peasants in the fields and the ruling classes controlling a specialist labour force in the cities. But they depended on one another, and upon the quality of leadership provided by the *Son of Heaven*—the Shang king.

The Chou

For five hundred years the Shang kings were equal to the task. Then, in 1027 B.C., the clan of Chou began to colonize the Shang territories. The Chou king built fortress cities to secure his new empire, an arrangement which depended upon the loyalty of his relatives and friends in the royal clan. He granted them control of the fortresses and surrounding lands in exchange for their political and military support. In theory, these *fiefs* remained the property of the king but in fact they soon developed into city states, kingdoms in miniature, and law and order declined in the land. 'More and more the feudal lords killed and warred with one another, without the Son of Heaven of Chou being able to prevent them.'† Moreover, this was not the only problem that developed. The spectacle of numerous states quarrelling among themselves was an open invitation to Mongolian and Siberian marauders pressing on the Chou frontiers in the north.

Confucius

Philosophers such as Confucius (551–479 B.C.) and Mencius (390–305 B.C.) tried to solve the problems that confronted the Chou dynasty. 'If a king is upright,' reasoned Confucius, 'all will go well without orders.' Personal virtue was therefore the primary requirement of a monarch—a quality rarely displayed by the rulers of the warring states. As far as good government was concerned, Confucius was sure that the essentials were: sufficient food, sufficient troops, and the confidence of the people. Of these, the last was the most important for 'a people without faith cannot survive'. But in seeking to define the nature of good government and to defend the feudal system of the Chou, Confucius was perhaps failing to take into account the many changes that were affecting the lives of the people. The rise of the merchant class, the new professional armies, the landowners who scorned the old fashioned fiefs and their customs, the peasants who worked for a wage and who paid their landlord taxes with a percentage of their rice or wheat crop—all of these new developments exposed the inefficiency and inadequacy of the later Chou rulers. The end came in 221 B.C. when one of the warring states, the Ch'in, conquered all China and established the rule of the first Emperor.

---

*Over 40,000 oracle bones have been excavated. About 3,000 Chinese characters can be identified and of these more than 1,000 have been deciphered.

†From a speech by Li-ssu, a remarkable minister in the Ch'in dynasty, quoted in D. Bodde's *China's First Unifier* (Hong Kong University Press, 1967).

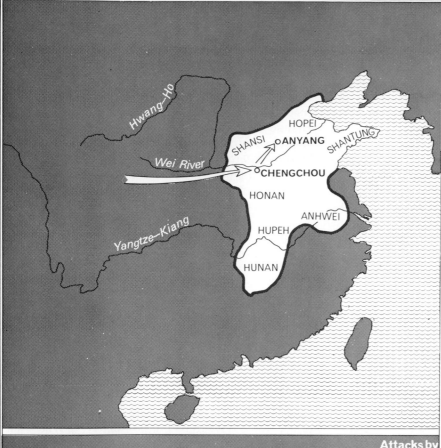

THE SHANG DYNASTY

☐ The unshaded area shows the extent of Shang influence; modern provincial names such as Anwhei indicate the location of recent excavations of Shang sites.

The unshaded area shows the extent of Shang influence; modern provincial names such as Anwhei indicate the location of recent excavations of Shang sites.

↗ Route followed by the early Shang clans and their two capitals Chengchou and Anyang. Anyang has been excavated in great detail.

CHARACTERISTICS OF THE TWO DYNASTIES

1. SHANG c. 1600–1027 B.C.
a. Knew how to make silk; used chopsticks; had cowries shells as money.
b. Royal succession was from brother to brother.
c. Human sacrifices were common at funerals. At one tomb in Shantung (excavated during 1966) 48 people had been sacrificed.

2. CHOU 1027–221 B.C.
a. Used ritual objects made of jade as well as the traditional bronze vessels.
b. Royal succession from father to son. Human sacrifice decreased.
c. Copper coins used for money.
d. Armies used iron weapons after about 500 B.C. – infantry and heavy cavalry tended to replace cumbersome chariots.
e. From about 400 B.C. some troops equipped with the crossbow.
f. Both Chou and Shang worshipped
   (i) The gods of nature &
   (ii) Ancestors.
Confucius refined their beliefs and reasoned that men should live in peace and harmony; there was a path or way (Tao) that men should follow. Confucius believed that man should live according to an ethical, disciplined code of conduct; 'Taoists' said that man should avoid imposed disciplines and live according to 'the way of nature'.
Obviously, the ideas of Confucius would appeal to the ruling class.

THE EMBLEM OF TAOISM—YIN and YANG
Yin is dark, passive and female.
Yang is light, active and male.
There is harmony between these forces.

THE CHOU DYNASTY

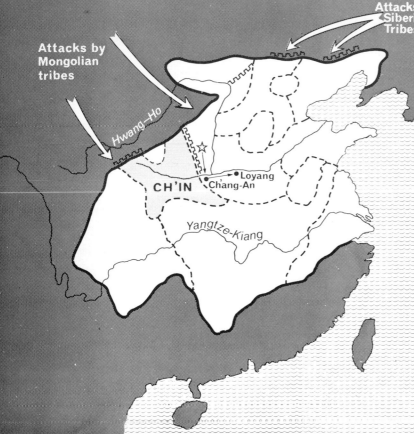

☐ The unshaded area shows the extent of Chou influence.
⌐⌐ Division of Chou territories into 'warring states'.
☆ Shensi (home of the Chou) and the route they followed to their main city states.
ᒥᒪᒥ Defensive walls built mainly between 450–290 B.C.

3 Ch'in and Han

The Ch'in, 221–206 B.C.

With the title Shih Hwang-ti (First Emperor), the Prince of Ch'in set about the systematic unification of the scattered lands that had once owed allegiance to the Chou kings. He divided his new empire into thirty-six commanderies, each controlled by an administrator in charge of civil affairs and a military governor in charge of the imperial garrisons. Both were directly responsible to the Emperor. In the north he ordered the walls to be linked into a continuous defensive system capable of protecting the Empire of Ch'in. With the building of the *Great Wall of Ch'in*—or China—it seemed, in the words of one ancient historian, that 'the world was finally united'.

Li-ssu

But it was a far from contented world. Local uprisings were common and although the military governors found them fairly easy to suppress the Emperor was anxious to eliminate them entirely. He turned to his Grand Councillor, Li-ssu, for advice. Li-ssu blamed the unsettled past and castigated the historians who pointed out that the misery of the present had its roots in the past: 'They excite and confuse the black haired ones'—the Ch'in expression for the mass of the people. Li-ssu advised the destruction of all historical records, except for those dealing with the Ch'in, with medicine and with agriculture. In 213 B.C. the Emperor ordered his administrators to begin the 'Burning of the Books'—and thousands of historical details, hand painted by scribes on slips of bamboo and wood, vanished for ever.

The Han Chinese and the expansion of China

The first Emperor died in 210 B.C. and after four years of chaos the Han Dynasty took charge of the Empire. From 206 B.C. to 220 A.D. the Han rulers imposed their vision on much of East Asia. They were military imperialists, determined to push China's frontiers to limits undreamt of by previous dynasties. They brought the northern tribes to heel, seized control of Central Asia's caravan routes and thrust deep into North Viet Nam. They built a network of fortress cities, initiated vast irrigation projects and undertook military campaigns beyond the Gobi Desert and into the Takla Makan. During four centuries the Han frittered away the strength and resources of the long-suffering peasants who had to shoulder the crushing burden of taxation and military service. A contemporary song captured some of the misery:

> At fifteen I went with the army, at fourscore I came home.
> On the way I met a man from the village, I asked him who was at home.
> 'That over there is your house, all covered with trees and bushes....'

In complete contrast to this were the splendours of the Han ruling classes. For example, when the Han buried Prince Liu-sheng and his wife Tou-wan they carved huge tombs in the side of a mountain and placed the bodies inside jade funerary suits—each of which was made of more than 2,000 jade plates sewn together with gold thread. Yet just one of the many bronze jugs they placed inside Tou-wan's tomb cost twice as much as a peasant farmer would have to pay in poll tax every year.* Then the Han sealed the tomb with a gigantic *cast iron* door—and made such a good job of it that when the archaeologists found it in 1968 they had to use dynamite to open it.

*The price tag was marked on the base of the jug!

Princess Tou-wan died in 104 B.C., nine years after her husband's death. They lived in the reign of Emperor Wu-ti, whose passionate aim was to breed the finest horses in Asia. The Han Chinese believed that the use of jade would preserve the bodies—but they were wrong. The jade suits and many of China's other archaeological treasures were on show in Paris and London during 1973–4.

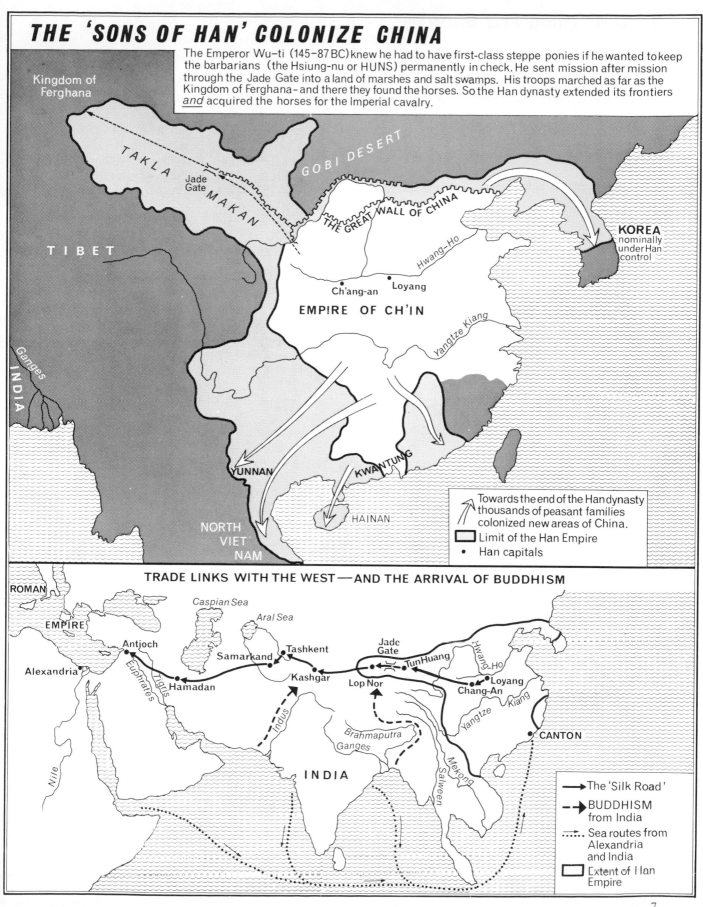

THE 'SONS OF HAN' COLONIZE CHINA

The Emperor Wu-ti (145–87 BC) knew he had to have first-class steppe ponies if he wanted to keep the barbarians (the Hsiung-nu or HUNS) permanently in check. He sent mission after mission through the Jade Gate into a land of marshes and salt swamps. His troops marched as far as the Kingdom of Ferghana – and there they found the horses. So the Han dynasty extended its frontiers *and* acquired the horses for the Imperial cavalry.

Kingdom of Ferghana

TAKLA MAKAN

Jade Gate

GOBI DESERT

THE GREAT WALL OF CHINA

TIBET

Hwang-Ho

KOREA
nominally under Han control

Ch'ang-an · Loyang

EMPIRE OF CH'IN

Yangtze Kiang

Ganges

INDIA

YUNNAN

KWANTUNG

HAINAN

NORTH VIET NAM

Towards the end of the Han dynasty thousands of peasant families colonized new areas of China.

☐ Limit of the Han Empire
• Han capitals

TRADE LINKS WITH THE WEST — AND THE ARRIVAL OF BUDDHISM

ROMAN

EMPIRE

Caspian Sea

Aral Sea

Antioch

Alexandria

Samarkand Tashkent

Jade Gate

Hwang-Ho

Euphrates

Tigris

Hamadan

Kashgar

Lop Nor

TunHuang

Loyang
Chang-An

Indus

Brahmaputra
Ganges

Yangtze Kiang

INDIA

Mekong

Salween

Nile

CANTON

→ The 'Silk Road'

⇢ BUDDHISM from India

┈┈ Sea routes from Alexandria and India

☐ Extent of Han Empire

4 Sui, T'ang and Sung

The Ch'in and the Han had been the creators of the imperial system. Now, over the next thousand years, three more dynasties made their own special contribution to the civilization of the Chinese people.

Sui, 589–618

This short-lived dynasty strengthened the northern walls and constructed a network of inland waterways, the most impressive of which was the Grand Canal. It was now possible for a river junk to load its cargo on the Yangtze-kiang and then carry it across China to one of the ports along the Hwang-ho. The only snag was that the trip might take twelve months! Strangely, a myth has grown up that the Chinese were not a maritime people. Yet they had already invented the stern rudder, the compass, the paddle wheel and buoyancy tanks. Treadmill-operated paddle boats were being used at the beginning of the seventh century to discourage pirate attacks upon defenceless river-craft.

The Sui dynasty modified the imperial system by introducing new forms of state examinations. Their aim was to attract talented people, irrespective of their social status, into the ranks of the scholarly mandarin class of officials—China's top civil servants. Candidates had to score very high marks in law, mathematics and Confucian philosophy.

T'ang, 618–907

Ironically, it was an official named T'ai-tsung who overthrew the Sui in 618 to found the dynasty of T'ang. Under this new dynasty China became the richest and most powerful empire in Asia with its frontiers—for a time, at least—stretching even further westwards than the limits attained by the Han. Two million people lived in the imperial capital of Ch'ang-an and the total population (the T'ang undertook triennial population surveys) topped 50 million. Culturally, China reached new peaks in painting, pottery, in the publication of printed books* and in the production of porcelain *objects d'art*. Then came the decline. By 751 advancing Arab armies had conquered most of the western empire while four years later An Lu-shan led a rebellion of the northern military governors and dealt so severe a blow to the T'ang dynasty that it never really recovered.

Sung, 960–1279

For the first time the centre of China's military and economic power began to shift away from the 'cradle of civilization' in the north to the lands around the Yangtze-kiang. The Sung built their main defence system south of the Yangtze; it was here that they began new irrigation and rice planting schemes, resettled refugee peasants and expanded the main centres of urban life. They certainly lived up to their motto: 'The south first, and then the north'.

City life

The Sung were famed for their well-ordered city life. Drummers sounded each hour of the night; reveille was at 0700 hours for everyone. Water-carriers, lantern-sellers, refuse-collectors and street-singers mingled in the streets with traders from distant provinces. Cookshops provided a wide range of dishes; inns selling brandy and rice wine offered merchants and officials plenty of relaxation. Buddhist priests had a busy day for part of their job was to supervise the city orphanage, hospital and graveyard. Fire brigade units, numbering a hundred men equipped with hoses, hatchets and grappling hooks, were on permanent stand-by while soldiers kept constant watch on the walls and main gates of the city.

Secret societies and peasant revolts

Secret societies, often composed of bandits, army deserters, the urban poor and unemployed, have existed throughout most of China's turbulent history. With colourful names such as the Yellow Turbans (these had helped to topple the Han dynasty), the Big Sword Society and the White Lotus, they attracted discontented peasants into their ranks and sometimes master-minded full-scale rebellions. One revolt in the south was named after Fang La, a bankrupt lacquer merchant. He won control of great tracts of countryside and effectively cut off food supplies to many cities during 1120. In an attempt to crush the Fang La rebellion the Sung foolishly weakened their northern defence perimeter so that, as thousands of imperial troops trudged southwards to deal with the rebels, the Mongol barbarians began to lay long-term plans for the conquest of the Chinese Empire.

---

*Ts'ai-hun, overseer of imperial factories to the Han Emperor, was manufacturing paper in 100 A.D. The earliest surviving printed book is the Diamond Sutra dating from 868 A.D.

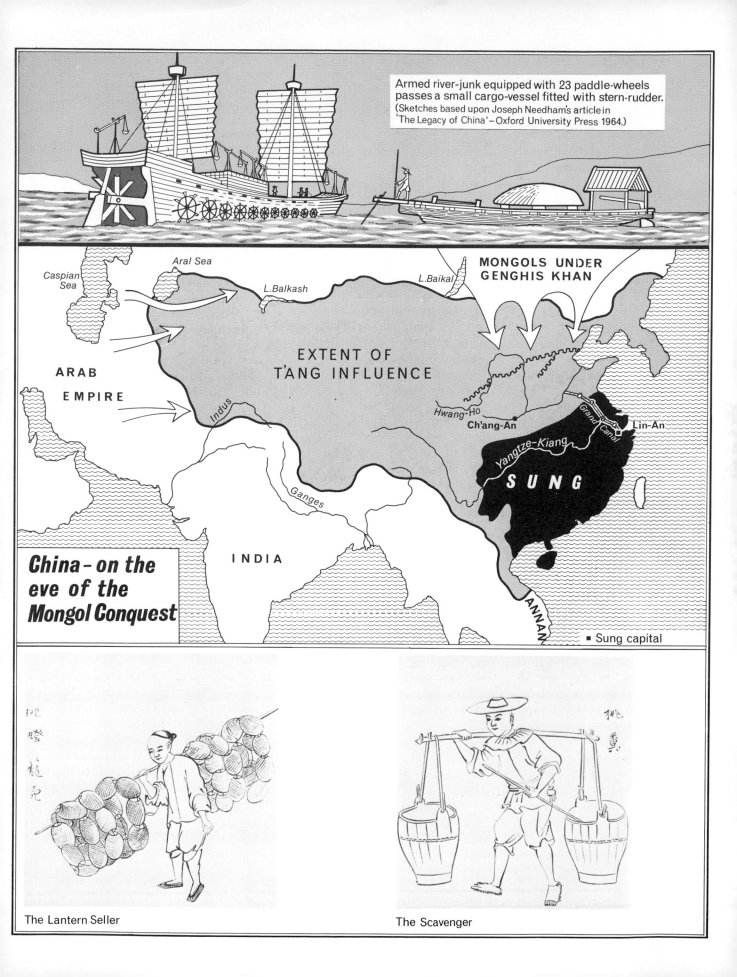

Armed river-junk equipped with 23 paddle-wheels passes a small cargo-vessel fitted with stern-rudder. (Sketches based upon Joseph Needham's article in 'The Legacy of China' – Oxford University Press 1964.)

Caspian Sea

Aral Sea

L.Balkash

L.Baikal

MONGOLS UNDER GENGHIS KHAN

ARAB EMPIRE

EXTENT OF T'ANG INFLUENCE

Indus

Hwang-Ho

Ch'ang-An

Grand Canal

Lin-An

Yangtze-Kiang

SUNG

Ganges

INDIA

China – on the eve of the Mongol Conquest

ANNAN

■ Sung capital

The Lantern Seller

The Scavenger

5 The Mongol conquest of China

Genghis Khan

In 1206 a great assembly of Mongol tribesmen elected their new leader or khan. The man they chose was Genghis Khan, a military genius who managed to weld his nomadic hordes into the most deadly cavalry armies the world had ever seen. In 1211 he led these armies across the Gobi Dessert into Northern China. It was a calculated risk. At least 150,000 Chinese soldiers stood in his way. High walls and deep moats defended most of the cities. Heavy catapults would bombard his tribesmen with missiles and even the most battle-hardened horses would shy during a cavalry charge if they came up against one of the Chinese flame-throwers. Yet Genghis Khan outwitted all the Chinese commanders during the campaigns of 1211—and again during 1213–14. Eventually, he sent two of his armies to attack Peking and the city surrendered in 1215. The Mongol troops swarmed over the walls, systematically destroyed and pillaged the buildings and had, according to the official Mongol historian, 'a most glorious slaughter'.

Kubilai Khan

A similar fate would have befallen the southern Sung but the death of Genghis Khan in 1227 reprieved them for half a century. During that time the three grandsons of Genghis Khan made the Mongol Empire even more powerful. Mangu, the Great Khan, ruled the imperial heartland of Mongolia; Hulagu controlled the Middle East; Kubilai was master of the North China Plain. In the 1260s Kubilai Khan moved his main base to Peking and in 1271 began the invasion of Southern China. After four years of fighting his Mongol cavalry occupied the Sung capital of Lin-an (Hangchow) and by 1279 they had wiped out the last of the Chinese resistance groups. Kubilai Khan, founder of the new dynasty of Ta Yuan, was now the Mongol Emperor of China.

The invasion of Japan

Back in 1274 Kubilai had made one disastrous attempt to occupy Japan. His assault troops landed on Tsushima and Iki where they came up against Japanese soldiers ready to fight to the last man. The main Mongol force managed to reach Kyushu but gathering storm clouds forced a hasty return to the landing craft. Kubilai deferred his next attack until after his victories in China. In 1281, 150,000 Mongols landed on Kyushu and fought non-stop for the next fifty-three days. Then, on 14 August 1281, a sudden typhoon sank most of the Mongol transports and the invasion failed. Not without reason did the Japanese name this typhoon *kamikaze*—the divine wind.

Pax Mongolica

By reputation the most barbaric of all Asian peoples, the Mongols were now in control of the most advanced civilization in the world. And though they naturally tried to fill all the top administrative posts in the Empire with their own people, they made very few changes in the traditional methods of Chinese government.* They reconstructed China's defences; extended the Grand Canal to link Peking with Hangchow; transformed battle-scarred Peking into the most beautiful city in Asia; and encouraged internal and international trade. But the Chinese people never accepted the Mongols and looked forward to the day when they would return to the northern steppelands. Nevertheless, the years between 1280 and 1300 were times of peace and prosperity both for China and for the lands which bordered the Silk Road. Hundreds of curious Christians—merchants, diplomats and missionaries—took advantage of this *Pax Mongolica* and set out on the long journey from the West to the court of Kubilai Khan and the legendary land of Cathay.†

The Western visitors

Two Franciscan friars had already made the journey to the Khan's first capital at Karakorum. One, Giovanni di Piano Carpini, went as early as 1245; Guillaume de Roubrouck travelled there in 1253 and discovered that the Chinese used paper money for trade and paintbrushes for writing, 'making in one figure the several letters containing a whole word'. But the most famous traveller was Marco Polo who from 1275 onwards not only visited the cities of Xanadu and Peking but also took a job with the Great Khan. Marco Polo was most impressed by the people of Hangchow. He admired their friendliness and civic spirit. Of course, they had some curious customs: Marco Polo was a merchant as well as a traveller and he was rather surprised to find that his Chinese counterparts always consulted a street astrologer before clinching their business deals. And although he described the people of Hangchow as peace-loving citizens, he did notice that they could not bear the sight of Mongol soldiers, 'believing that it is through them that they have been deprived of their own natural kings and lords'.‡

*They abolished the selection examinations, however!
†The Western term for China.
‡From *The Travels of Marco Polo* translated by R. E. Latham (Penguin, 1958) p. 191.

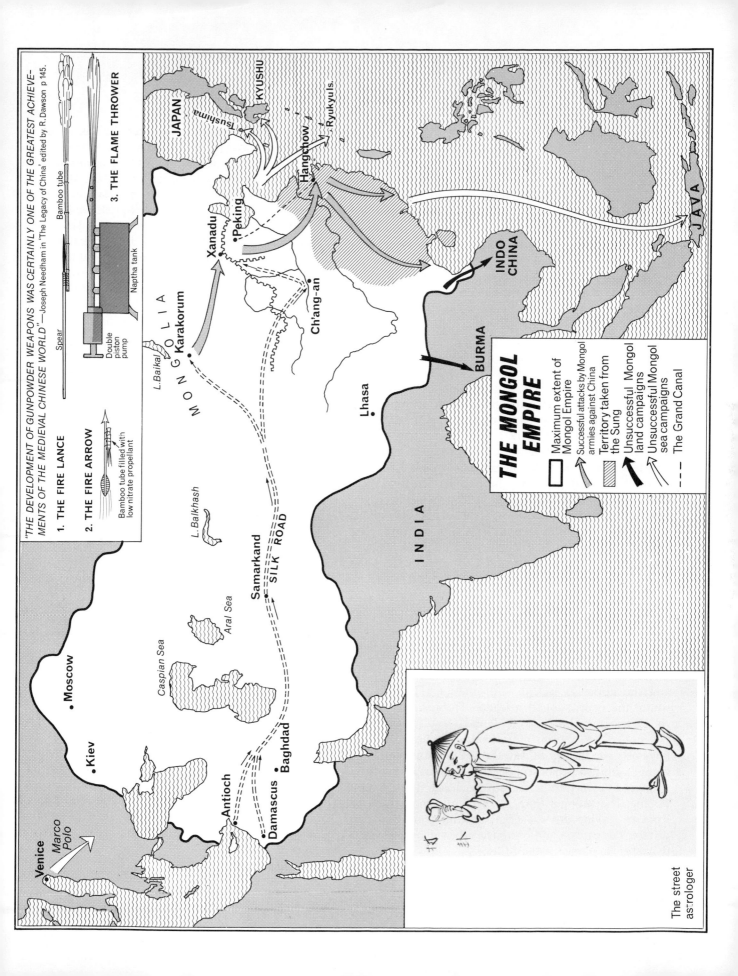

"THE DEVELOPMENT OF GUNPOWDER WEAPONS WAS CERTAINLY ONE OF THE GREATEST ACHIEVE-
MENTS OF THE MEDIEVAL CHINESE WORLD" —Joseph Needham in 'The Legacy of China' edited by R. Dawson p.145.

1. THE FIRE LANCE

Spear

Bamboo tube

2. THE FIRE ARROW

Bamboo tube filled with
low nitrate propellant

3. THE FLAME THROWER

Naptha tank

Double
piston
pump

THE MONGOL EMPIRE

- Maximum extent of Mongol Empire
- Successful attacks by Mongol armies against China
- Territory taken from the Sung
- Unsuccessful Mongol land campaigns
- Unsuccessful Mongol sea campaigns
- - - The Grand Canal

Venice

Marco Polo

Moscow

Kiev

Antioch

Damascus

Baghdad

Caspian Sea

Aral Sea

L. Balkhash

Samarkand

SILK ROAD

L. Baikal

M O N G O L I A

Karakorum

Xanadu

Peking

Ch'ang-an

Lhasa

INDIA

BURMA

INDO CHINA

JAPAN

KYUSHU

Tsushima

Hangchow

Ryukyuls.

JAVA

The street
astrologer

6 Ming: the last of the native Chinese dynasties

The mandate to govern

Chinese ideas about the duties and responsibilities of the Son of Heaven—the Emperor—were rooted in the political ideas of Confucius. Because Heaven cared for the welfare of the people it had given the Emperor the mandate to govern. If he governed well, Heaven would send fine weather, bumper crops and everyone would be happy. But if he turned out to be a corrupt or incompetent ruler, Heaven would send droughts, famines, earthquakes and floods. At that point, the people had the right to rebel, remove the mandate from the offending Emperor and hand it to his successor who would establish his own dynasty.

The time of troubles

Shun-ti (1333–68), the last of the Mongol Emperors, was an unpopular ruler. He put up the taxes, swamped the country with worthless paper currency and conscripted reluctant peasants for work on various irrigation projects. And to make matters worse, a series of appalling disasters coincided with his reign. Droughts caused serious food shortages in Northern China. The food shortages turned to famine during 1334 and the next two years saw violent earthquakes and widespread floods. Millions of Chinese died—though not all succumbed to the violence of the elements. Stalking through the densely populated areas of China, India and Central Asia came the most dreaded killer of all—the Black Death.

The expulsion of the Mongol Emperor

Long years of suffering provoked the peasantry into rebellion and the Mongol troops were hard-pressed to retain control of the cities, let alone the countryside. At first the uprisings lacked co-ordination. Then, in the south, the people found a leader. He was Chu Yuan-chang, a former Buddhist monk and a soldier of fortune. He unified the peasant movements; cut the vital canal links between the capital and the rice lands around Che-kiang; and then began to liberate Southern China from Mongol rule. In 1368 he was strong enough to march on Peking. The Mongol Emperor promptly fled across the frontier, leaving the way clear for Chu Yuan-chang to occupy the capital and establish a brand new Chinese dynasty. He named it the Ming.

Keeping the Mongols at bay

Chu Yuan-chang ruled China for the next thirty years.

He made valiant attempts to re-open the Silk Road and sent his armies on expeditions against the Mongol khans. He patched up the northern frontier, occupied Manchuria and transformed Korea into a vassal state of China. In the hope that a secure and peaceful northern frontier might persuade merchants to risk sending valuable caravans along the Silk Road, the later Ming Emperors adopted similar policies. But it took them years to pacify the Mongols, who persisted in attacking the Ming Empire. For example, the Mongols swarmed across the Great Wall in 1449, captured the Emperor and besieged Peking. Luckily for the Chinese, the Mongol armies of the fifteenth century were not of the same calibre as those who had followed Genghis Khan. Eventually, the Ming did succeed in checking the Mongols; they also persuaded them to honour a treaty of peace and friendship. However, by the time this happened—in 1571—threats from a completely different quarter were already challenging the Ming.

Threats from the sea

China's longing to re-establish her trade links with India and Arabia had prompted a series of remarkable sea voyages. Under the command of a senior Ming official named Cheng-ho, Chinese fleets sailed south to Malacca in 1403. Two years later, Cheng-ho's junks began to voyage as far as Ceylon, East Africa and the Arabian Sea. But it was Malacca that was to be the main centre of Oriental trade and over the next hundred years Chinese merchants flocked to Malaysia, Sumatra and Java.* Inevitably, so famous an *entrepôt* was bound to attract European explorers and in 1509 six Portuguese carracks dropped anchor in Malacca's busy roadstead. Soon the Portuguese were searching for the land they called Cathay and in 1514 their ships were in Canton harbour. There were quarrels between the Europeans and the Chinese port officials and during 1522 the Portuguese came off worst in a brief sea battle outside the harbour. Far more dangerous than the Portuguese were the fleets of Japanese pirates. Between 1550 and 1570 they terrorized the coast from the Shantung Peninsula right down to the island of Hainan. Hangchow and Ningpo went up in flames and for a time the huge city of Nanking† was under threat of destruction from marauding Japanese fleets.

*Part of the Empire of Sri-Vijaya.
†The Ming Emperors had originally chosen Nanking as their capital because it seemed safe from attacking Mongols. They resided in their 'Southern City' (the meaning of 'Nanking') from 1368 to 1402 and then moved to Peking.

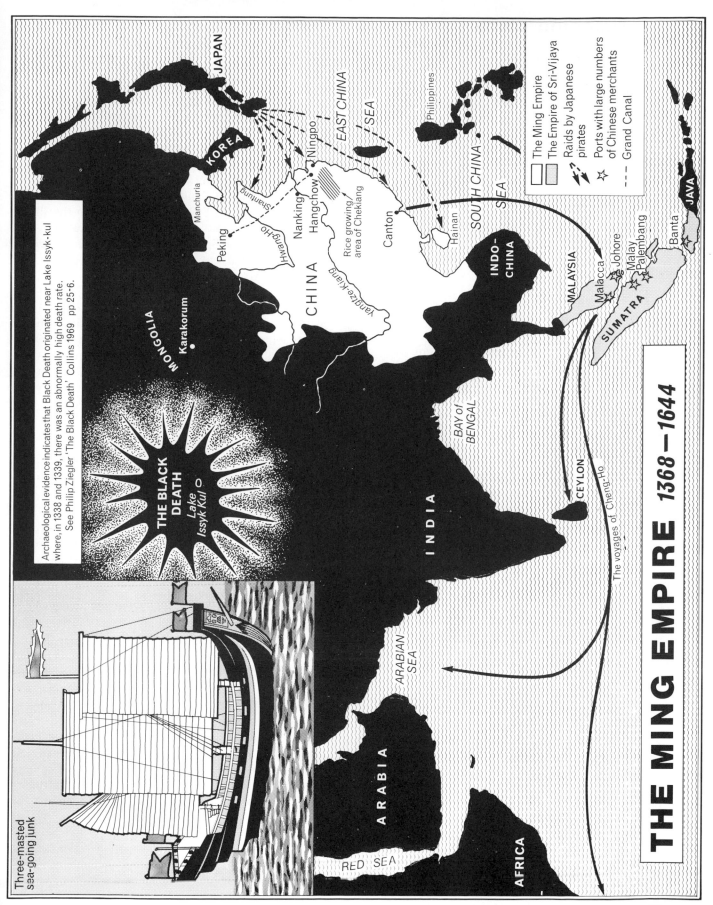

THE MING EMPIRE 1368—1644

Legend:
- The Ming Empire
- The Empire of Sri-Vijaya
- Raids by Japanese pirates
- Ports with large numbers of Chinese merchants
- --- Grand Canal

Three-masted sea-going junk

Archaeological evidence indicates that Black Death originated near Lake Issyk-kul where, in 1338 and 1339, there was an abnormally high death rate.
See Philip Ziegler 'The Black Death' Collins 1969 pp 25-6.

THE BLACK DEATH
Lake Issyk Kul

JAPAN

KOREA

Manchuria

MONGOLIA
Karakorum

Peking

Shantung

Hwang-Ho

Nanking
Hangchow
Ningpo

CHINA

Yangtze-kiang

Rice growing area of Chekiang

EAST CHINA SEA

Philippines

Canton

Hainan

SOUTH CHINA SEA

INDO-CHINA

MALAYSIA
Malacca

Johore
Malay
Palembang
Banta

SUMATRA

JAVA

INDIA

BAY OF BENGAL

CEYLON

The voyages of Cheng-Ho

ARABIAN SEA

ARABIA

RED SEA

AFRICA

7 Changing China

The population increase

Between 1400 and 1600 China's population rose from 70 million to 140 million people. During these two centuries the Chinese people enjoyed a higher standard of living, due mainly to the quantity and quality of foodstuffs available. In effect, China experienced an agricultural revolution.

New crops

There is a saying in China that the precious things in life are not pearls and jade but the five grains: wheat, barley, millet, soybeans and rice. Rice had become the staple diet and accounted for 70 per cent of food production. Just before the Ming period began a new strain of rice had arrived from Indo-china. Known as Champa rice, it had two distinct advantages: it needed less water for growing, and it matured in a hundred days. Not only could a farmer anticipate two crops each year but he could also cultivate the hillsides, and by 1450 the landscape was taking on a new appearance as peasants transformed the hills into terraced paddies. Then during the 1550s came the 'American crops': sweep potatoes, Irish potatoes, maize and peanuts. Once the peasants realized that these crops would flourish in the uplands they trekked into the undeveloped regions and established thousands of new farming communities. It was an heroic task and the peasants achieved it without benefit of mechanical aids— 'the Chinese peasant's main weapon in his struggle with new land was crops'.* Unfortunately, his over-enthusiastic deforestation of the hillsides caused so much erosion that the rivers silted up and flooded the valleys far more seriously than they had done before.

The new city of Peking

Marco Polo had been amazed by Peking: 'the whole city is arranged in squares like a chessboard ... in a manner so perfect that it is impossible to give a description that should do it justice.' Under the Ming Emperors, Peking grew into the most beautiful city in Asia. And when the Ming added a huge suburban settlement zone, it became one of the biggest. With its temples, pagodas, palaces and merchants' houses, markets, theatres, baths and a myriad of street traders, Peking was the unrivalled capital of Chinese civilization.

Newcomers

Despite their early brush with the war junks, the Portuguese persisted in their trade with China. For a time they had access to Ningpo, Foochow and Amoy until, in 1545, their arrogant behaviour forced the Chinese to expel them. Suitably contrite, the Portuguese pleaded for at least one trading station and in 1557 the Chinese relented and allowed them to build a colony on the isthmus of Macao. Meanwhile, Spanish colonists from the Philippines were trying to break into the lucrative China trade—in 1586 the Spaniards actually contemplated the invasion of China, but they abandoned the project after the ill-fated Armada sailed against England in 1588. Some newcomers, at least, arrived in the name of peace—notably the Jesuits led by Matteo Ricci. He reached Canton in 1582 and impressed the Chinese with his interest in their scientific and astronomical equipment. In 1601 the Chinese allowed him to live in Peking where he worked side by side with leading Chinese scientists. Their interest, however, was not entirely academic. They were very keen to learn about European firearms and especially the methods used to cast reliable, heavy cannons. The Emperor was very anxious about the security of his north-east frontier.

New conflicts: Korea

For many years the Japanese had been harassing China's ports and coastal trade. Now, under the leadership of the war-lord Hideyoshi, Japan tried to gain a foothold on the Asian mainland. An invasion force of 200,000 men crossed the Straits of Tsushima and occupied Pusan, Seoul and Pyongyang. Chinese troops countered by crossing the frozen Yalu in January 1593 to begin six years of fighting in the Korean peninsula. They were lucky in having the help of an extraordinary Korean admiral named Yi Sun-sin. He had developed a new warship or 'tortoise boat' which was an armoured version of one of his galleys. It had rounded decking impervious to Japanese missiles; it had iron rams fitted fore and aft. According to some accounts, the tortoise boats sank seventy Japanese ships in a single engagement!† In the land battles, the Ming generals contrived to contain the Japanese—only to face the grim prospect of another attack from the north-east, this time from *Manchu* tribesmen whose leaders were one day destined to be the rulers of all China.

*Ping Ti-ho, quoted by Keith Buchanan on p. 22 of his *The Transformation of the Chinese Earth* (Bell and Sons, 1970).
†See, for example, Richard Storry's *A History of Modern Japan* (Pelican, 1961) p. 52.

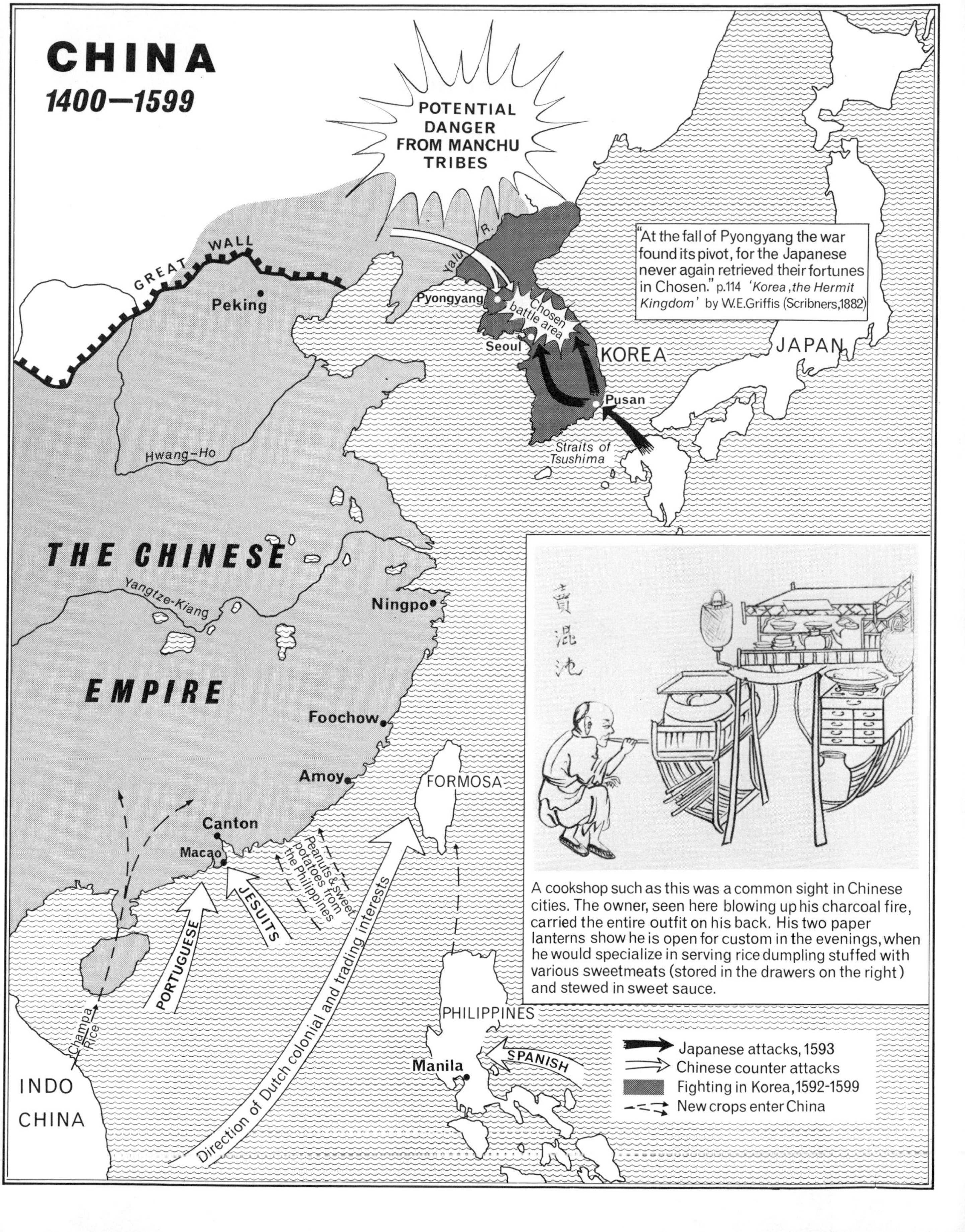

CHINA
1400—1599

POTENTIAL
DANGER
FROM MANCHU
TRIBES

GREAT WALL

Peking

Yalu R.

Pyongyang

Chosen
battle area

Seoul

KOREA

Pusan

*Straits of
Tsushima*

Hwang-Ho

"At the fall of Pyongyang the war
found its pivot, for the Japanese
never again retrieved their fortunes
in Chosen." p.114 *'Korea, the Hermit
Kingdom'* by W.E.Griffis (Scribners,1882)

JAPAN

THE CHINESE

Yangtze-Kiang

EMPIRE

Ningpo

Foochow

Amoy

FORMOSA

Canton

Macao

*Peanuts & sweet
potatoes from
the Philippines*

JESUITS

PORTUGUESE

*Champa
Rice*

Direction of Dutch colonial and trading interests

**INDO
CHINA**

PHILIPPINES

Manila

SPANISH

賣混沌

A cookshop such as this was a common sight in Chinese
cities. The owner, seen here blowing up his charcoal fire,
carried the entire outfit on his back. His two paper
lanterns show he is open for custom in the evenings, when
he would specialize in serving rice dumpling stuffed with
various sweetmeats (stored in the drawers on the right)
and stewed in sweet sauce.

➤	Japanese attacks, 1593
⇨	Chinese counter attacks
▬	Fighting in Korea, 1592-1599
- ⤳	New crops enter China

Further Reading

Theme 1—The Ancient Empire

Spread

1.	Michael Ridley	*Treasures of China*	The Dolphin Press, 1973
2.	Arthur Cotterell and David Morgan	*China: An Integrated Study*	Harrap, 1975
3.	Bamber Gascoigne	*The Treasures and Dynasties of China*	Jonathan Cape, 1973
4.	Werner Eichhorn	*Chinese Civilization*	Faber and Faber, 1969
5.	Wilfrid Blunt	*The Golden Road to Samarkand*	Hamish Hamilton, 1973
6.	Keith Buchanan	*The Transformation of the Chinese Earth*	Bell, 1970
7.	Donald Macintyre	*Sea Power in the Pacific*	Arthur Barker Ltd., 1972

The Great Wall of China.

THEME 2

Ch'ing: The Rise and Fall of the Manchu Empire, 1644–1912

Secret societies, peasant rebellions and Manchu invaders all combined to bring about the decline and fall of the Ming, China's last *native* dynasty. In their place, the victorious Manchus founded the Ch'ing dynasty and in many ways became more Chinese than the Chinese themselves. Manchu Emperors were obsessed with the cultivation of China's ancient culture and with the preservation of past glories. Yet at the same time they had to contend with problems entirely beyond their experience—and proved to be totally unsuited to the challenge.

When the Manchu Emperors first came to China's 'Dragon Throne', the country's population was increasing at an unprecedented rate. But they made no attempt to adjust the economy accordingly and China's limited farmland was unable to cope with the demand for food. It was not long before the peasants began to suffer from the uncontrolled population explosion and in particular from its *economic* side effects. At the same time, missionaries roamed the land in their quest for 'rice Christians'; western merchants bargained for tea, silk and art treasures; foreign gun-boats appeared in imperial waters; peasant uprisings threatened the entire fabric of government.

Two risings in particular heralded the doom of the Manchu Empire: the Taiping Rebellion and the Boxer Revolt. Their new ideas challenged traditional forms of government and made an immediate appeal to young Chinese intellectuals. Conscious of the pressing need to assert 'Chinese nationalism', they supported men such as Sun Yat-sen, founder of the *Kuomintang* or Nationalist Party. For they resented the humiliation that had been heaped upon China during the Opium Wars, during the clash with Japan in 1894–5 and during the more recent aftermath of the ill-fated Boxer Revolt. Eventually, on 1 January 1912, Sun Yat-sen proclaimed the creation of the Republic of China and the Manchus stepped down in favour of a President as the ruler of all China.

8 The Manchu conquest of China

The Manchu bannermen

During the years 1618–26 well-organized *banners** of Manchu cavalry soldiers surged across China's north-eastern frontier. Some swung round the edge of the Ever-White Mountains into battle-scarred Korea and forced this unfortunate kingdom to capitulate in 1637. Elated by this success and aided by Mongol tribesmen and disaffected Chinese from within the Ming Empire, the banners intensified their assault upon China. They smashed through the Great Wall and marched on Peking. Here, in 1644, the last Ming Emperor committed suicide and the Manchus proclaimed their new dynasty—the Ch'ing.

Coxinga

The Manchu attacks had caused chaos inside China and it was some time before the Ch'ing Emperors could introduce a stable government. First they had to undertake a systematic advance towards the south, setting up their garrisons and persuading—or compelling—local populations to transfer allegiance to the Ch'ing. They met a determined opponent in Kok Seng-ya (better known as Coxinga) who harassed the over-extended Manchu forces for many years. Though they managed to defeat him at the Battle of Nanking (1659) this did not deter Coxinga. He shipped his surviving forces across to Quemoy, the Pescadores and, finally, to Taiwan. Thousands of Chinese emigrants were already living on this lovely off-shore island (the Portuguese always called it *Formosa*, which means 'the beautiful') where Dutch settlers had been creating a flourishing colony ever since 1623. Coxinga soon defeated the Dutch but the island was not the haven he hoped it would be.† Across the Straits of Formosa came the Manchu fleets, whittling away at his bases and persuading his junk captains to desert. It was all over by 1683 when Taiwan, for the first time, became part of the rapidly expanding Chinese Empire.

Manchu influence

The Manchus were aliens, cousins of the Mongols. Their language, customs, writing and costume were different from those of the native Chinese. Yet, apart from their insistence that everybody should adopt the Manchu 'pig-tail', they made no serious effort to change the Chinese life style. Instead, they tried to improve the *quality* of life by injecting into a corrupt and inefficient imperial government better standards and new enthusiasms. In the long run, China gained tremendous benefits from Man-

chu rule and the credit for this goes mainly to the Emperors K'ang Hsi and Ch'ien Lung. Both were ardent imperialists and under their leadership more people and more lands came under direct Chinese influence than in any previous dynasty.

China's new contacts

Despite the appalling terrain and climate, Russian pioneers had been pushing eastwards at roughly the same time as the Manchus had invaded China. Cossack frontiersmen clashed with Manchu border patrols from 1650 onwards and in 1689 Emperor K'ang Hsi negotiated the Treaty of Nerchinsk, the first of many attempts to stabilize Sino–Russian frontiers. This soon proved inadequate and a supplementary Treaty of Kiakhata defined the border even more closely in 1728.‡ Ch'ien Lung (1735–99) was more ambitious. He settled colonists in Sinkiang, moved troops into Tibet to combat Gurkha invasions from Nepal and forced Annam and Burma to recognize Manchu overlordship. Such extensive influence convinced most Chinese that their Empire was indeed the centre of the world and far superior to all the other lands and kingdoms that fringed its frontiers.

An ever-increasing population

Eighteenth-century statistics are notoriously misleading; nevertheless, it seems likely that China's population almost doubled between 1700 and 1800. Certainly, Ch'ien Lung was deeply conscious of his responsibility towards the teeming millions and the need to protect them against the ravages of flood and famine. He authorized programmes of public works to guarantee peasants a chance of paid employment during times of crisis. Simultaneously, he exploited the 'American crops' introduced during the Ming period and encouraged farmers to grow more wheat and, wherever possible, to plant cash-crops such as cotton, sugar-cane and indigo. His foresight provided the people with a long period of internal peace, better food production and a variety of domestic industries. These were certainly important factors behind the extraordinary increase in population from about 160 million in 1700 to around 300 million in 1800.

*A banner was a division in the Manchu armies led by an outstanding general called Nurhachi.

†Coxinga died on Taiwan shortly after defeating the Dutch. His son Cheng Ching ruled the island until 1661.

‡The Manchus and Russians could not understand one another's languages. They enlisted the help of the Jesuits in Peking; and both Treaties were written in Latin!

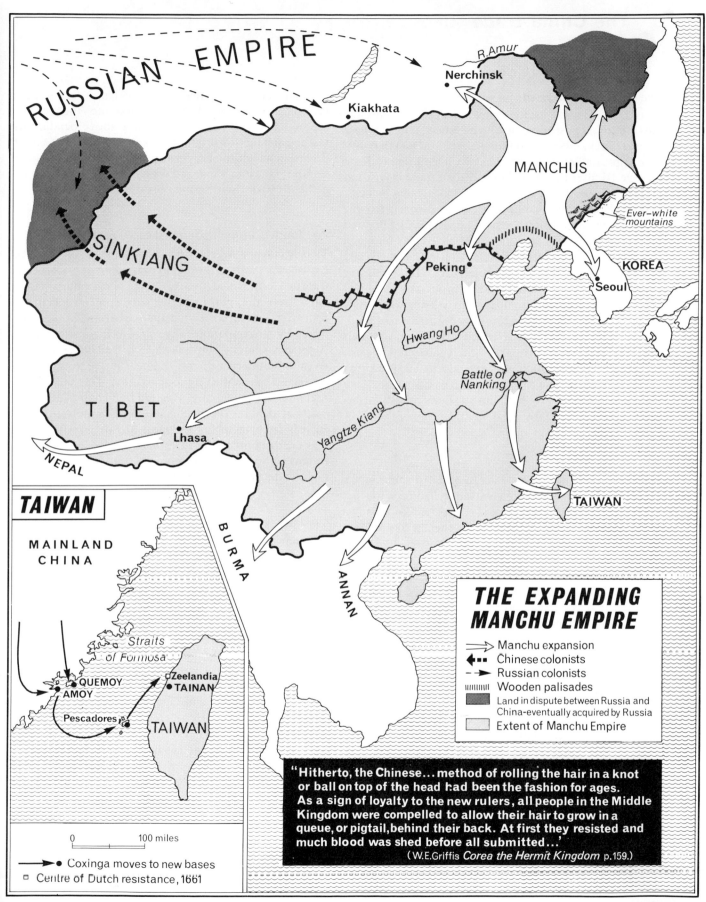

RUSSIAN EMPIRE

Nerchinsk

R. Amur

Kiakhata

MANCHUS

Ever-white mountains

SINKIANG

Peking

KOREA

Seoul

TIBET

Hwang Ho

Lhasa

Battle of Nanking

Yangtze Kiang

NEPAL

BURMA

TAIWAN

ANNAN

TAIWAN

MAINLAND CHINA

Straits of Formosa

QUEMOY

AMOY

Zeelandia
TAINAN

Pescadores

TAIWAN

0   100 miles

→● Coxinga moves to new bases
▢ Centre of Dutch resistance, 1661

THE EXPANDING MANCHU EMPIRE

⟹ Manchu expansion
◀▪▪▪ Chinese colonists
- - ▶ Russian colonists
ⅢⅢ Wooden palisades
▨ Land in dispute between Russia and China-eventually acquired by Russia
░ Extent of Manchu Empire

"Hitherto, the Chinese... method of rolling the hair in a knot or ball on top of the head had been the fashion for ages. As a sign of loyalty to the new rulers, all people in the Middle Kingdom were compelled to allow their hair to grow in a queue, or pigtail, behind their back. At first they resisted and much blood was shed before all submitted...'
(W.E.Griffis *Corea the Hermit Kingdom* p.159.)

9 The China trade

The Chinese attitude

A condescending attitude towards *all* types of trade was the traditional posture struck by members of the Chinese ruling classes and the most famous expression of that attitude appeared in a letter written by Ch'ien Lung to King George III after the arrival of a British trade delegation in 1793. Ch'ien Lung accepted the royal gifts—clocks, guns and telescopes—simply because so much trouble had been taken to bring them so far. But, as he pointed out, 'There is nothing we lack ... We have never set much store on strange or ingenious objects, nor do we need any more of your country's manufactures.' But ordinary Chinese thought differently and thousands accepted voluntary banishment by emigrating to lands where they could live up to their reputation of being a nation of shopkeepers. Luzon (the Chinese called it Lu-sung) was their favourite target and this part of the Philippines became the first major centre of the China trade; for even Peking's courtiers were willing to exchange their silks, tea, chinaware and rhubarb for high-grade silver mined in faraway Spanish America.

The traders arrive

European merchants were equally keen to share in the commerce of China. Portuguese traders had been the first on the scene but the British (who had backed Coxinga in the vain hope that he would win them a foothold on the mainland) soon followed them, as did the Dutch, Swedes, Danes and Spaniards. By the time the first American ship sailed into Canton,* the Emperor had decreed (1757) that not only must all trade be channelled through that particular port but the *factors* or traders must confine themselves to *factories* leased from local landlords.

The China they found

Hemmed into these little compounds—the Chinese called them *hongs*—the American and European traders soon found that dealing with local officials could lead to trouble. The Emperor, cocooned rather more palatially inside his *Forbidden City*, made no direct contact with the 'foreign devils'. Instead, he used his *censors* (senior civil servants) to conduct Canton's commerce on behalf of the Son of Heaven. It was the censor's job to report regularly on the situation in Canton and teams of messengers mounted on relays of fast horses took a mere twenty days to carry his letters to Peking. Here the Emperor would review the situation with his Grand Council, reach a decision and send his orders back to Canton. Everything depended first, on the censor's report—and civil servants were not above bending the truth or telling downright lies—and second, on the interpretation which the Emperor placed upon it. Misunderstanding was inevitable and soon the traders were at loggerheads with the Chinese port officials.

The Emily *and the* Lady Hughes

Two accidents highlighted the problem. In 1784 the British ship *Lady Hughes* fired a salute as she entered Canton—and killed two Chinese. The captain had to hand over the guilty gunner; a report went to the Emperor, who decreed that the barbarian should suffer death by strangulation. Then, in 1821, a sailor on the American vessel *Emily* knocked a fruit-seller into the river—and the lady drowned. The Chinese took him prisoner and he too died by strangulation. This sort of summary justice made the Western merchants extremely wary of dealing with officialdom, especially after the British discovered that the most lucrative import of all was the drug *opium*. The Emperor expressly forbade the import of opium and repressed attempts by native Chinese to grow the poppies in Yunnan.

Commissioner Lin

His action simply increased the demand for illegally imported opium and the British and Chinese merchants decided to bribe the local mandarins to turn a blind eye to this new smuggling racket. It was an evil trade, virtually monopolized by the British who had vast acreages of poppy fields in Bengal. The drug did untold damage to China physically, morally as well as financially—for China paid out vast quantities of silver bullion for 'this pernicious article'.† The Emperor threatened to punish severely any mandarin caught buying or smoking the drug; but this did not make any impression upon the corrupt civil servants. He therefore decided to give to Commissioner Lin Tse-hsu the job of putting an end to the trade once and for all. Lin had already made his mark in Hunan and Hupeh where he had closed down hundreds of opium dens. Now, in 1839, he arrived in Canton to do battle with the 'foreign devils'.

*In 1784. Hopefully named the *Empress of China*, it was a converted privateer, a veteran of the American War of Independence, 1775–83.
†Warren Hastings' phrase. But it was he who, as Governor of Bengal, authorized opium shipments to China.

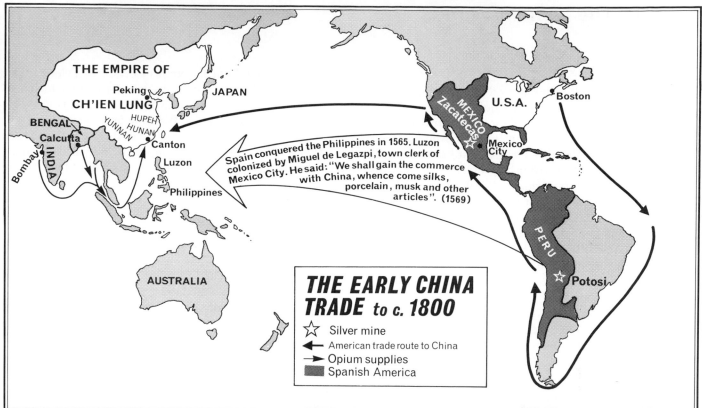

THE EMPIRE OF
CH'IEN LUNG
Peking
JAPAN
HUPEH
HUNAN
YUNNAN
Canton
Luzon
Philippines
BENGAL
Calcutta
Bombay
INDIA
AUSTRALIA

U.S.A.
Boston
MEXICO
Zacatecas
Mexico City
PERU
Potosi

Spain conquered the Philippines in 1565. Luzon colonized by Miguel de Legazpi, town clerk of Mexico City. He said: "We shall gain the commerce with China, whence come silks, porcelain, musk and other articles". (1569)

THE EARLY CHINA TRADE to c. 1800

☆ Silver mine
← American trade route to China
→ Opium supplies
▨ Spanish America

The Opium Trade with China to 1839

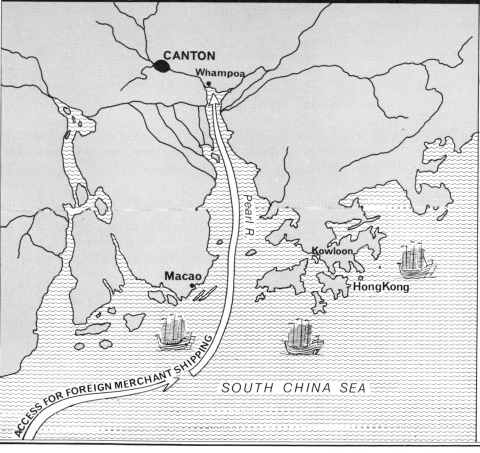

CANTON
Whampoa
Pearl R.
Kowloon
Macao
HongKong
ACCESS FOR FOREIGN MERCHANT SHIPPING
SOUTH CHINA SEA

THE APPROACH TO CANTON

Firms such as Jardine & Matheson used opium clippers - the first one to sail was the **Red Rover** *in 1829 - to bring chests of opium up the Pearl River as far as Whampoa. Mandarin cruisers*

stood by to prevent Chinese smugglers from bringing *in the drug, but in general these armed vessels did not interfere with the foreign merchants. The opium clippers then transferred their illicit cargo - usually at night - to fast Chinese galleys rowed by about forty tough desperadoes. These vessels brought the opium ashore. In 1837 when a mere 230 foreigners were living in the Canton* **hongs,** *40,000 chests of opium were delivered to China and the quantity imported was increasing every year.*

10 The 'Opium Wars'

Lin's failure, 1839

Within a week of his arrival in Canton, Lin began to blockade the factories. It would end, he said, when the foreigners surrendered their stockpiles of opium. So, when the British eventually handed over 20,000 chests of opium, Lin believed he had won a great victory. Events soon proved him wrong. During July some British and American sailors accidentally killed a villager in a fist-fight. Lin asked the British to try the culprits and then hand over the murderer—but the British claimed that they could not decide who had actually killed the China-man. Again, Lin resorted to a blockade and forced the British community to seek refuge on ships anchored off Hong Kong. His elation soon turned to horror when he discovered that the ships were being used as the new headquarters of the opium trade! He ordered his war junks to intercept food supplies ferried by Chinese boatmen to the British ships—and promptly lost four junks to the guns of Royal Navy frigates. This was open war and it marked the failure of the policies of Commissioner Lin.

The First Anglo-Chinese War, 1839–42

Once news of these events filtered back to London, the British government made it clear that although it disapproved of the opium trade it was bound to protect the lives of British citizens overseas. For Foreign Secretary Palmerston this meant sending in gun-boats; a demonstration of force would persuade Emperor Tao-kuang to accept foreigners as equals and perhaps open trade with the whole of China. An expeditionary force duly arrived in 1840, deposited two regiments on Chusan and then sailed north to the Taku forts to deliver Palmerston's point of view to the Emperor. But as it seemed impossible to make contact with the Son of Heaven, a diplomatic solution evaded everybody. The British therefore attacked along the coast and threatened Nanking. Tao-kuang decided it was time for 'soothing the barbarians' and instructed Commissioner Chi-ying to negotiate the Treaty of Nanking (1842). Britain gained Hong Kong, a cash indemnity to make up for the loss of opium in 1839 and permission to trade at five 'treaty ports': Canton, Amoy, Foochow, Ningpo and Shanghai.

A rash of treaties

In 1843 the British signed the Treaty of the Bogue which granted them the status of 'most favoured nation' in China. This meant that, in the event of China's negotiating treaties with other nations, Britain would automatically enjoy the same advantages as those conferred upon, say, the U.S.A. In fact, America's President Tyler had just appointed Caleb Cushing as his envoy to China and Cushing arrived on the U.S.S. Brandywine in 1844. He travelled to the village of Wanghia and signed America's first trade treaty with China. Later that year the French signed the Treaty of Whampoa by which Tao-kuang agreed to tolerate Christian churches within the Chinese Empire.

The Arrow incident, 1856

Chinese mandarins often pleaded ignorance of the Nanking Treaty and interfered with Western commerce whenever they could. Their most famous intervention was in 1856 when they arrested the crew of the Arrow, a lorcha flying the British flag. Palmerston—now Prime Minister—thought this was the last straw: 'this violation in regard to the lorcha is not the first or the only one that has occurred, but part of a deliberate system to strip us step by step of our treaty rights ...' Once more the gun-boats moved into action.

The Second Anglo-Chinese War, 1856–60

British forces, aided by French units, silenced the guns of the Taku forts—Peking's first line of defence—and compelled the Chinese to sign the Treaty of Tientsin (1858). This gave the Europeans extra trading rights and actually legalized the opium trade. But because Emperor Hsien-feng refused to tolerate Western ambassadors in his capital the fighting continued. A Mongol prince named Sang-ko-lin-chin (British soldiers always called him Sam Collinson!) rebuilt the Taku forts and defied the Allies until 1860 when they managed to overwhelm the main Chinese defences.

The Convention of Peking, 1860

Chinese resistance soon came to an end. Throughout the conflict peasant revolts had distracted the main Imperial armies; the Emperor had already fled to Mongolia. Leisurely, the invaders first looted the Summer Palace and then set fire to it. Lord Elgin, Queen Victoria's special envoy to China, did not try to stop this—he thought it would hit the Emperor where it hurt the most. He entered the capital in triumph and there signed the Convention of Peking. China agreed to pay another indemnity and add Tientsin to the list of treaty ports. The Convention was supposed to place relationships between China and the West 'on a sound footing and insure the continuance of peace for a long time'. It opened up China to foreign trade and ended her long period of isolation.

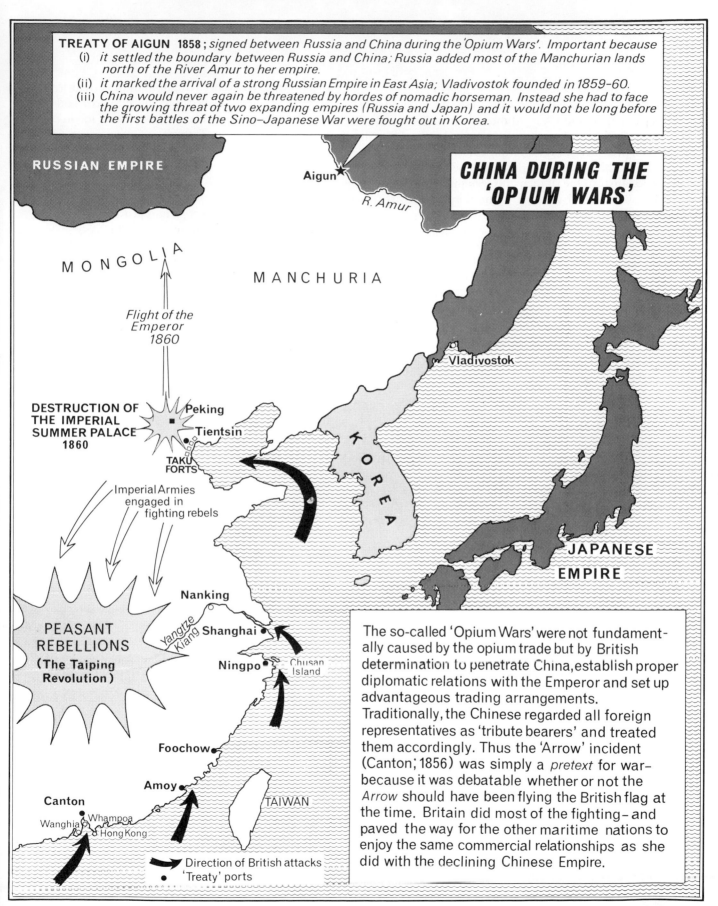

TREATY OF AIGUN 1858; *signed between Russia and China during the 'Opium Wars'. Important because*
  (i)   *it settled the boundary between Russia and China; Russia added most of the Manchurian lands north of the River Amur to her empire.*
  (ii) *it marked the arrival of a strong Russian Empire in East Asia; Vladivostok founded in 1859-60.*
  (iii) *China would never again be threatened by hordes of nomadic horseman. Instead she had to face the growing threat of two expanding empires (Russia and Japan) and it would not be long before the first battles of the Sino–Japanese War were fought out in Korea.*

RUSSIAN EMPIRE

Aigun

R. Amur

CHINA DURING THE 'OPIUM WARS'

M O N G O L I A

M A N C H U R I A

Flight of the Emperor 1860

Vladivostok

DESTRUCTION OF THE IMPERIAL SUMMER PALACE 1860

Peking

Tientsin

TAKU FORTS

Imperial Armies engaged in fighting rebels

KOREA

JAPANESE EMPIRE

Nanking

Yangtze Kiang

Shanghai

PEASANT REBELLIONS (The Taiping Revolution)

Ningpo

Chusan Island

Foochow

Amoy

TAIWAN

Canton

Wanghia   Whampoa
         Hong Kong

Direction of British attacks

'Treaty' ports

The so-called 'Opium Wars' were not fundamentally caused by the opium trade but by British determination to penetrate China, establish proper diplomatic relations with the Emperor and set up advantageous trading arrangements. Traditionally, the Chinese regarded all foreign representatives as 'tribute bearers' and treated them accordingly. Thus the 'Arrow' incident (Canton; 1856) was simply a *pretext* for war- because it was debatable whether or not the *Arrow* should have been flying the British flag at the time. Britain did most of the fighting- and paved the way for the other maritime nations to enjoy the same commercial relationships as she did with the declining Chinese Empire.

11 The Taiping Revolution, 1850–64

Hung Hsiu-chuan

Christianity was making a rather curious mark upon the internal history of China at the same time as the 'Opium Wars' were being fought out along her battered coastline. In the provinces of Kwangtung and Kwangsi there lived the Hakka people—warlike, independent and fiercely nationalistic. One of them, a schoolmaster named Hung Hsiu-chuan, had gleaned a smattering of Christianity from missionary pamphlets. He then had a severe illness and experienced hallucinations which left him convinced that he was a nineteenth-century version of Jesus Christ whose mission was to liberate China from the rule of the foreign Manchu dynasty. By 1847 Hung and his followers (known as the 'God-worshippers') controlled Kwangsi and had the beginnings of a revolutionary programme. Hung promised that all land would belong to the people, surplus crops would be stored for deficiency areas and women would have the same status as men.

The revolution begins

Armed resistance to the Manchu Emperor began in 1850 and in 1851 Hung announced the coming of the 'Heavenly Kingdom of the Great Peace'—the *Taiping Tien Kuo*, which gave the revolution its name. Hung attacked along the valley of the Yangtze and occupied Nanking in 1853, making it the capital of the *Taiping Kingdom*. Hung then despatched two armies to liberate the rest of China and by 1860 the 'God-worshippers' had brought a third of China under their control.

The generals

Taiping and Manchu leaders alike made use of Western experts during the later stages of the revolution. Best known is Charles 'Chinese' Gordon who fought for the Emperor. One Englishman who entered Hung's service was Augustus Lindley. Known to the Chinese as Lin-Le, he was only twenty when he began fighting Gordon's troops. He actually captured one of Gordon's paddle-steamers, renamed it the *Taiping* and commissioned it as the flagship of the revolutionary navy! The leading Taiping commander was General Li whose guerrilla warfare tactics have been much admired by modern Chinese leaders. The Emperor's outstanding general was Tseng Kuo-fan. As a senior mandarin back in 1852, Tseng had warned the Emperor of the dangerous condition of the Chinese peasantry—the serious shortage of agricultural land due to an exploding peasant population; the heavy taxes imposed irrespective of the size of harvest; the corrupt officials; the misery caused by famine and flood. Tseng was describing the underlying causes of the Taiping Revolution: the millions of peasants who fought and died for the 'Heavenly Kingdom of the Great Peace' did so because they believed that the Emperor had already lost the Mandate of Heaven. It was time for his dynasty to make way for the Taiping.

Defeat

By 1860 the chances of a Taiping victory seemed quite good. Anglo-French troops had just entered Peking, the Emperor had fled to Mongolia and the country seemed to be without effective government. However, the Taiping revolutionaries had not anticipated the reaction of the Western powers. The British were especially worried that the Taiping might capture all of the Treaty ports and, since trade was more important to them than anything else in China, they decided to give the Emperor just enough military aid to defeat the 'God-worshippers'. Gordon took control of a rabble of mercenaries—optimistically named the Ever-Victorious Army—and marched south to link forces with Tseng Kuo-fan. General Li held them up for two years but in 1863 Gordon managed to capture the key base of Soochow. His troops then besieged Nanking and the city surrendered in 1864. The revolution that had ravaged China for fourteen years was over. Twenty million Chinese had died in what has been described as 'probably the biggest civil war in history'.[*] Hung committed suicide; General Li was beheaded; 'Chinese' Gordon received the rank of Imperial Field Marshal; Lindley came home to England to write a book.[†]

The significance of the revolution

More than anything else, the Taiping revolution demonstrated the potential power of the Chinese peasantry. Given iron discipline on the part of everyone—from leader down to the humblest private soldier—the peasants could achieve anything. But they would have to be properly equipped and properly led by military experts if they were ever to bring down a dynasty that resorted to Western methods of attack. The fact that the Emperor himself had lost control of his armies during the revolution was irrelevant; it had simply meant that all power had passed to the Imperial generals and that Tseng Kuo-fan, capable and sympathetic though he was, emerges as the first of a long line of *Chinese* war-lords whose soldiers owed allegiance to them rather than to their Emperor.

[*]Keith Buchanan in his *The Transformation of the Chinese Earth* (Bell, 1970) p. 24.

[†]He called it *The History of the Taiping Revolution* and had it published in 1866. Nearly a hundred years later (in 1962) the Chinese published a new edition of it in Peking.

THE CLASH of IDEOLOGIES

CHINA DURING THE TAIPING REVOLUTION 1850—1864

The landowners and civil servants believed in the traditional Chinese values. They were strict Confucians, conservative and hostile to any radical change—though willing to consider reform where it seemed beneficial. Tseng Kuo-fan was typical of these men and he sought to educate his troops—most of whom he enlisted from within the rich province of Hunan—in Confucian beliefs. The soldiers saw that they were defending law and order and therefore fought for their new Emperor, Tung-chih, who ascended the imperial throne in 1862.

KOREA

●PEKING

NANKING

SOOCHOW

Yangtze Kiang

HUNAN

TAIWAN

KWANGTUNG

KWANGSI

THE TAIPING AND WOMEN'S LIBERATION

Traditional China regarded women as subordinate to men. The Taiping saw men and women as equal. They allowed women to enter civil service examinations and serve in the Taiping armies. The practice of *footbinding*–common in China for nearly a thousand years– was illegal.
However, the Taiping did require all women to marry– and the marriage ceremony was very similar to a church wedding in the Western world.

The Taiping creed was based on a Western, imported religion. All 'God-worshippers' had to demonstrate their hostility towards traditional Confucian beliefs and Manchu law:

(i) by accepting Hung as their leader appointed by God.

(ii) by wearing hair-styles of the pre-Manchu period i.e. they abandoned the shaven head and pigtail.
This was why Tseng Kuo-fan always told his troops they would be fighting a lot of "long-haired rebels"!

■ Extent of Taiping influence

12 The missionaries

The Jesuit mission to Peking, 1601–1773

Though they were by no means the first Christian missionaries to operate in China, the Jesuits—members of the Society of Jesus—were the first to make a lasting impression on the Chinese Emperors. They arrived in Peking under the leadership of Matteo Ricci, determined to convert the Son of Heaven and his courtiers to the Catholic faith. The Emperor had little respect for the Jesuits as priests but he did recognize their skills as architects, astronomers and mathematicians. Jesuit mapmakers produced terrestrial globes to demonstrate the sphericity of Planet Earth;* Jesuit architects drew the designs for the Summer Palace—destined to be looted and destroyed by European invaders at the end of the Opium Wars. The priests remained in Peking until 1773 when the Pope suppressed their Society. By then they had converted about 300,000 Chinese. But they failed to convert the scholars and when the Jesuits left China the Confucian beliefs that had dominated the Empire for centuries remained unchanged.

The Protestant missionaries

Between the signing of the Treaty of Nanking (1842) and the Convention of Peking (1860), British and American missionaries preached the Gospel and built their hospitals and schools within the confines of the growing number of treaty ports. When the Taiping Revolution began in 1850 many of these missionaries saw the hand of God at work and trusted that the revolution would herald the mass acceptance of Christianity in China. They sent home glowing reports and in 1853 the *British and Foreign Bible Society* was sufficiently impressed to print one million copies of a Chinese version of the New Testament. However, it was soon obvious that the Taiping view of Christianity was a freak development in Chinese history and the missionaries withdrew their support. Once the fighting was over, the more adventurous workers moved outside the treaty ports and, by the end of 1866, the newly-formed *China Inland Mission* had penetrated several provinces. Meanwhile, Scottish and Irish missionaries were pushing north into Manchuria. It seemed that Christianity was making a many-sided attack upon Confucian China.

The Tientsin Massacre, 1870

Various Catholic missions were active in the 1860s and one party of French priests made their way into Szechwan where they struck fear into village populations totally unprepared for their arrival. Christian teaching about life in the Bible lands meant nothing to peasants who practised ancestor-worship. The few who became converts ran the risk—if they accepted free food hand-outs from the missionaries—of being condemned as 'rice-Christians' by contemptuous neighbours. Some missionaries were blind to the Chinese point of view and their insensitivity provoked the 1870 Tientsin Massacre. French Sisters of Mercy working in the city took a special interest in the welfare of orphans. They built an orphanage but unwisely offered cash to Chinese who brought along an 'orphan' child in need of care. Local citizens became suspicious and regarded the foreign women as kidnappers in disguise. When they gathered outside the orphanage a frightened French consul opened fire—so they rushed the orphanage, killed ten nuns and several other foreigners. Inevitably, Western gun-boats steamed into Tientsin, thus ending the brief period of good relations between China and Europe.

The missionary failure

Undeterred by the massacre, missionary societies began to step up their efforts to convert the Chinese. They sent in women workers during the Shansi famine (1877–8) to comfort distraught mothers and educate fatherless children. Welfare work, however, did not appease the Chinese. In 1891 rioters destroyed an American Methodist school in Nanking; during 1895 widespread violence forced the missionaries out of Szechwan; and in May that year, near Kucheng in Fukien Province, nine missionaries and two of their children died in 'one of the worst missionary massacres of modern times'.† Clearly, the missionaries had not achieved their long-expected breakthrough. Even they were conscious of failure. Arnot Reid, who travelled through China during the 1890s, commented that it was only their abiding faith in God that saved them from complete mental breakdowns. China's population ran into hundreds of millions of people; but the annual rate of conversion numbered only a few hundred people. It was a drop in the ocean: 'measured by ordinary human probability, this work is wasted'.‡

*They seemed unaware that Chinese scholars had discussed this likelihood in 200 B.C. See *Chinese and Japanese Maps* (British Museum Publications Ltd., 1974).
†This was Marshall Broomhall's description in his *The Chinese Empire* (Morgan and Scott, 1907) p. 32.
‡From *Peking to Petersburg* by Arnot Reid (Arnold, 1899) p. 80.

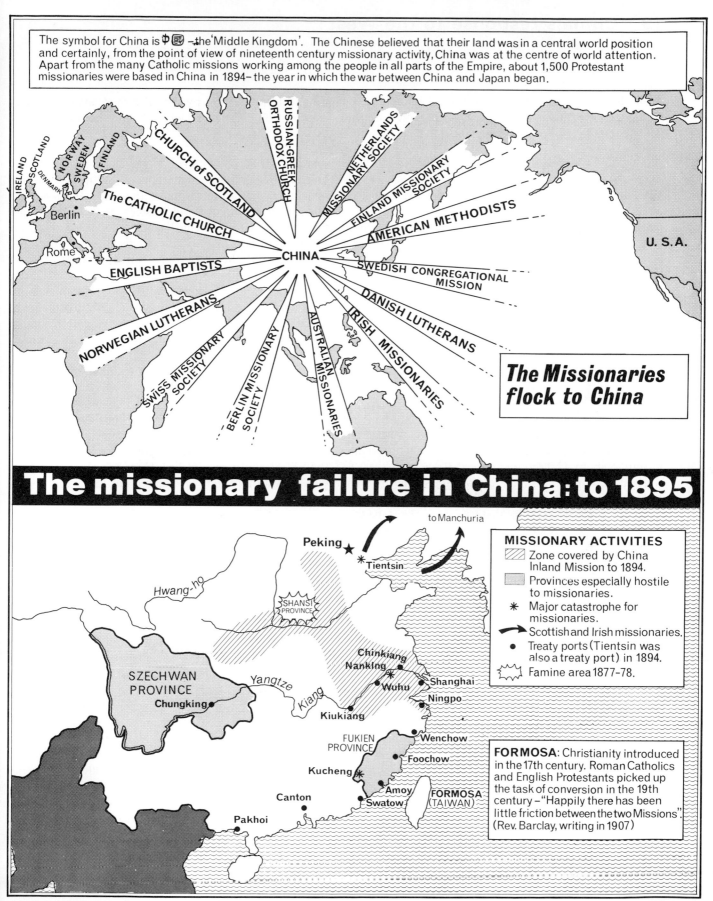

The symbol for China is 中国 – the 'Middle Kingdom'. The Chinese believed that their land was in a central world position and certainly, from the point of view of nineteenth century missionary activity, China was at the centre of world attention. Apart from the many Catholic missions working among the people in all parts of the Empire, about 1,500 Protestant missionaries were based in China in 1894 – the year in which the war between China and Japan began.

RUSSIAN-GREEK ORTHODOX CHURCH

CHURCH of SCOTLAND

NETHERLANDS MISSIONARY SOCIETY

FINLAND MISSIONARY SOCIETY

AMERICAN METHODISTS

The CATHOLIC CHURCH

Berlin

Rome

CHINA

U.S.A.

SWEDISH CONGREGATIONAL MISSION

ENGLISH BAPTISTS

DANISH LUTHERANS

NORWEGIAN LUTHERANS

SWISS MISSIONARY SOCIETY

BERLIN MISSIONARY SOCIETY

AUSTRALIAN MISSIONARY

IRISH MISSIONARIES

IRELAND SCOTLAND NORWAY SWEDEN DENMARK FINLAND

The Missionaries flock to China

The missionary failure in China: to 1895

to Manchuria

Peking ★

✳ Tientsin

Hwang-ho

SHANSI PROVINCE

Chinkiang

Nanking

Wuhu

Shanghai

Ningpo

SZECHWAN PROVINCE

Yangtze Kiang

Chungking

Kiukiang

Wenchow

FUKIEN PROVINCE

Foochow

Kucheng ✳

Amoy

Swatow

FORMOSA (TAIWAN)

Canton

Pakhoi

MISSIONARY ACTIVITIES

▨ Zone covered by China Inland Mission to 1894.

▧ Provinces especially hostile to missionaries.

✳ Major catastrophe for missionaries.

➤ Scottish and Irish missionaries.

• Treaty ports (Tientsin was also a treaty port) in 1894.

⚡ Famine area 1877–78.

FORMOSA: Christianity introduced in the 17th century. Roman Catholics and English Protestants picked up the task of conversion in the 19th century – "Happily there has been little friction between the two Missions". (Rev. Barclay, writing in 1907)

27

13 China's response to the West

After the end of the first 'Opium War' in 1842 some Chinese tried, in their different ways, to come to terms with the West. Very few succeeded.

The emigrants

Traditionally, the Emperors had always discouraged emigration, regarding it as an act of betrayal punishable by death. This had not deterred the millions of Chinese who had settled in South-East Asia—especially in the Malay States and the Dutch East Indies. It was during the second half of the nineteenth century that the attractions of Australia and America began to lure fresh waves of Chinese emigrants.

(a) *Australia:* After convict labour ended in New South Wales (1840) local employers began hiring unskilled labour in the newly established treaty ports. By 1850 they were shipping coolies from Amoy and Hong Kong at the rate of 3,000 a year. Unfortunately for the employers, the arrival of the Chinese coincided with the gold-strikes in Victoria. Most of the coolies deserted their masters and headed straight for the diggings. By 1860 the Australians were anxious about the size of their Chinese community—about 42,000—and passed *Restriction Laws* to prevent further entry. In fact most Chinese did not want to stay in Australia; but while they were there they had to suffer unnecessary humiliation. Australians neither liked nor understood their extraordinary capacity for hard work, their independence and their general tight-fistedness. There were race riots in some mining communities and the widespread feeling against Asians persuaded the state governments to adopt a policy of 'Keep Australia White'.

(b) *The United States:* the Chinese were even worse off when they arrived in 'the land of the free'. Gold strikes in California (1848–9) enticed thousands to America—and they kept coming long after the gold rush was over. Most took jobs on the new Pacific railroad projects and when these ended in 1869 they congregated in *chinatowns* in various parts of the U.S.A. and the Caribbean. Race riots were common. In 1890 a thousand white men burnt down Los Angeles' Chinatown and killed twenty-five Chinese. Discrimination went on even in the rural areas and all Chinese suffered from the American fear that the Asians would eventually take over the U.S.A. There was talk of the *Yellow Peril*: it was the duty of all Americans, according to some newspapers, 'to aid in the good work of ridding the States of the Chinese now here, and of preventing any more from coming'.* Already, in 1882, the Americans had passed strict immigration laws to control the Asian influx—but by then they had acquired a substantial Chinese element in their multinational society.

The Self-Strengthening Movement

Other Chinese believed that the Empire should strengthen itself from within by the study and adoption of western knowledge and western methods of manufacture. The scholar Feng Kuei-fen (1804–74) urged the Emperor to set up translation schools in Canton and Shanghai and the government did indeed establish a school of languages and science in Shanghai. Feng wanted to do much more than this—China must learn the secret of western strength so she could control the barbarians. China must build arsenals and shipyards in all the treaty ports. For the time being, of course, she must buy her 'solid ships and effective guns' abroad. After industrialization she would be able to make them herself. To emphasize his point Feng drew attention to Japan—'a little country', he called her, 'yet she knows how to exert her energy to become strong'. So China's best students went off to study in Japan, Britain and the U.S.A. and for a time it seemed that the government had adopted the Self-Strengthening policy. However, the mood soon passed and there were few lasting results.

The failure to modernize

For example, work began on a rail link between Shanghai and Woosung† in 1875—China's first railway. The local peasants insisted that the steel road was disturbing the *fen shui*—spirits that lived in earth and water—so they tore up the track, chopped down the telegraph poles and forced the line to close in 1877. Consequently, there was no true railway development in China until the very end of the century. Other western-inspired efforts to build modern textile factories came to nothing because the Chinese workers smashed the spinning and weaving machines at every opportunity. Nevertheless, despite hostility and a great deal of financial corruption in high places, the government did manage to allocate some money to buy guns and warships. By 1894 China had the nucleus of a respectable navy which included two battleships, some armoured cruisers and a few torpedo boats. She also hired the services of Captain W. M. Lang, R.N., to teach Chinese sailors the secrets of modern gunnery and naval tactics.

*Quoted on p. 63 of Richard Van Alstyne's *The United States and East Asia* (Thames and Hudson, 1973).
†Woosung is a mile or two north of Shanghai.

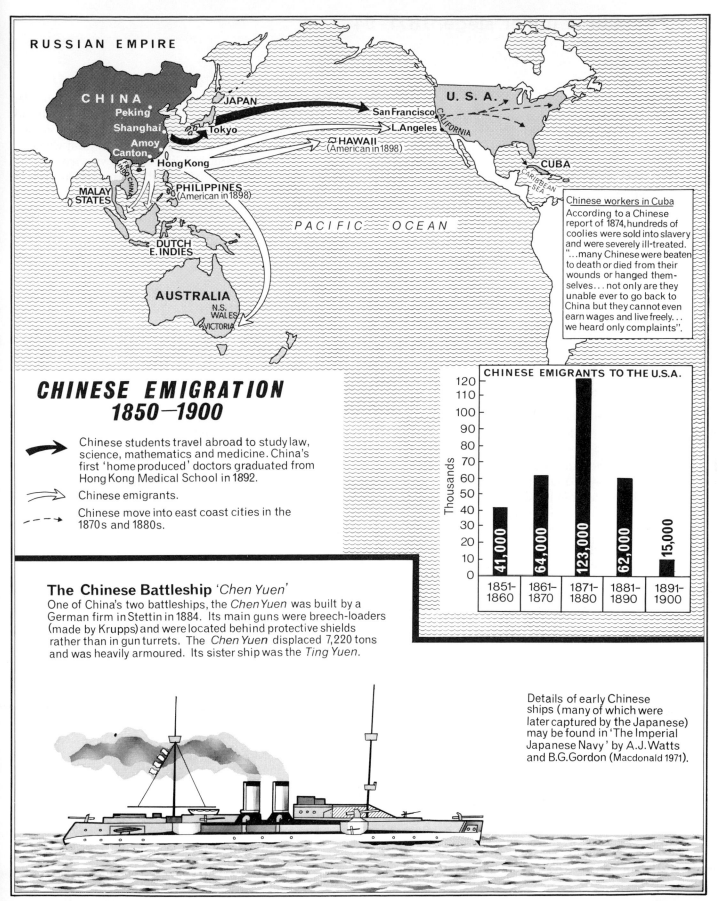

RUSSIAN EMPIRE

CHINA
Peking
Shanghai
Amoy
Canton
Hong Kong

JAPAN
Tokyo

MALAY STATES

PHILIPPINES
(American in 1898)

DUTCH E. INDIES

AUSTRALIA
N.S. WALES
VICTORIA

PACIFIC OCEAN

HAWAII
(American in 1898)

San Francisco
L. Angeles
CALIFORNIA

U.S.A.

CUBA
CARIBBEAN SEA

Chinese workers in Cuba
According to a Chinese report of 1874, hundreds of coolies were sold into slavery and were severely ill-treated. "...many Chinese were beaten to death or died from their wounds or hanged themselves... not only are they unable ever to go back to China but they cannot even earn wages and live freely... we heard only complaints".

CHINESE EMIGRATION 1850–1900

➜ Chinese students travel abroad to study law, science, mathematics and medicine. China's first 'home produced' doctors graduated from Hong Kong Medical School in 1892.

⇨ Chinese emigrants.

⇢ Chinese move into east coast cities in the 1870s and 1880s.

CHINESE EMIGRANTS TO THE U.S.A.

Period	Thousands
1851–1860	41,000
1861–1870	64,000
1871–1880	123,000
1881–1890	62,000
1891–1900	15,000

The Chinese Battleship 'Chen Yuen'

One of China's two battleships, the *Chen Yuen* was built by a German firm in Stettin in 1884. Its main guns were breech-loaders (made by Krupps) and were located behind protective shields rather than in gun turrets. The *Chen Yuen* displaced 7,220 tons and was heavily armoured. Its sister ship was the *Ting Yuen*.

Details of early Chinese ships (many of which were later captured by the Japanese) may be found in 'The Imperial Japanese Navy' by A.J. Watts and B.G. Gordon (Macdonald 1971).

14 China under siege, 1871–94

Warning signs ignored

The weakness of the Self-Strengthening Movement was that it failed to communicate to the mass of the people any sense of urgency. They did not seem to comprehend the fact that the land was besieged by predatory nations who, if they were not allowed to develop trade with the inland provinces, were quite capable of thrusting themselves and their armies upon the Chinese people. They were already carving up Africa and it might not be long before they partitioned China into a collection of foreign spheres of influence. But the Empress Dowager Tzu-Hsi seemed to have no inkling of the danger. Since 1861 she had been the effective ruler of the Empire but as she had no knowledge of the outside world she relied upon her war-lord adviser, Li Hung-chang, for news of events taking place on the imperial frontiers. There was no shortage of news. Most of China's traditional tributary states were in the process of being occupied by 'foreign devils'!

Viet Nam: lost to France, 1885

One of these tributary states was Viet Nam. For years the French had been systematically occupying Cochin-China and now they were hoping to open up a trade route between Saigon and the Chinese province of Yunnan. Viet Nam stood in the way. Ever since 1865 it had been the base for marauding 'Black Flags'—survivors from the Taiping armies—and twice, in 1873 and in 1882, the French had clashed with these renegades. When Li Hung-chang told the Empress Dowager of these events she ordered Chinese troops into Viet Nam and they were soon in action against the French. But the fighting developed into a conflict that the Empress Dowager could not afford. The French attacked on all sides—along the Yangtze, in the Pescadores and in Taiwan. French ships destroyed the newly-built Foochow naval squadron and then, to the horror of the Empress Dowager, blockaded the canal routes so that the annual convoy of tribute boats could not get through to Peking. She managed to save face when Chinese troops in North Viet Nam won an unexpected victory at Lang-son and the French readily agreed (by the 1885 Treaty of Tientsin) to evacuate Taiwan and the Pescadores. In return, Li Hung-chang had to sacrifice Viet Nam and watch it become an unwilling part of the French colonial empire.

Burma: lost to Britain, 1886

Meanwhile, the British were also trying to build a trade route into Yunnan via Bhamo in Upper Burma. Though China claimed it as a tributary state, the British needed it to make their dream of a Shanghai–Bhamo rail link come true. A survey team set off from Bhamo in 1875 under the command of a Captain Margery but when the local Chinese tribesmen heard that he was scouting for a railway they ambushed and killed him in 1876. Though this dampened their ardour for a rail link with China it did not deflect the British from their intention to acquire Burma. Despite constant raids from Chinese irregular troops over the next ten years, the British formally annexed Upper Burma in 1886.

Russia moves into Manchuria

Russia's main interest was to win an ice-free port with access to the Pacific and the China Seas. Tsar Alexander II (1855–81) believed that the first task was to build road and rail links with Vladivostok, opened as a *partially* ice-free port in 1861. A chance to improve Russia's influence in the Far East came in the 1870s. For years the Russians had endured chaos along the frontier with Sinkiang province. Trade had fallen off and Chinese guerrillas were constantly galloping across the border to raid Russian settlements. By 1871 the Russians had had enough. They marched up the Ili valley and sorted out the troublemakers on Chinese soil. They stayed in the Ili region for ten years and to get rid of them the Chinese had to concede navigation rights on Manchuria's river systems. With this to encourage them the Russians built new roads and in 1891 made a start on the Trans-Siberian Railway. It meant that from now on China would have to contend with Russian pressure along the entire northern frontier.

Outbreak of war with Japan, 1894

Between 1875 and 1880 Japan forced her way into two more of China's tributary states. The first was Korea, compelled to sign a trade treaty with Japan in 1876; the second was the string of islands called the Ryukyus, annexed by Japan in 1880. China therefore had good reason to dislike the Japanese and there was a risk of war in 1882 when Korean rioters burnt down the Japanese legation in Seoul. Both sides sent troops to Korea and then agreed to withdraw them with the promise that they would not return unless there was more lawlessness in the peninsula. Japanese secret agents deliberately arranged for this to happen in 1894. China sent 2,500 soldiers to Asan; simultaneously, a Japanese invasion force of 8,000 troops steamed into Chemulpo harbour. By 1 August 1894 both sides were formally at war.

THE EROSION OF CHINA'S FRONTIER SYSTEM BY FOUR POWERFUL NATIONS

① Imperial Russia
② Britain
③ France
④ Imperial Japan

① IMPERIAL RUSSIA

MANCHURIA

R. Amur

MONGOLIA

Lake Balkhash

R. Ili

Liao Ho

Vladivostok

④ IMPERIAL JAPAN

KOREA
C
Seoul
Asan

SINKIANG

Peking ★
Tientsin

C H I N A

RYUKYUS

Shanghai

T I B E T

KIANG
YANGTZE

Foochow

② BRITAIN—from India and Bengal

Battle of Lang-son 1885

P
TAIWAN

YUNNAN

Bhamo

Calcutta

UPPER BURMA

INDIA

VIET NAM

Saigon

COCHIN CHINA

③ FRANCE—from Cochin-China

C = Chemulpo
P = Pescadores
Ili region occupied by Russia 1871–81
Tributary state

31

15 The Sino–Japanese War, 1894–5, and the degradation of China

The Battle of the Yalu River, 1894

Chinese and Japanese ships had already clashed in the Yellow Sea six days before the official declaration of war. Three light cruisers of the Imperial Japanese Navy intercepted and seriously damaged the *Tsi-Yuen* returning from Korea on 25 July. And on the same day they sank the troopship *Kowshing* carrying 12,000 Chinese soldiers. These preliminary actions high-lighted China's biggest problem in fighting a war in Korea. As the roads connecting the two countries were in an abominable condition China would have to win command of the sea if she hoped to reinforce her fighting men in Korea. So, when the next big convoy left Port Arthur in August it had as its escort Admiral Ting's fleet of two battleships and eight cruisers. They all made port safely but as Ting set course for home he ran into the main Japanese battle fleet on patrol at the mouth of the Yalu River. In the fight that followed the Japanese sank or disabled six of Ting's warships. Li Hung-chang was appalled when he heard the news. He had always supported the Self-Strengthening Movement and was the leading advocate of naval strength—against the expressed wish of the Empress Dowager who would much rather spend her subjects' taxes on restoring the Summer Palace than on buying warships in Europe. But in its very first battle the fleet had failed to stop the enemy. China hadn't a chance of winning the war now.

Defeat

Her army in Korea was well equipped and reasonably well trained; it included some of Li Hung-chang's personal regiments. But it was far too small to stop the Japanese invaders and by the end of September it had retreated beyond the Yalu, thus allowing the Japanese to enter Manchuria. But while this was happening, another Japanese task force sent units ashore behind Port Arthur and on the Shantung peninsula. Once Port Arthur was captured the Japanese were in a position to launch a pincer attack upon Peking—by which time the Empress Dowager appreciated the gravity of the situation. She ordered Li Hung-chang to sue for peace and the Japanese agreed to hold talks. At first the Empress Dowager refused to let Li leave for Japan as she held him responsible for China's defeat. But the Japanese insisted that a man of his stature must represent China at Shimonoseki and Li eventually signed the peace treaty there in April 1895.

The Treaty of Shimonoseki, 1895

China had to recognize that Korea was no longer a tributary state but an independent kingdom. Moreover, she had to cede to Japan the island of Taiwan, the Pescadores and the Liao-tung peninsula. This last clause infuriated Tsar Nicholas II because at the tip of the peninsula was the one place he prized above anything else—the ice-free harbour of Port Arthur. He quickly canvassed support from France and Germany and then pointedly advised the Japanese to withdraw from Liao-tung. Resentfully, the Japanese complied. Of course, this delighted the Chinese who saw Russia as their new-found friend. In fact, in 1896 Li Hung-chang visited Moscow for the Tsar's coronation and signed the secret Sino–Russian Treaty which gave the Russians the right to build a railway across Heilungkiang and Kirin as far as Vladivostok.

China's degradation

Grateful though she was for the so-called 'Triple Intervention' by Russia, Germany and France, China was certainly not expecting the flood of requests for land concessions, mining rights and trade facilities that came pouring out of these and other European countries after 1895. For example, the Germans used the murder of two missionaries in Shantung (1897) as an excuse for commandeering the Kiaochow territories; Russia took Port Arthur in 1898; France claimed Kwangsi as a French sphere of influence; Britain wanted control of the Yangtze and the *New Territories* north of Hong Kong. These seemingly unending encroachments by foreigners plus the recent defeat by Japan rankled in the minds of many Chinese and had a certain unifying effect upon the people. Not all Chinese believed in supporting the Ch'ing Dynasty against the foreigners. Some could say, as the professional revolutionary Sun Yat-sen* did say, 'From 1885, that is from the time of our defeat in the war with France, I set before myself the object of the overthrow of the Ch'ing Dynasty and the establishment of a Chinese Republic on its ruins.' But the time was not ripe and his first attempt at revolution (in Canton 1895) ended with the arrest and execution of most of his friends. Most Chinese simply wanted to drive the foreigners away and tended to support a secret anti-foreigner society called the League of Harmonious Fists—the Boxers.

*Son of a Chinese peasant; educated in the West and a qualified doctor.

CHINA DURING THE LAST YEARS OF THE NINETEENTH CENTURY

RUSSIA

HEILUNGKIANG

MANCHURIA

MONGOLIA

•Kirin

Vladivostok

SEA OF JAPAN

Tokyo□

Yalu R.

LIAO-TUNG

1894

KOREA

•Seoul

JAPAN

Port Arthur

Peking•

Wei-hai-wei

SHANTUNG

YELLOW SEA

Shimonoseki

Kiaochow

Hwang-Ho

CHINA

Nanking
1899

Soochow 1896

Hangchow
1896

Yangtze Kiang

Santuaho 1899

to JAPAN 1895

"The Sino-Japanese War of 1894–5... was the turning point of the whole history of the Far East; Japan, as a result of victory, emerged as the master of the East; China, the victim of the war, suffered the agony of being brought to the brink of partition by the Western Powers."   Frederick Foo Chien in 'The Opening of Korea' (Shoe String Press 1967 p.3)

TAIWAN

PESCADORES

KWANGSI
PROVINCE

Canton
Scene of Sun Yat-sen's abortive revolutionary attempt in 1895

Hong Kong

'NEW TERRITORIES'

FRENCH
INDO-
CHINA

Kwangchow-wan

→ Japanese attacks 1894–5.
⇢ Threatened pincer movement, 1895.
--→ Proposed Russian railway development.
Battle of the Yalu River 1894.
Leased Territories after 1898:
1. **Port Arthur** (Russia)
2. **Wei-hai-wei** (Britain)
3. **Kiaochow** (Germany)
4. **'New Territories'** (Britain)
5. **Kwangchow-wan** (France)
☆ Important treaty ports opened 1895–99.

33

16 The Boxer Uprising, 1900

The cause of the trouble

During the 1890s the Boxers were openly displaying banners calling on people to join the 'patriotic militia' dedicated to the destruction of all foreigners—who, of course, included the ruling Manchu dynasty. The Boxers were anti-Christian and had the curious notion that they were invulnerable to bullets. They had no time for anyone who tried to come to terms with the foreign devils and were totally unimpressed by the *Hundred Days of Reform* carried out in 1898 by Emperor Kuang-Hsu, especially after his fearsome aunt, the Empress Dowager, clapped him in jail for his impudence. Nor were they convinced by the *Open Door* policy suggested by America in 1899 in order to open all parts of the country to free trade and thus reduce the tendency to partition China into spheres of influence. Plenty of Chinese were ready to support the Boxers for there was currently a great deal of social distress due to flooding on the Hwang-ho. Even the Empress Dowager gave them her blessing in the hope that the Boxers would stop the foreign take-over of China. By 1900 the new motto of the Boxers was 'Support the Ch'ing and eliminate the foreigners'.

The siege of the legations, 1900

Nestling inside the great Tartar Wall in Peking were the buildings that housed the eleven foreign legations. Rumours were already flying around that the Boxers had begun their rebellion in Shantung and were tearing up the newly built railway lines outside the capital. On 17 June 1900 the Boxers entered the capital. Three days later they had killed the German ambassador, Baron von Ketteler, and set siege to the legations. At night time the more fanatical Boxers made their sorties across 'no man's land': one was 'a mere boy of fifteen who had stripped naked and smeared himself all over with oil after the manner of Chinese thieves ... armed only with matches and a stone bottle of kerosene with which he purposed to set buildings on fire'.* Another had 'a long red tunic edged with blue ... his head tied up in the regulation *bonnet rouge*. Round his waist he also girded on a blue cartridge belt of cloth, with great thick Martini bullets jammed into the thumb holes.'† But the Boxers failed to capture the legations and soon crowds of Chinese soldiers and Manchu *bannermen* arrived to take their place. Even the hard-pressed defenders admired the spectacle: 'There were jackets and tunics of every colour, trouserings of blood red embroidered with black dragons; great two-handed swords in some hands, men armed with bows and arrows mixing with Kansu horsemen who had modern carbines slung across their backs. There were blue banners, yellow banners embroidered with black, white and red flags, both triangular and square ... but of the Boxers there was not a sign.'‡

The relief

Despite their continuous attacks, the Chinese troops seemed reluctant to mount a full-scale assault and after fifty-five days of siege warfare an international relief force commanded by the German General von Waldersee entered the Imperial capital. There had been surprisingly few casualties among the Europeans although in the countryside 200 missionaries and 3,000 converts died at the hands of the Boxers. Now it was the turn of the Empress Dowager to feel afraid and on 15 August 1900 she escaped from the Forbidden City in a cart and took refuge in Sian. The Imperial Palace lay empty—an open invitation to the foreign looters.

China's punishment: the International Protocol, 1901

The siege of the legations had caught the imagination of the Western world and it was not long before Boxer charms were on sale and newspapers and magazines ran bloodthirsty accounts of Boxer atrocities. There was not a shred of sympathy for China when the Western powers imposed the International Protocol on the country in 1901. Once more Li Hung-chang had to preside over China's humiliation, expressing formal regret for the murder of the German minister. He agreed that China should pay an indemnity of 450 million taels (1 tael was equal to £0.15 in 1901) and promised that any Chinese who joined an anti-foreign society would be executed.

China's surrender

China was now firmly in the hands of the foreign capitalists—banks, shipping firms, mining, insurance and railway companies. Permanently in debt (only America waived her share of the indemnity), China could no longer oppose the flood of missionaries and merchants who poured through scores of treaty ports into the interior. Western gun-boats patrolled the rivers, western soldiers guarded civilian settlements. And in the midst of everything the Empress Dowager bounced back into power and resumed residence in Peking. Clearly, anyone who wanted to help China now must first overthrow the dynasty she represented.

*B. L. Putnam Weale, *Indiscreet Letters from Peking* (Hurst and Blackett, 1907) p. 163.
†ibid., p. 81.
‡ibid., p. 110.

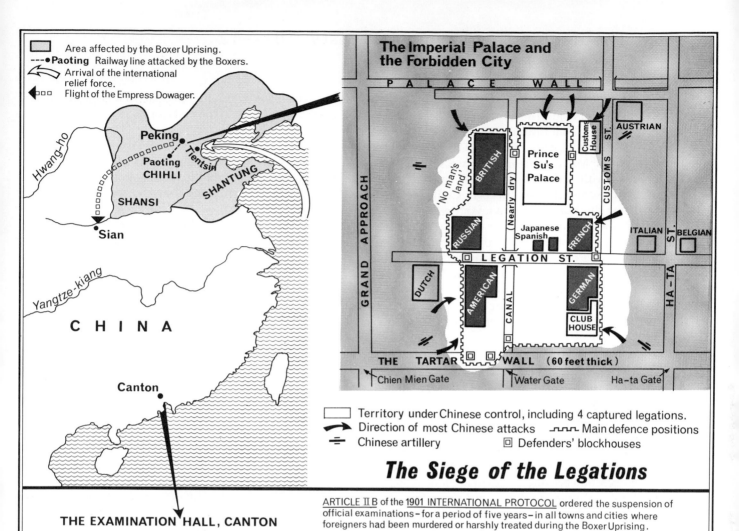

Area affected by the Boxer Uprising.

- - - •Paoting Railway line attacked by the Boxers.

Arrival of the international relief force.

Flight of the Empress Dowager.

Hwang-ho

Peking

Tientsin

Paoting
CHIHLI

SHANSI

SHANTUNG

Sian

Yangtze-kiang

C H I N A

Canton

The Imperial Palace and the Forbidden City

P A L A C E   W A L L

'No man's land'

BRITISH

Prince Su's Palace

Customs House

AUSTRIAN

GRAND APPROACH

(Nearly dry)

RUSSIAN

Japanese Spanish

FRENCH

ITALIAN ST.

BELGIAN

CUSTOMS ST.

LEGATION ST.

DUTCH

AMERICAN

CANAL

GERMAN

CLUB HOUSE

HA-TA

THE   TARTAR   WALL   (60 feet thick)

Chien Mien Gate | Water Gate | Ha-ta Gate

☐ Territory under Chinese control, including 4 captured legations.

Direction of most Chinese attacks   ⌐⌐⌐ Main defence positions

Chinese artillery   ☐ Defenders' blockhouses

The Siege of the Legations

ARTICLE II B of the 1901 INTERNATIONAL PROTOCOL ordered the suspension of official examinations – for a period of five years – in all towns and cities where foreigners had been murdered or harshly treated during the Boxer Uprising.

THE EXAMINATION HALL, CANTON

Hundreds of candidates were sealed into these little cells for examinations which lasted several days !

This salesman would sell to anxious relatives the 'ROLL OF HONOUR' – copies of the examination results.

17 The end of the Manchu Dynasty, 1911–12

Belated reforms

In a frantic effort to hold her empire together the Empress Dowager displayed a radical change of heart. She entertained Western diplomats; promised to outlaw footbinding; permitted Manchus to marry Chinese; and in a massive break with the past abolished the examinations which had supplied the Imperial Civil Service with officials for the last 2,000 years. And when Japan beat Russia in the War of 1904–5 she ordered Yuan Shih-kai to supervise the modernization of the army and sent her most promising officers* to be trained by the Japanese. But time was running out of 'Old Buddha'—her nickname in Northern China—and she died in 1908, as did her nephew the Emperor Kuang-Hsu. His successor was two-year-old Pi-yu whose father, Prince Chun, became Regent.

Sun Yat-sen, prophet of revolution

Born into a peasant family in 1866, Sun Yat-sen had the good fortune to have a brother who lived in Hawaii. When he was twelve, Sun joined his brother, went to a mission school and became a Christian. He returned to China to find that his parents had used match-makers to find him a peasant girl as a bride. Married before he was eighteen, Sun became a student at Hong Kong Medical School and graduated as a doctor in 1892. But his heart was in politics, not medicine. In 1895 he tried his hand at revolution. It was a fiasco and he was soon on the run from the Chinese secret service. He spent most of the next sixteen years in exile, travelling the world, preaching revolution and persuading expatriate Chinese businessmen to contribute cash to the revolutionary cause. Secret society members, bandits and students returning from abroad bore the brunt of revolutionary activities in China and it was to co-ordinate their work that Sun founded the *Tung Meng Hui* (Revolutionary Alliance Party) while he was living in Japan. It frequently tried to mount revolutions between 1905–10 but never succeeded. Sun promised the fruits of revolution with his *Three Principles of the People* and his *Five Power Constitution* but it seemed that he had no idea of how to start the revolution in the first instance.

The revolt begins, 10 October 1911

Between 1908 and 1911 the Manchus encouraged European firms to build China's new railways—a policy which infuriated the population of Szechwan. Prodded into action by the Revolutionary Alliance, the peasants rose in revolt. This gave the city-based conspirators their chance—and then in the midst of eager preparations one of their bomb factories exploded in Hankow (9 October 1911). In rushed the police, who discovered a list of revolutionaries which included the names of local militiamen. Rather than risk decapitation, the soldiers mutinied† and to their amazement found they had won control of the entire conurbation of Wuhan. Backed by the peasants in the countryside, the Revolutionary Alliance seized power in the provinces of Central and Southern China. And when the Manchus summoned Yuan Shih-kai and the army to restore law and order the wily old general stayed in the Peking area and began negotiations with the rebels.

The creation of the Chinese Republic, 1912

Sun Yat-sen was in America when all this was happening. He received a coded telegram giving him all the news but as he had sent on to Denver his trunk containing the codebook he could not read the telegram for a fortnight! He made a leisurely return trip to China and arrived in Shanghai on Christmas Eve 1911. The revolutionaries had patched up a truce with Yuan Shih-kai; now they elected Sun as Provisional President. On 1 January 1912 he proclaimed the creation of the Chinese Republic. He held office for six weeks, stepping down in favour of Yuan Shih-kai when the Manchus named him as their successor at the time of the Emperor's abdication (13 February 1912). Sun Yat-sen withdrew from politics (Yuan made him, ironically, Director of Railways) and the new President set about the destruction of the young Republic so that he could found, in true Chinese tradition, a brand new dynasty.

*One of these was Chiang Kai-shek.   †The next day, 10 October.

Immaculately attired, wearing 'butterfly' hair styles, the matchmakers display their two trade-marks: big umbrellas and tiny feet. All Chinese took them most seriously.

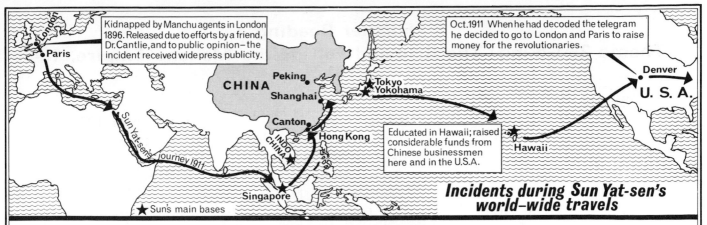

Kidnapped by Manchu agents in London 1896. Released due to efforts by a friend, Dr. Cantlie, and to public opinion — the incident received wide press publicity.

Oct. 1911 When he had decoded the telegram he decided to go to London and Paris to raise money for the revolutionaries.

Educated in Hawaii; raised considerable funds from Chinese businessmen here and in the U.S.A.

★ Sun's main bases

Incidents during Sun Yat-sen's world-wide travels

SUN YAT-SEN'S POLITICAL IDEAS

The three principles of the people
1. Principle of nationalism i.e. freedom.
2. Principle of people's rights i.e. democracy.
3. Principle of 'the people's livelihood' —
   a vague idea which he later interpreted as involving the 'equalization of land rights' i.e. a form of socialism.

The five power constitution
1. EXECUTIVE i.e. a President.
2. LEGISLATIVE i.e. a Congress or Parliament.
3. JUDICIARY i.e. a Supreme Court.
4. EXAMINATION SYSTEM: traditional Chinese idea — a career in the civil service would be open to all who passed the examination.
5. CENSORIAL SYSTEM: officials would be employed to investigate and expose government corruption.

Sun Yat-sen envisaged three post-revolutionary stages:
1. A period of military rule, lasting about 3 years.
2. Then elections would be held to create a provisional, representative government. This would govern for 3 years.
3. After 6 years CONSTITUTIONAL GOVERNMENT would begin.

SINKIANG (still remote from mainstream of Chinese politics. Its name means "new frontier".)

OUTER MONGOLIA (declared itself independent of China, 1912.)

Russian penetration 1900-1905

MANCHURIA

Japanese penetration 1905-11 (Japan annexed Korea in 1910)

TIBET (declared itself independent of China 1912.)

☆ Conurbation of Wuhan comprising cities of Hankow, Hanyang and Wuchang, in Hupeh Province.
■■▶ Early forays into China by revolutionaries.
– –▶ Yuan Shih-kai's troops.
■ Under Japanese control/influence
▨ Provinces supporting the revolution.
⁂ Main area of fighting, 1911.

THE 1911 REVOLUTION
(Called the "Double Tenth" as it began on the tenth day of the tenth month.)

Further Reading
Theme 2—Ch'ing: The Rise and Fall of the Manchu Empire, 1644–1912

Spread

8.	F. C. Jones	*China: Part I*	Arrowsmith, 1937
	J. Spence	*Emperor of China: Self-portrait of K'ang-hsi*	Cape, 1975
9.	Charles Meyer and Ian Allen	*Source Materials in Chinese History* (Unit 1)	Warne and Co., 1970
10.	Edgar Holt	*The Opium Wars in China*	Putnam, 1964
11.	Jean Chesnaux	*Peasant Revolts in China 1840–1949*	Thames and Hudson, 1973
	Jen Yu-wen	*The Taiping Revolutionary Movement*	Yale University Press, 1973
12.	C. R. Boxer	*Jesuits at the Court of Peking 1601–1775*	*History Today*, pp. 580–89, 1957
13.	Van Alstyne	*The United States and East Asia*	Thames and Hudson, 1973
	Griffith Taylor	*Australia*	Methuen, 1968
	Meyer and Allen	*Source Materials in Chinese History* (Unit 3)	Warne and Co., 1969
14.	Michael Edwardes	*The West in Asia*	Batsford, 1967
15.	Donald Macintyre	*Sea Power in the Pacific*	Arthur Barker Ltd., 1972
16.	Victor Purcell	*The Boxer Uprising*	Cambridge University Press, 1963
17.	Robert Bruce	*Sun Yat-sen*	Oxford University Press, 1969

Street scenes: the barber and the collector of human hair.

THEME 3

Nationalist China

Nationalist China was a far from happy land and it soon fell victim to war-lord rule and to fresh demands from the Japanese invader. In the hope that they might promote the cause of democracy in their own country by joining the Allies in the First World War, the Chinese declared war on Germany. But when peace came the old 'concessions' remained in force and China had gained precisely nothing. There was protest from the newly-formed Chinese Communist Party, and Sun Yat-sen took immediate steps to revitalize the ailing Kuomintang. But he died in 1925, to be succeeded by Chiang Kai-shek who for the next fifty years conducted a personal crusade against Communism. Perhaps it is true, as some have said, that in Chiang Kai-shek's China between 1928 and 1937 'a new nation was coming into being and attracting towards itself the loyalty of most Chinese people'*; perhaps it is true that Chiang's China might have developed into Asia's first Western-style democracy; and perhaps it is true that it was the Japanese invasions of 1931 and 1937 that really destroyed Nationalist China.

But it is certain that Chiang's constant harrying of his Communist opponents created an implacable foe which eventually won the struggle for the 'hearts and minds of the people'. Of course, Chiang was never under any illusions about the power of the Communists—their tenacity and single-mindedness were obvious to all during the 1935 Long March. And as he put it himself: 'The Japanese are a disease of the skin; the Communists are a disease of the heart.' So everything had to be subordinated to the anti-Communist struggle. Perhaps it is in Chiang Kai-shek's own order of priorities that the real cause of the destruction of Nationalist China may be found.

*Henry McAleavy in his review of Emily Hahn's *China Only Yesterday* (*History Today*, December 1963, pp. 878–9).

18   China under the war-lords

The unhappy Republic

The upheavals of 1911–12 had left the Chinese people with few tangible benefits. They had merely exchanged their Manchu rulers for President Yuan Shih-kai, a crafty and ambitious war-lord who did not bother to conceal his intention of becoming Emperor. A brand new Western-style parliament had assembled in Peking, but Yuan had hamstrung its powers by banning Sun Yat-sen's revolutionary party—now named the *Kuomintang*. Any Kuomintang member who dared oppose the President ran the risk of assassination by Yuan's secret agents. It was not long before Sun Yat-sen fled to Japan* where he began planning yet another revolution against those who ruled in Peking.

The threat from Japan

Now it was Japan's turn to take advantage of the young Republic. With the European powers embroiled in the First World War, Japan saw that the time was ripe to win a foothold on the Chinese mainland. On 27 August 1914 she declared war on Germany, promising to help the Chinese by attacking the Germans living in their concession at Kiaochow. Japanese troops landed in the Shantung Peninsula during September and soon captured the German naval base at Tsingtao. But once the fighting was over the Japanese showed no inclination to leave China; they wanted to hold on to the peninsula, together with its newly constructed railway system. In January 1915 they made their position crystal clear by presenting President Yuan with their *Twenty-One Demands*. Not only did the Japanese wish to take over existing German rights in Shantung, but they also proposed to convert their own industrial and commercial interests in Southern Manchuria into outright economic control of the region.

The rebellion against Yuan, 1915–16

Yuan felt that he was in no position to defy the aggressive Japanese and he agreed to many of the Twenty-One Demands. In fact he was far more interested in his immediate self-advancement and by December 1915 he was confident enough to announce that he would ascend the Imperial Throne in the New Year. This was the last straw: his meek acceptance of many of the Twenty-One Demands had enraged the people; they were certainly not going to let Yuan put the clock back by restoring the Imperial system. Yunnan province was the first to rebel; Kwangsi, Kwangtung and Kweichow followed suit. After

some indecisive fighting in central China, Szechwan and Hunan rose in revolt. Yuan retreated to Peking, where he died of a heart attack on 6 June 1916.

The war-lords take over

Yuan's death meant that effective power now fell into the hands of hundreds of war-lords. Some were rich and powerful; some were petty tyrants. They levied taxes with great enthusiasm, raised private armies, made war against their rivals and negotiated their own treaties. Some toyed with the idea of becoming Emperor; others wanted to restore the Manchus—and one actually managed to put Pu-yi (who had abdicated in 1912) back on the throne in 1917 although the restoration of the Manchu Emperor lasted only a week! Another war-lord became dictator of Manchuria—with Japanese support. Sun Yat-sen soon found out the position for himself when he set up his headquarters in Canton during 1917. He was entirely dependent upon the goodwill of the local war-lord; when he lost that goodwill Sun had to seek shelter in the Shanghai International Concession. For the next decade the war-lords were the rulers of China. They were not all especially evil men, but they showed little concern for the welfare of the people. Their interminable military campaigns wrecked many a harvest and caused an immense amount of human suffering.

China at war with Germany, 1917–18

It seems incredible that, at this stage in her history, China should choose to fight Germany.† Nevertheless, she hoped that by allying herself with Britain, France and America she would gain their support against Japanese encroachment. So her hopes were high, first when the war ended in 1918, and then when the Allies met in 1919 to settle the Versailles Treaty. But to her horror, the Allies only paid lip-service to the principles of Chinese sovereignty and Chinese territorial rights. They let Japan keep her gains while they themselves retained *their* pre-war concessions along the coast and up the Yangtze-kiang. The Chinese were disgusted; their allies had betrayed them. Students led a nationalist demonstration—the *Fourth of May Movement*—which sparked off nation-wide strike action. One well-organized strike disrupted Changsha in 1919; its leader was a young teacher named Mao Tse-tung.

*In Japan he married Chingling Soong—though he neglected to divorce his first wife.
†China's one belligerent act was to send coolies to France where they dug Allied trenches along the Western Front.

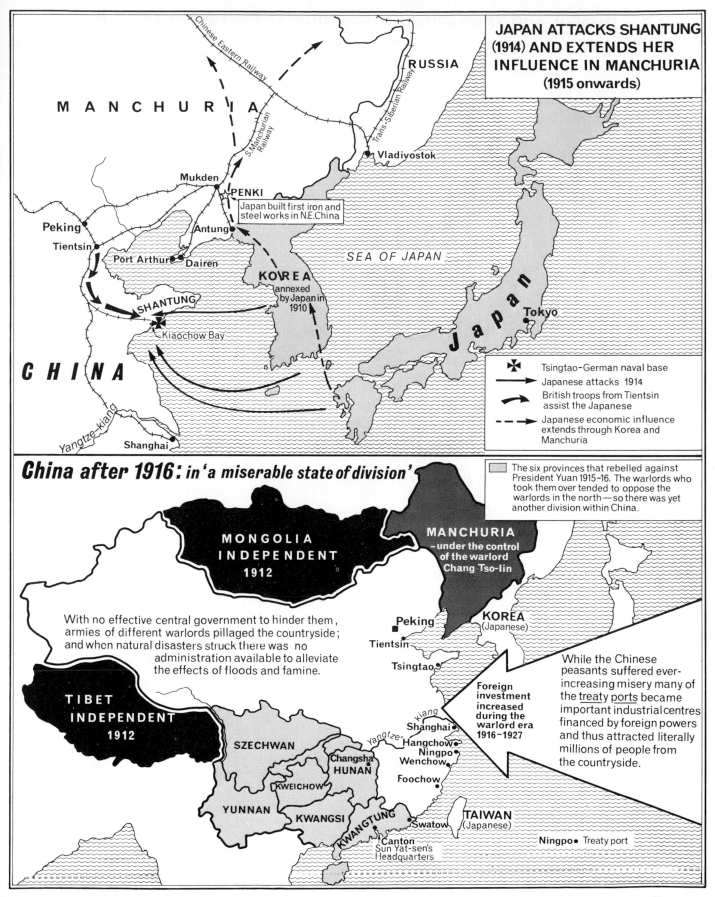

JAPAN ATTACKS SHANTUNG (1914) AND EXTENDS HER INFLUENCE IN MANCHURIA (1915 onwards)

M A N C H U R I A

Chinese Eastern Railway

Trans-Siberian Railway

S. Manchurian Railway

RUSSIA

Vladivostok

Mukden

PENKI

Japan built first iron and steel works in N.E.China

Peking

Tientsin

Antung

Port Arthur • Dairen

KOREA
annexed
by Japan in
1910

SEA OF JAPAN

SHANTUNG

Kiaochow Bay

Japan

Tokyo

C H I N A

Yangtze-kiang

Shanghai

✠ Tsingtao-German naval base
→ Japanese attacks 1914
➔ British troops from Tientsin assist the Japanese
⇢ Japanese economic influence extends through Korea and Manchuria

China after 1916: in 'a miserable state of division'

The six provinces that rebelled against President Yuan 1915–16. The warlords who took them over tended to oppose the warlords in the north—so there was yet another division within China.

MONGOLIA
INDEPENDENT
1912

MANCHURIA
–under the control
of the warlord
Chang Tso-lin

With no effective central government to hinder them, armies of different warlords pillaged the countryside; and when natural disasters struck there was no administration available to alleviate the effects of floods and famine.

Peking

KOREA
(Japanese)

Tientsin

Tsingtao

TIBET
INDEPENDENT
1912

Foreign
investment
increased
during the
warlord
era
1916–1927

While the Chinese peasants suffered ever-increasing misery many of the treaty ports became important industrial centres financed by foreign powers and thus attracted literally millions of people from the countryside.

SZECHWAN

Yangtze-kiang

Shanghai

Hangchow
Ningpo
Wenchow

Changsha
HUNAN

KWEICHOW

Foochow

YUNNAN

KWANGSI

KWANGTUNG

Swatow

TAIWAN
(Japanese)

Canton
Sun Yat-sen's
Headquarters

Ningpo • Treaty port

19 Russia and the Chinese Communist Party—the C.C.P.

Founding the Party, 1920–21

Mao Tse-tung was one of many young Chinese caught up in the protest against the Versailles Treaty. He had already joined various socialist study groups at Peking University,* groups which by 1920 had become highly receptive to the propaganda flowing out of Moscow, capital of the world's first Communist state. Already the Comintern had arranged to print a Chinese translation of the *Communist Manifesto*; it also despatched Gregory Voitinsky† to create the nucleus of a Chinese Communist Party. The logic of Marx and Engels appealed to the Confucian-trained minds of Chinese intellectuals and one of them, Chen Tu-hsiu, welcomed Voitinsky with open arms. Together they founded the first Communist Party cell in Shanghai and by the end of 1920 similar cells had sprung up not only in other Chinese cities but also among Chinese students overseas. Clearly, there was enough support to warrant the creation of a Chinese Communist Party and on 1 July 1921 the C.C.P. held its First National Congress in Shanghai.

Communist–Kuomintang links, 1922–3

Though the Russians had been instrumental in founding the C.C.P. they preferred, for the time being, to support Sun Yat-sen's Kuomintang—the KMT. Russia's Far Eastern interests would be best served by the emergence of an independent Chinese Republic and the KMT, properly handled, seemed to have the best chance of defeating the war-lords and ejecting the foreign imperialists. That was why the Comintern sent Adolf Joffe, its most skilled negotiator, to China in 1922. After weeks of tough bargaining Sun finally agreed (in January 1923) to co-operate with the Soviet Union and the newly-formed C.C.P. He would return to his revolutionary base at Canton, await Soviet military aid and then establish KMT control over Southern China. No one knows how far Sun intended to take his policy of co-operation with Russia. He was certainly disenchanted with Britain and America who had refused to give him any kind of backing; and he strongly admired the highly centralized Soviet system of government, believing it to be far superior to Western-style democracy. Whatever his private aims may have been, Sun was certainly doing well out of the Russian connection. Chiang Kai-shek went off to Moscow in 1923 to study the Soviet Red Army; the Comintern loaned their best political adviser, Mikhail Borodin, to Sun and also sent General Vassily Blücher to advise on military training. Comintern agents congregated in Canton where Sun was allowing C.C.P. members to join the KMT as private individuals. Their skill as propagandists among the people provided a new weapon in the KMT armoury—and by the end of 1923 Sun controlled *Peasant Associations* in many parts of Kwangsi, Kwangtung and Fukien.

1924: a revitalized KMT

For the first time since his resignation as President in 1912 Sun seemed to be in control of events. With Borodin's help he organized a spectacular KMT National Congress in Canton. He described the KMT programme as one of alliance with Russia, alliance with the CCP and alliance with the people; he expounded his Three Principles of the People and offered them as a new ideology capable of uniting the Chinese people against all their enemies. Every day that passed saw an increase in his power and influence. Chiang Kai-shek returned from Moscow to establish, with Blücher's help, the Whampoa Military Academy. Chiang supervised the military training programme for the officer cadets while Chou En-lai looked after their political indoctrination. In October, the first Russian freighters laden with war supplies arrived in Canton. Sun was sure that the time had come for a visit to the northern war-lords to convince them, from his new-found position of strength, of the wisdom of allying themselves with the KMT. Borodin urged him to stay in the south but Sun was adamant. In November he went north to meet the war-lords.

The death of Sun Yat-sen

When Sun left Canton he was already dying from cancer. He reached Peking but was far too ill to hold the all-important conference with the war-lords. He realized that he had only a month or two to live, knew that the revolution was incomplete but was confident that sufficient groundwork had been done. Now it was up to those who took his place. In his last message to Moscow he said: 'I leave behind me a party which ... will be allied to you in its historical task of liberating China ... My charge to the KMT before all is that it shall continue to promote the cause of the national revolutionary movement for the emancipation of China, which has been degraded by imperialism into a semi-colonial country...' Sun Yat-sen, the first great Asian nationalist, died on 12 March 1925.

*Mao had worked there as an assistant librarian.
†Secretary of the Communist International (Comintern) Far Eastern Bureau.

THE EMERGENCE OF THE CHINESE COMMUNIST PARTY

☆ CCP cells founded in 1920. Mao Tse-tung set up the Changsha Communist group when he was teaching in Hunan First Provincial Normal School.

■ Provinces under KMT control 1923-4.

FROM MOSCOW–
SOVIET SUPPORT
FOR THE CCP

SOVIET UNION

OUTER
MONGOLIA

MANCHURIA

Peking
Tientsin ☆
Tsinan ☆

KOREA

JAPAN

COMMUNIST
CELL FORMED BY
CHOU FU-HAI

CHINA

TIBET

Wuhan ☆

Changsha ☆

Shanghai

SOVIET AID
TO THE KMT.

FUKIEN

KWANGSI
KWANGTUNG
Canton ☆

CANTON

Whampoa

IN PARIS–
COMMUNIST
CELL FORMED
BY CHOU EN-LAI

SHANGHAI

MOUTH OF THE
YANGTZE-KIANG

British and
U.S. Sectors

Italian
Sector

Japanese
Sector

Whangpoo River

French
Sector

Original
walled city

THE COMMUNIST FIRST
NATIONAL CONGRESS
MET IN A GIRLS' SCHOOL
IN THE FRENCH
CONCESSION ON
1 JULY 1921.

THE SHANGHAI INTERNATIONAL SETTLEMENT

The settlement was made up of a number of 'concessions' which were areas of land leased by the Chinese to foreign countries at a very low rental. Chinese law did not operate inside these territories – and this was the cause of the long-standing Chinese complaint about the evil of 'extra-territoriality'. Concessions were in effect colonies and this is why the CCP referred to Britain, France etc. as 'imperialist powers'. Foreign consuls who ran the concessions had their own troops and police forces.

In 1863 the British and Americans combined their concessions in Shanghai to form the International Settlement. By 1921 Shanghai had a population of 3·5 million Chinese. It was China's most valuable port (though she did not control its trade) and a growing centre of manufacturing and ship-building industries. It was the easiest city in which to form trade unions and the CCP organised some of its first strikes and demonstrations there.

Communist historians refer to the years of outward harmony between the KMT and the C.C.P. (1923–7) as the *First United Front*. But this unity, fragile from the very beginning, was in jeopardy even before the Northern Expedition began.

'Pei Fa!' 'March North!'

During the early months of 1926 this cry could be heard on the lips of KMT and C.C.P. supporters alike—but for very different reasons. The C.C.P. was working towards a Communist revolution and had been busily forming Peasant Associations south of the Yangtze-kiang so that, by June 1926, it had enrolled about eight million peasants. If the C.C.P. could persuade these peasants to join up with a Northern Expedition against the war-lords and *then* support a Communist uprising against the KMT a united Soviet China would emerge. Chiang Kai-shek, the new leader of the KMT Nationalists, also wanted to march north—but his aim was to pre-empt a Communist take-over. If he could win over the war-lords and secure the support of the landowners, the better-off peasants and the city merchants, then he could create a Nationalist Republic of China, united under his personal rule. Both political parties were staking a great deal on the outcome of the Northern Expedition.

The Northern Expedition: Stage I, 1926–7

Two armies left Canton in July 1926. Commanded by Generalissimo Chiang Kai-shek and spear-headed by his Whampoa-trained officers, these armies advanced on Changsha and Wuhan. One army, with many C.C.P. sympathizers in its ranks, besieged Wuhan; Chiang diverted the other towards Nanking and Shanghai. Fanning out ahead of these armies were agents of the KMT Political Department who systematically roused the Peasant Associations against war-lords and foreign missionaries alike. At the same time other agents such as Chou En-lai were lurking in the cities, ready to organize strikes, sabotage factories and attack foreign concessions. These were very effective tactics: many war-lords joined the KMT armies while the British had to evacuate their concessions at Hankow and Kiukiang and bring in 20,000 troops to defend the Shanghai International Settlement. Wuhan soon fell to the western army and radical KMT members joined with the C.C.P. to set up a government in Hankow. To the east, Chiang—aided by Chou En-lai's resistance fighters—marched into Shanghai. It was

March 1927; he had conquered most of Southern China in less than a year.

The White Terror

Chiang now devised a brutal plan to rid himself of the Communist threat. He adopted a policy of mass extermination—the so-called White Terror. For Chiang it was simply a matter of survival; if he did not get the Communists now they would get him later.* So, in the early hours of 12 April 1927, KMT soldiers pounced on all the Communists they could find in Shanghai and executed them on the spot. Soon the White Terror spread along the Yangtze valley—but the Communists refused to surrender the cities without a fight. At Nanchang,† Swatow and Chaochow they fought bitter battles with the Nationalists—and lost every one. It all seemed hopeless and Mao Tse-tung, despite adverse criticism from his colleagues, decided to abandon the urban proletariat and put his faith in the peasantry. From his hide-out in Chingkangshan he watched his friends in the Red Army fight and lose the battle for the cities in southern China. And as they withdrew Chiang Kai-shek began to dissolve the trade unions and peasant associations that had contributed so much to his military victory.

The Northern Expedition: Stage II, January–July 1928

A week after the Shanghai Massacres Chiang had replaced the Hankow government with his new Nationalist government based on Nanking. In January 1928 he proclaimed Nanking (which means *Southern Capital*) to be the new capital of the Nationalist Republic of China. Then, for the next five months he fought a most difficult campaign against not only the hostile war-lords but on one occasion an interfering Japanese army. Finally, on 4 June 1928, his troops entered Peking. The city (whose name means *Northern Capital*) received a new name—Peiping or *Northern Peace*. It was not an apt name as Northern China was soon under attack. On 18 September 1931 the Japanese Army invaded Manchuria with profound results for the Nationalists, for the Communists and for the whole world.

*Theodore H. White discusses this simple explanation in his *China: the Roots of Madness* (B.B.C. Publications, 1970) pp. 54–5.

†The C.C.P. celebrates the Nanchang Uprising (led by mutinous soldiers of the 24th Division of the Nationalist Eleventh Army on 1 August 1927) as the anniversary of the founding of the Chinese Red Army.

THE NORTHERN EXPEDITION 1926–28

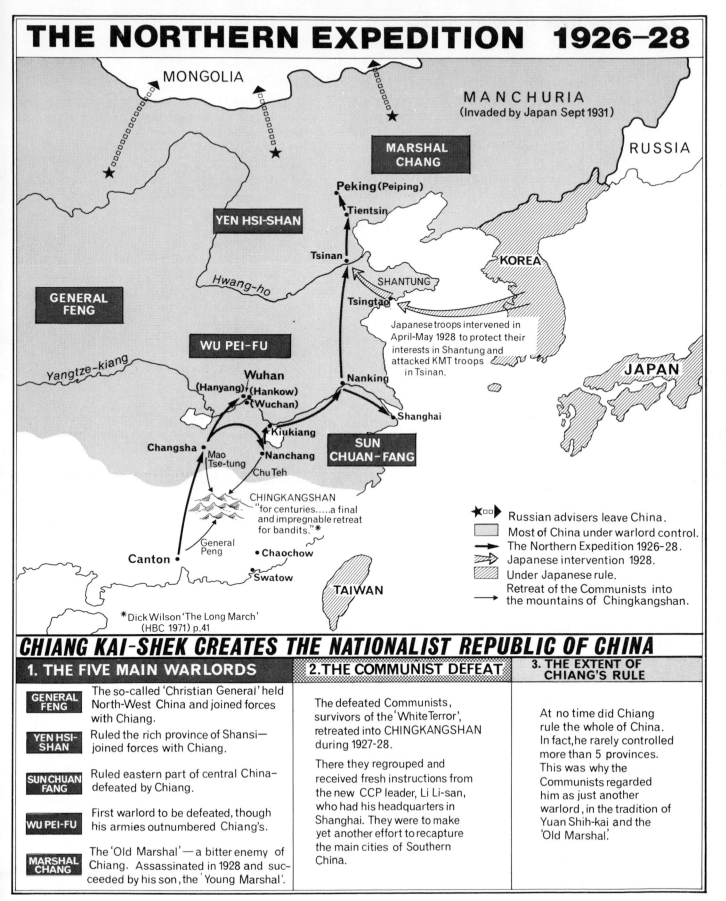

MONGOLIA

MANCHURIA
(Invaded by Japan Sept 1931)

RUSSIA

MARSHAL CHANG

Peking (Peiping)

Tientsin

YEN HSI-SHAN

Tsinan

KOREA

SHANTUNG

Tsingtao

Hwang-ho

GENERAL FENG

Japanese troops intervened in
April-May 1928 to protect their
interests in Shantung and
attacked KMT troops
in Tsinan.

WU PEI-FU

JAPAN

Yangtze-kiang

Wuhan
(Hanyang)
(Hankow)
(Wuchan)

Nanking

Shanghai

Kiukiang

Changsha

Mao
Tse-tung

Nanchang

SUN CHUAN-FANG

Chu Teh

CHINGKANGSHAN
"for centuries.....a final
and impregnable retreat
for bandits."*

★□□▶ Russian advisers leave China.

☐ Most of China under warlord control.

➡ The Northern Expedition 1926-28.

⇗ Japanese intervention 1928.

▨ Under Japanese rule.

→ Retreat of the Communists into
the mountains of Chingkangshan.

General
Peng

Canton

Chaochow

Swatow

TAIWAN

*Dick Wilson 'The Long March'
(HBC 1971) p.41

CHIANG KAI-SHEK CREATES THE NATIONALIST REPUBLIC OF CHINA

1. THE FIVE MAIN WARLORDS

GENERAL FENG	The so-called 'Christian General' held North-West China and joined forces with Chiang.
YEN HSI-SHAN	Ruled the rich province of Shansi— joined forces with Chiang.
SUN CHUAN FANG	Ruled eastern part of central China– defeated by Chiang.
WU PEI-FU	First warlord to be defeated, though his armies outnumbered Chiang's.
MARSHAL CHANG	The 'Old Marshal'—a bitter enemy of Chiang. Assassinated in 1928 and succeeded by his son, the 'Young Marshal'.

2. THE COMMUNIST DEFEAT

The defeated Communists, survivors of the 'White Terror', retreated into CHINGKANGSHAN during 1927-28.

There they regrouped and received fresh instructions from the new CCP leader, Li Li-san, who had his headquarters in Shanghai. They were to make yet another effort to recapture the main cities of Southern China.

3. THE EXTENT OF CHIANG'S RULE

At no time did Chiang rule the whole of China. In fact, he rarely controlled more than 5 provinces. This was why the Communists regarded him as just another warlord, in the tradition of Yuan Shih-kai and the 'Old Marshal.'

45

21 The loss of Manchuria

The constant challenge

While the 'orthodox' Li Li-san was still running the C.C.P., the Red Army was under orders to capture the southern cities. Therefore, on 27 July 1930, General Peng, Chu Teh and Mao Tse-tung sallied forth to attack Changsha and Nanchang—with dismal results. Nationalist armies tore them to pieces and forced the survivors back into their hideouts. However, this abortive Communist uprising was important in that it crystallized Chiang Kai-shek's priorities: if he hoped to retain the support of the landowners and merchants and see the day when Chinese Nationalists would drive the foreigners from the treaty ports, then he must first eliminate those who challenged his personal leadership. Most dangerous of all were the Communists, so their extermination must take priority over everything else.

The first three extermination campaigns, 1930–31

Chiang sent 50,000 men into the mountains during the first extermination campaign (December 1930). It was a disaster—he lost an entire division in an ambush at the beginning of the offensive. In April 1933 he committed another 150,000 troops—but 90,000 of them promptly deserted to the Reds! But in July he managed to assemble 300,000 soldiers and by sheer weight of numbers and intensity of firepower he sapped the enemy's strength. Before long the Red Army was fighting for its life outside Juichin—headquarters of Mao Tse-tung. Then, without warning, the whole situation changed: Japanese troops invaded Manchuria.* Chiang hastily returned to Nanking, taking his best combat troops with him.

The Japanese invasion of Manchuria

Just before midnight on 18 September 1931 a bomb exploded on the South Manchurian Railway (S.M.R.) track. Claiming that this was the work of Chinese saboteurs, the Japanese Kwantung Army—which guarded part of the S.M.R.—occupied Mukden, Antung and Changchun. An outraged Chiang Kai-shek appealed for help to the League of Nations which sent out the Lytton Commission to investigate the rights and wrongs of this sudden Manchurian crisis. It was not difficult to understand why the Japanese had invaded Manchuria: they had invested huge sums of money in industrial developments there; the country had reserves of oil, bauxite (for aluminium), coal, iron ore and foodstuffs, all of which could provide jobs and living-space for an expanding Japanese population already hard-hit by the 1929 world economic crisis. Moreover, Manchuria was an ideal springboard for a future attack upon China.

The Battle of Shanghai, 1932

World interest in the Manchurian crisis became acute when the Japanese launched their savage assault upon Shanghai in 1932. Shanghai was the busiest port in Asia, and Britain, for example, was always ready to defend it 'just as though it were a British possession'.† Consequently, the world press covered the battle in detail and censured the Japanese carrier-bombers for their indiscriminate raids on the civilian suburbs, but praised Chiang Kai-shek's Nineteenth Route Army for its valiant resistance to the Japanese marines and soldiers swarming off warships anchored in the Whangpoo River. After parts of Shanghai had been flattened by air attack and naval gunfire, the British managed to arrange a cease-fire on board H.M.S. *Kent* and fighting in the city stopped on 3 March.

The creation of Manchukuo

Meanwhile, the Lytton Commission had reached Manchuria where it saw at first-hand that the Nationalist government had lost control of the entire region. It appeared that Chiang Kai-shek was unwilling to commit himself to a major war against Japan; he was ready to accept the loss of China's most important industrial region if this would allow him to concentrate his military talents upon the extermination of the Communists. No other country was prepared to lend China a hand and this meant that the Japanese could go ahead and set up the puppet state of Manchukuo in place of Manchuria. Japan made Pu-yi (the last of the Manchu Emperors) ruler of Manchukuo and recognized the country's 'independence' in September 1932. And when the Lytton Commission published its indictment of Japanese aggression, the Japanese simply resigned from the League of Nations (1933). Chiang Kai-shek signed an ignoble truce with Japan in the same year.

The significance of the loss of Manchuria

Japan had delivered a body blow both to China and the prestige of the League of Nations. But she had also diverted Chiang Kai-shek's attention from Kiangsi and had thus given the Communists just enough time to regroup their forces before the ever-eager Generalissimo returned to try out some new tactics in the fourth and fifth extermination campaigns.

*Japan had guaranteed China's territorial integrity by the 1922 Nine Power Treaty.
†British Foreign Office memo quoted by Christopher Thorne, *The Limits of Foreign Policy* (Macmillan, 1973) p. 48.

U.S.S.R.

SOUTHERN SAKHALIN

Chinese Eastern Railway

MANCHURIA —

MANCHUKUO

MONGOLIA

JEHOL PROVINCE

Changchun

• Vladivostok

Mukden

SEA OF JAPAN

Hwang-ho

PEKING (Peiping) •

Antung

Tientsin

Port Arthur

NATIONALIST

KOREA

JAPAN

• Tokyo

CHINA

KWANTUNG — formerly the Liaotung Peninsula and leased by Japan from China.

The Emperor did not know that the Kwantung Army planned to invade Manchuria. He commented: "The Army's interference and its wilfulness...we must view with apprehension".

Nanking •

Yangtze-kiang

1932

SHANGHAI

Changsha •

• Nanchang

Kiangsi Province

Juichin

THE BATTLE OF SHANGHAI 1932

• Liuho

Japanese fleet— including an aircraft carrier.

All this area occupied by Japanese troops

WOOSUNG

Canton •

TAIWAN

Woosung Creek

Whangpoo River

Jap.Sector

Walled City

French concession

NATIONALIST CHINA 1930–33

COMMUNIST AND JAPANESE ATTACKS

- - - → Communist attacks 1930.
——→ Japanese attacks 1931–2.
+ + + + SOUTH MANCHURIAN RAILWAY.
Extermination campaigns.
Communist-held territory.
Manchuria–captured by the Japanese

☐ International Settlement.
——→ Japanese attacks.
Main battle area.

0   miles   5

22 The Long March

The fourth and fifth extermination campaigns

Even before he had signed his truce with Japan, the impatient Chiang had begun an extermination campaign against the small Oyuwan Soviet near Wuhan and by August 1933 he was ready to attack the Reds in Kiangsi. He now had modern equipment at his disposal: his engineers built roads into the mountains; some of his divisions were motorized; he had artillery and a few aircraft.* He also had some new ideas—though the brains behind them belonged to some retired German army officers. One of them, General von Seeckt, had devised 'scorched earth' barbed wire and blockhouse tactics to encircle the Reds and thwart the guerrilla units which usually scored successes by ambushes and hit-and-run raids. Von Seeckt blockaded the Reds, starved them of food, ammunition and medical supplies and deprived them of contact with the local peasantry. These highly successful tactics drew the Reds out into the open and they unwisely risked a pitched battle at *Kuangchang* (April 1934) where they suffered heavy casualties.†

Break-out

Some Red Army units managed to fight their way out of von Seeckt's trap between July and September but most were left behind, burdened down by more than 20,000 wounded comrades and a leadership which had no easy answer to their problem. There seemed to be one solution only: abandon the base in Kiangsi and try to set up another one elsewhere. The three main leaders, Li Teh, Chou En-lai and Mao Tse-tung, had no precise spot in mind but they all agreed they should try to make early contact with the Russians. The break-out began on 16 October 1934 amidst great secrecy. Six thousand troops stayed behind to cover the escape and to deceive the enemy into thinking that the Red Army was still in position. It was a month before Chiang discovered the deception.

The saga of the Long March 1934–5

Having escaped from the beleaguered Kiangsi Soviet, the marchers had no clear idea of their ultimate destination. They trudged westwards trying to keep ahead of the Nationalists who, once they realized that the Reds had tricked them, were relentless in their pursuit. Pitched battles—the first major clash was at the crossing of the *River Hsiang*—artillery bombardments and constant air attacks all took their toll of the Long Marchers. Eventually they reached Tsunyi where they decided that the man best fitted to lead them was Mao Tse-tung; from then on he was known as Chairman Mao. He led his people to the banks of the Yangtze-kiang and ferried the Red Army across in an operation lasting eight days. After that he had to face an even greater challenge—the crossing of the Tatu, a river which flowed through deep mountain gorges. There were no ferries and just one bridge was left. This was the *Luting bridge* composed of thirteen huge chains from which the Nationalists had removed most of the wooden planking. Against a hail of machine-gun fire the 'Twenty-two heroes of Tatu' led the assault and captured the bridge. Then the entire Red Army warily crossed the slender bridge suspended high above the raging Tatu River. On went the Long Marchers, across snow-covered mountain ranges 16,000 feet high, into lands populated by wild tribesmen, through the swamps of the *Great Grasslands* and into Shensi, a poverty-stricken province in north-western China. About 7,000 of Mao's 'ragged skeletons' finished the Long March, a feat of endurance unparalleled in the history of the world.

The significance of the Long March

Undertaken in the most heroic circumstances, the Long March ensured the survival of the Chinese Communist Party and the emergence of Mao Tse-tung as its 'supreme leader and father figure'.‡ Since 1935 the Long March has become a legend, the epic story of an army of courageous peasants and soldiers who placed their national and political ideals above their own selfish interests. Americans have their own tale of human fortitude in the story of Washington's troops at Valley Forge in the harsh winter of 1777–8; the British remember the heroism of the 'Few' who, in the dark days of 1940, fought and won the Battle of Britain. Today Chinese children, whether they live in the People's Republic, in South-East Asia or in the West, learn the story of the Long March as the supreme example of the struggle for an ideal.

*Chiang hired Colonel Jouett to head an American Military Mission to China. Jouett built up the Nationalist Air Force by training 350 pilots at the Hangchow Aviation Academy.

†The battle was fought on the advice of Li Teh. He was in fact a German named Otto Braun who represented the Comintern in Kiangsi. He was the only European to complete the Long March.

‡Dick Wilson, *The Long March* (Hamish Hamilton, 1971) p. 277.

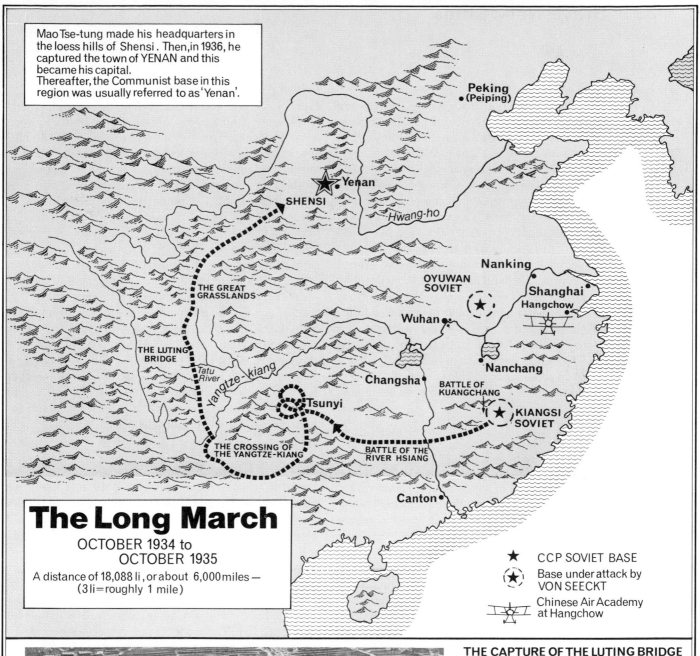

Mao Tse-tung made his headquarters in the loess hills of Shensi. Then, in 1936, he captured the town of YENAN and this became his capital.
Thereafter, the Communist base in this region was usually referred to as 'Yenan'.

Peking (Peiping)

Yenan

SHENSI

Hwang-ho

THE GREAT GRASSLANDS

Nanking

OYUWAN SOVIET

Shanghai
Hangchow

THE LUTING BRIDGE

Tatu River

Yangtze-kiang

Wuhan

Tsunyi

Changsha

Nanchang

BATTLE OF KUANGCHANG

KIANGSI SOVIET

THE CROSSING OF THE YANGTZE-KIANG

BATTLE OF THE RIVER HSIANG

Canton

The Long March

OCTOBER 1934 to OCTOBER 1935

A distance of 18,088 li, or about 6,000 miles —
(3 li = roughly 1 mile)

★ CCP SOVIET BASE

⍟ Base under attack by VON SEECKT

✈ Chinese Air Academy at Hangchow

THE CAPTURE OF THE LUTING BRIDGE

Platoon Commander Ma Ta-chiu stepped out, grasped one of the chains, and began swinging hand over hand towards the north bank. The platoon political director followed, and after him the men. As they swung along, Red Army machine guns laid down a protective screen of fire and the Engineering Corps began bringing up tree trunks and laying the bridge flooring... Ma Ta-chiu was the first to be shot into the wild torrent below. Then another man and another. The others pushed along.... and threw their hand grenades in the midst of the enemy...The bridge became a mass of running men with rifles at the ready... The enemy retreated...
Agnes Smedley *The Great Road*
(MRP 1956) p.321.

23 'Brave New China'

The New Life Movement, 1934

As the Communists retreated from Kiangsi so Chiang Kai-shek was left master of the richest part of China—the valley of the lower Yangtze-kiang. Here he set out to weld the peasants and the townsfolk into a single people, a nation owing its loyalty to the government in Nanking. With great enthusiasm, Chiang publicized his *New Life* movement—a propaganda campaign designed to build national unity through a programme of health education. He sent teams of teachers into the five provinces under his control; they were to urge the people to be 'clean, dignified, simple and honest'. Chiang argued that once the people had built up their self-respect they would develop a sense of responsibility. And once they had that he was ready to lend them government funds so they could band together into *co-operatives* and begin to help one another. In 1935 he introduced loans for rural collectives and this was so successful that he extended it to small *industrial co-operatives* three years later. So there were at least some signs that a 'New China' was gradually taking shape.

Modernization

Chiang was anxious that his New China should take on some of the outward signs of a modern, progressive state. It was difficult to develop heavy industry, especially since the Japanese had occupied Manchuria where the biggest factories were located. Moreover, even the experts were pessimistic about the chances of China going through a Western-type industrial revolution. 'The limiting factor', wrote Tawney in 1932, 'is not coal but iron. The growth of an iron and steel industry of considerable dimensions is hardly possible in China.'[*] Chiang therefore imported his most urgent needs. Nazi Germany provided military equipment; Fascist Italy sent technicians to build a Fiat aircraft factory in Nanchang; the U.S.A., impressed by Chiang's marriage to an Americanized Chinese and by his conversion to Methodism,[†] supplied not only goods and technical assistance but also a great deal of charitable aid. Chiang was able to concentrate on modernizing the communications system. He installed long-distance telephone and telegraph facilities, built new railways—including a link between Canton and Peiping (Peking)—and introduced civil airline services. Travelling time between Shanghai and Chungking—usually six weeks by river junk—now took six hours by 'plane.

Chiang Kai-shek's priorities

Japan was keeping a watchful eye on these developments. A resurgent China, well-equipped and well-led, would resist a Japanese attack in the future. Time was therefore not on the side of Japan if she wished to extend her commercial and political interests in China. Yet time was not on the side of Chiang Kai-shek either. His armies were still harassing the Communists (who had already declared war on Japan) and foreign observers such as Edmund Clubb were already predicting a social revolution in China if the Nanking government continued to ignore the plight of the mass of the people. There had been a serious famine in north China since 1930, and when the Hwang-ho overflowed its dykes in 1931 the floodwaters carried away seed-corn, fodder, animals and entire farms. Yet Chiang seemed reluctant to devote his main energy to this sort of problem and continued to send his armies against the Reds. One British writer living in China at this time later commented that, rather than help the millions of suffering Chinese, 'Chiang Kai-shek seemed determined to expend all the resources of the land in exterminating his political opponents.'[‡]

The Sian kidnapping, 1936

An extraordinary event occurred in 1936: Chiang was kidnapped by his own soldiers. He had for some time been worried by the low morale among Nationalist troops sent to fight against the Reds. In December 1936 he flew up to Sian to discuss the situation with the Young Marshal. Shortly after he landed pro-Communist troops arrested him and ordered him to stop fighting the Reds and unite the whole country against the real enemy—Imperial Japan. At first Chiang refused—so his captors threatened to kill him. Mao Tse-tung, who was probably stage-managing the whole affair, arranged for Chou En-lai to fly in and 'negotiate' the Generalissimo's release. So, after a fortnight of captivity, a badly shaken Chiang returned to Nanking, having given a half-hearted promise to join forces with the Reds. He was soon very glad he had done this; in July 1937 Japan launched a full-scale attack upon Nationalist China.

[*]R. H. Tawney, in his *Land and Labour in China* (Allen and Unwin, 1932).
[†]He became a Methodist in 1930; he married Soong Mei-ling whose sister had married Sun Yat-sen.
[‡]Winifred Galbraith, *The Chinese* (Pelican, 1942) p. 91.

TWO EXAMPLES OF CHIANG KAI-SHEK'S PROPAGANDA

AN ANTI-COMMUNIST LEAFLET DROPPED BY 'PLANE

Generalissimo has personally come to save you... Only the brigand leaders, Chuh Teh and Mao Tse-tung, will be killed.... rise up quickly and kill all the red brigands in order to regain your freedom. Brigand soldiers, come quickly to join the Revolutionary (i.e. Nationalist) Army. Each brigand soldier who comes with a rifle will be rewarded. Red brigands are low and mean.

Quoted by O. Edmund Clubb in his report originally written in 1932 and published by Columbia U.P. in 1968 as *'Communism in China'*

THE NEW LIFE MOVEMENT

The aim of the NEW LIFE MOVEMENT is to teach the Chinese citizen to appreciate life as it is. Its actual purpose is to revive the four traditional and fundamental virtues of Chinese civilization: etiquette, justice, integrity and conscience....a healthy people can produce a sound government.... Cleanliness and elegance (the proper use of handkerchiefs) are strictly compulsory. It is not rare to see the highest local authorities clean the streets to set an example for the population.

'Source Materials in Chinese History' by Meyer & Allen (Warne & Co.1970) pp. 102-3.

CHINA 1937– on the eve of war with Japan

- ◄— Foreign aid.
- ◄---- Chiang's flight to Sian.
- ▨ Flooded areas during the early thirties.
- ► Direction of Russia's interests.
- Under Japanese control.
- ◄ Direction of Japanese expansion.
- ※ Jehol—ceded to Manchukuo in 1933.

Generalissimo Chiang Kai-shek

THE GENERALISSIMO'S UNLIKELY ALLIES

① The Russians supported him as Chinese leader because Stalin believed that he was the only man capable of uniting China against attack from Japan—and Stalin was afraid of future Japanese penetration of Mongolia.

② Similarly, Mao Tse-tung was ready to form a SECOND UNITED FRONT (announced in 1937) with the Nationalists because he knew that Japan would soon exploit the weakness of a DIVIDED China. This was the motive behind the Sian kidnapping.

24 The Japanese onslaught

The incident at the Marco Polo Bridge

Historians frequently assert that the Second World War may be dated from the Japanese attacks on China. Some choose the occupation of Manchuria 1931–3; others are more explicit and state: 'The Second World War began in the Far East on the night of 7–8 July 1937.'* On that night Chinese soldiers—possibly with good reason—fired at a Japanese infantry company on manoeuvres near the Marco Polo Bridge west of Peiping. Within a few days the Japanese government had ordered its front-line air, land and naval units—equipped with some of the most potent military weapons then available—into action against the Chinese. Their objective was the capture of Peiping, the occupation of the North China Plain and the penetration of the valley of the Yangtze-kiang. Expecting an easy victory, they were startled to encounter fierce Chinese resistance.

The Second United Front, 1937

Chinese self-confidence grew out of two significant developments. The first was the signing of a *Non-Aggression Pact* with Russia in August 1937; the second was the announcement in September that the Communists and the Nationalists would form, in view of the common danger, a *United Front* against Japan. For the first time the Chinese people could anticipate supplies of modern weapons from a friendly power—the Russians despatched hundreds of aircraft to defend Northern China—as well as a *co-ordinated* military defence system for the whole country. Clearly it was impossible to stop the Japanese onslaught immediately but it should be possible to slow it down. So Chiang Kai-shek's troops put up a spirited, though unsuccessful, defence of Shanghai before retreating first to Nanking and then to Hankow. Mao Tse-tung's armies beat the Japanese at a pitched battle near Pinghsinkuan and a Nationalist force won an unexpected victory at Taierhchwang. Unfortunately, this new-found unity was not enough. The Japanese kept advancing and the Nationalists, engaged in a fighting retreat, moved their capital to Chungking.

Western reaction to undeclared war

Many British and American warships were serving on the 'China station'. Traditionally, they were there to keep the peace and to make the country safe for trade. But the devastating Japanese onslaught was a headache for the flimsy gun-boats patrolling China's river systems. In a strictly legal sense, there was no war between China and Japan. Both sides referred to the 'China Incident' or the 'Sino–Japanese Incident'. Japan did not want to arouse unnecessary hostility among the commercial nations, and Chiang Kai-shek did not want to lose American military supplies—the U.S.A. was usually unwilling to supply arms to warring nations during the 'thirties. So the gun-boats had to do their best to help the terrified civilian population and at the same time dodge the bombs and shells that fell around them. One British gun-boat, H.M.S. *Ladybird*, suffered hits in 1937 and when a Japanese plane sank the U.S.S. *Panay* there was the momentary danger of war flaring between America and Japan.

Changes in Japanese strategy

It was not long before the Japanese realized that Chiang Kai-shek could hold out as long as he was in receipt of supplies from Russia and the Western powers. They therefore decided to challenge the Russians in Mongolia, occupy China's vulnerable ports in the south and bomb all the routes to Chungking. Gradually, Japan's commitments in China would increase and she would eventually try to destroy the commercial and imperial power of both Britain and the United States. But the 'day of infamy'—Pearl Harbor, 7 December 1941—was still more than three years in the future and until that day China would have to fight alone.

*See *The Royal Navy and the Sino–Japanese Incident 1937–41* by Martin Brice (Ian Allan, 1973) p. 11.

Royal Navy gunboat H.M.S. *Tern*: designed to operate on the Upper Yangtze as far as Chungking, she is seen here making speed through the Yangtze gorges (1931). She was destined to be scuttled during the defence of Hong Kong 1941–2.

CHINA SUFFERS A NEW KIND OF WAR

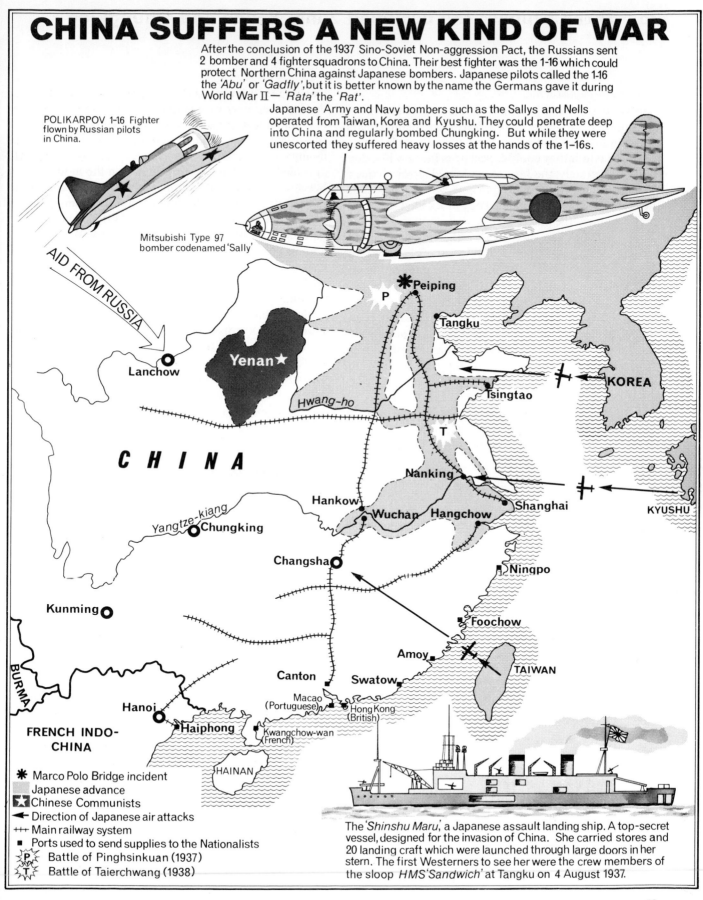

After the conclusion of the 1937 Sino-Soviet Non-aggression Pact, the Russians sent 2 bomber and 4 fighter squadrons to China. Their best fighter was the 1-16 which could protect Northern China against Japanese bombers. Japanese pilots called the 1-16 the 'Abu' or 'Gadfly', but it is better known by the name the Germans gave it during World War II — 'Rata' the 'Rat'.

Japanese Army and Navy bombers such as the Sallys and Nells operated from Taiwan, Korea and Kyushu. They could penetrate deep into China and regularly bombed Chungking. But while they were unescorted they suffered heavy losses at the hands of the 1-16s.

POLIKARPOV 1-16 Fighter flown by Russian pilots in China.

Mitsubishi Type 97 bomber codenamed 'Sally'

AID FROM RUSSIA

Lanchow

Yenan ★

Hwang-ho

P ✳ Peiping

Tangku

KOREA

Tsingtao

T

CHINA

Nanking

Shanghai

KYUSHU

Hankow

Wuchan Hangchow

Yangtze-kiang Chungking

Changsha

Ningpo

Kunming

Foochow

Amoy

TAIWAN

Canton

Swatow

Macao (Portuguese)

Hong Kong (British)

BURMA

Hanoi

Haiphong

Kwangchow-wan (French)

FRENCH INDO-CHINA

HAINAN

✳ Marco Polo Bridge incident
Japanese advance
🟦★ Chinese Communists
◄— Direction of Japanese air attacks
+++ Main railway system
■ Ports used to send supplies to the Nationalists
P Battle of Pinghsinkuan (1937)
T Battle of Taierchwang (1938)

The 'Shinshu Maru', a Japanese assault landing ship. A top-secret vessel, designed for the invasion of China. She carried stores and 20 landing craft which were launched through large doors in her stern. The first Westerners to see her were the crew members of the sloop HMS 'Sandwich' at Tangku on 4 August 1937.

25   Three Chinas: the occupied zone, Yenan and Chungking

Japanese-occupied China

'Kill all, destroy all, burn all': the ferocious attacks by the Imperial Japanese armed forces on Shanghai and Nanking in 1937 had given the Chinese people a taste of the behaviour they could expect from the new invaders. Quite deliberately, the Japanese adopted terror tactics in the belief that this was the quickest way of persuading the Nationalists to surrender. They blockaded the coastline, occupied the major ports and captured Hainan Island so that by the end of 1939—the year in which the Second World War began for most of Europe—the Japanese controlled the main lines of communication and the industrial cities of eastern China. But the Japanese had failed to dominate the rural areas and it was not long before Nationalist and Communist guerrilla units began operating behind enemy lines. Yet whenever they attacked a blockhouse or blew up an ammunition train the Japanese immediately took reprisals against the civilian population. It was this indiscriminate use of terror that intensified the hatred that most peasants felt towards the Japanese and drove them into the arms of the most famous guerrilla leader of all—Mao Tse-tung. In the long run, Japanese terror helped to guarantee a Communist victory in China.

Yenan

In the short term, however, Mao's prospects were not so bright. He had plenty of men in Yenan, for thousands of peasants arrived to join the Red Army—now renamed the Eighth Route Army. Others swarmed to join the New Fourth Army stationed just north of the Yangtze-kiang. But the Communists engaged in very little fighting with the Japanese. Mao preferred to perfect his system of government in Yenan—now renamed the Border Region—and to recruit supporters from among the millions of peasants living in the occupied zone. Mao knew that his most dangerous enemy was still Generalissimo Chiang Kai-shek and that an attack from him was just as likely as an attack from the Japanese.

Chungking

As soon as Chiang Kai-shek reached the relative safety of Chungking, the fragile Nationalist–Communist *Second United Front* began to fall apart. Chiang was far more interested in reducing Mao's military power than he was in expelling the Japanese invader. In fact, during 1939–40 he actually sent his best divisions northwards to blockade the Communists and prevent military supplies from

reaching their bases. At the same time, he tried to entice the Japanese ever westwards, to over-extend their lines of communication* and make them vulnerable to guerrilla attack. It was a war of attrition in which the Generalissimo was prepared to 'trade space for time'. He appealed to the Chinese to join him in the mountains of Szechwan and several millions trekked across country to rally round the man who had established himself as the defender of *Free China*, the man most fitted to take charge of China's destiny. He convinced many Westerners—among them President Roosevelt—of the truth of this. Certainly, all the Nationalist propaganda—ably managed by Madame Chiang Kai-shek†—was highly impressive. A Chinese industrial revolution had begun in Szechwan; geologists had found rich iron ore deposits in Yennan and Kweichow; 400 dismantled factories were arriving from the east to provide the nucleus of chemical plants, steel works, cotton mills and paper factories. Specialist plants for manufacturing truck tyres, gas masks and synthetic petrol were mushrooming—tempting targets for the Japanese bombers that roamed at will over south-west China.‡

The situation in 1940

For the British and their allies, this was the year of Dunkirk, the fall of France and the Battle of Britain. Obviously, Japan need not fear a Western intervention in China! She had already tested her strength against the U.S.S.R. during 1938—9 and had been mauled very badly in the battles around Nomonhan. So she was contenting herself with the occupation of French Indo-China, the exploitation of China's wealth—and coping with any false moves by Mao Tse-tung. Mao did in fact launch a guerrilla war against the Japanese in the summer of 1940 (the so-called *Hundred Regiments Offensive*) but soon regretted the move when fierce enemy counterattacks killed thousands of his soldiers. Stalemate seemed to have arrived in China. There were two contestants for political supremacy. One was poised in the hills of Yenan; the other in the mountains of Szechwan. Both were salting away arms and equipment for the inevitable confrontation and, for the time being, made no *significant* effort to liberate their country from the Japanese invader.

*Just as Wellington had done when fighting the French in the Peninsula War 1808–14.
†Hurst and Blackett published her *China Shall Rise Again* in 1940—a typical example of her considerable skill as a propagandist.
‡Especially after 19 August 1940 when the Japanese began using their new Zero fighters as bomber escorts.

STALEMATE IN CHINA 1940

THE EXTENT OF RUSSIAN INVOLVEMENT IN THE 'CHINA INCIDENT'
Stalin consistently supported Chiang Kai-shek and sent the Nationalists military aid by land (via Lanchow) and by sea (via Rangoon and Haiphong). He was anxious to prolong the Sino-Japanese conflict – for this would divert the aggressive Japanese Army from Mongolia and the Soviet territories bordering the Sea of Japan. His policy was fairly successful: there was one clash over possession of a hill called Changkufeng in 1938; while 1939 saw serious Japanese defeats at the hands of the Soviet Red Army and Air Force around the wastelands of Nomonhan. But from 1940 until 8 August 1945 (when Stalin declared war on Japan) there was peace along Russia's Asian frontiers.

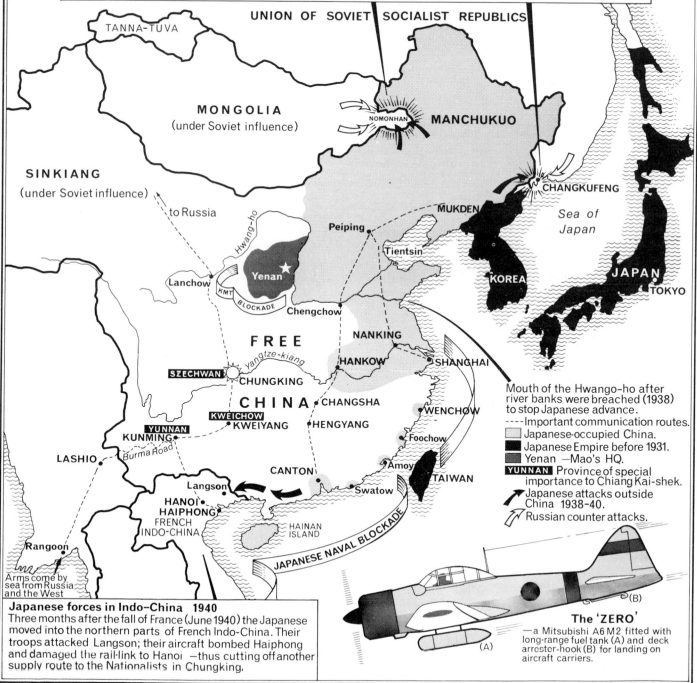

UNION OF SOVIET SOCIALIST REPUBLICS

TANNA-TUVA

MONGOLIA
(under Soviet influence)

NOMONHAN

MANCHUKUO

SINKIANG
(under Soviet influence)

to Russia

CHANGKUFENG

MUKDEN

Sea of Japan

Hwang-ho

Peiping

Tientsin

KOREA

JAPAN

Lanchow

KMT BLOCKADE

Yenan

TOKYO

Chengchow

NANKING

FREE

HANKOW

SHANGHAI

SZECHWAN

Yangtze-kiang

CHUNGKING

CHINA

CHANGSHA

WENCHOW

KWEICHOW

KWEIYANG

HENGYANG

Foochow

YUNNAN

KUNMING

LASHIO

Burma Road

Amoy

CANTON

TAIWAN

Swatow

Langson

HANOI
HAIPHONG
FRENCH
INDO-CHINA

HAINAN ISLAND

Rangoon

Arms come by sea from Russia and the West

JAPANESE NAVAL BLOCKADE

Mouth of the Hwango-ho after river banks were breached (1938) to stop Japanese advance.

- - - - Important communication routes.

Japanese-occupied China.

Japanese Empire before 1931.

Yenan —Mao's HQ.

YUNNAN Province of special importance to Chiang Kai-shek.

Japanese attacks outside China 1938-40.

Russian counter attacks.

The 'ZERO'
—a Mitsubishi A6 M2 fitted with long-range fuel tank (A) and deck arrester-hook (B) for landing on aircraft carriers.

Japanese forces in Indo-China 1940
Three months after the fall of France (June 1940) the Japanese moved into the northern parts of French Indo-China. Their troops attacked Langson; their aircraft bombed Haiphong and damaged the rail-link to Hanoi —thus cutting off another supply route to the Nationalists in Chungking.

26　Life in Yenan and the emergence of Maoism

Between 1937 and 1942 Mao Tse-tung created a new society amidst the loess hills of Yenan. It was a peasant society with unique military, egalitarian and democratic characteristics.

A people's war

War dominated everything in the Border Region and permeated every activity. When the peasants gathered in the harvest, the soldiers helped; when the soldiers dug new gun emplacements, the peasants lent a hand. No distinction existed between the ordinary people and the soldiers for they held one another in mutual respect. This in itself was a revolutionary change, for the peasants usually feared and despised the military. But now, to quote one Communist commander*, 'The people are the water, the soldiers of the Eighth Route Army are the fish—the fish cannot live without water.' Every peasant understood why he was at war and what his contribution should be. An American journalist† who visited a Communist village reported that 'Every approach, every trail was heavily mined ... Even the village entry was mined. The villagers moved about nonchalantly, as though oblivious of death underfoot. Everyone carried a weapon of some sort—a rifle on his back, a potato masher grenade at his hip ... even the little boys and girls wore dummy grenades dangling from their waists.'

An egalitarian society

Equality between soldiers and peasants extended to the sexes. Men *and* women joined the executive committees of the Peasant Associations; men *and* women went out on guerrilla raids; men *and* women spun the cotton; while women took the lion's share of patrol work, sentry duty and the all-important job of carrying supplies to the fighting units:

> *Sending grain to the army*
> *The mule carts are lined up.*
> *Load the grain and fodder!*
> *Let's go without delay*
> *The Fighting Eighth is waiting.*‡

Democracy in action

Decision making was a democratic affair in Yenan—though once a decision was made it was binding upon everyone. Soldiers had their elected committees to supervise unit funds; Peasant Associations had similar arrangements so that everyone shared in the fruits of production. Taxes and rents payable to the Border Government and to local landlords tumbled drastically and Yenan increasingly offered an attractive, if frugal, way of life to its inhabitants. Soon they created their own folklore, their own songs and dances. They attracted some remarkable visitors such as Ho Chi Minh and Dr. Bethune, a Westerner whose memory the Chinese still revere. Norman Bethune was a Canadian who organized the first mobile blood banks in the Spanish Civil War. He went to China in 1938 to run the first mobile surgical hospitals which saved the lives of hundreds of Communist soldiers. Dr. Bethune died in China (1939) after contracting blood poisoning and the Communists erected a tomb in his honour and built teaching hospitals to perpetuate his name.

Maoism

By radically changing the ideas of Marx and Lenin about the nature of revolution, Mao Tse-tung created a new ideology—Maoism. Marx and Lenin had regarded the *urban proletariat*—the industrial workers—as the true agents of revolution. The uneducated, badly-organized peasants were simply allies of the revolution. Mao disputed this; in China, it was the peasantry who provided the main revolutionary force. All that was needed was determined leadership—and an easily understood ideology. The C.C.P. could provide the leadership; the ideology must grow out of a selfless dedication by the masses to the idea of revolution. No one must stray from the path which led to the victorious revolution: a peasant must watch out for political shortcomings among his comrades; he must also be able to identify his own weaknesses, confess to them and strive to put them right. Through this sort of self-criticism and self-improvement everybody could serve the revolution. But this was not all. As revolution was a very serious business, a struggle between classes, it called for a 'protracted war'. This war would be waged from the villages—Mao always called them 'the bastions of the revolution'—against the Japanese invaders and the Nationalists who always based themselves upon the towns and cities.

---

*Peng Te-huai.
†He was Harrison Forman who wrote *Report from Red China* quoted by Jean Chesnaux in *Peasant Revolts in China 1840–1949* (Thames and Hudson, 1973) pp. 133–4.
‡Women's song quoted in *China: a world so changed* by C. P. Fitzgerald and Myra Roper (Nelson and Heinemann Educational Books, 1972) p. 110.

'SNOW' — *a poem by Mao Tse-tung*

The northern scene:
A thousand leagues locked in ice,
A myriad leagues of fluttering snow
On either side of the Great Wall
Only one vastness to be seen.....
Such is the beauty of these mountains
          and rivers
That has been admired by unnumbered
          heroes—
The great emperors of Ch'in and Han
Lacking literary brilliance,
Those of T'ang and Sung
Having but few romantic inclinations,
And the prodiguous Genghis Khan
Knowing how to bend his bow and
         shoot at vultures.

All are past and gone!
For men of vision
We must seek among the present
        generation.

*(For this poem and others by
Mao Tse-tung see 'The Penguin Book
of Socialist Verse' edited by Alan Bold
(Penguin 1970) pp.170-78)*

YENAN – and its famous landmark, an old pagoda. nestling amidst the loess hills which (said Mao), "like waxen elephants, plod on the plain".

YENAN — MAO'S HEADQUARTERS

The famous eight rules of the Eighth Route Army:

1. Speak politely to the people & help them whenever you can.
2. Return doors and straw matting to the owners.
3. Pay for any damage that you cause.
4. Pay a fair price for any goods you buy.
5. Be sanitary-establish latrines well away from houses.
6. Don't take liberties with the womenfolk.
7. Don't ill-treat prisoners.
8. Don't damage the crops.

In addition to Yenan there were five other major Communist bases organised on similar lines to Mao's H.Q.

1. WUTAI MOUNTAINS BORDER REGION
2. EAST SHANTUNG BORDER REGION
3. LOWER YANGTZE BORDER REGION
4. NORTHERN SHANSI BORDER REGION
5. TAIHANG MOUNTAINS BORDER REGION

〜〜 Great Wall
      Areas under Japanese control

MAO TSE-TUNG'S WRITINGS IN YENAN—AND HIS RULES FOR FIGHTING A GUERRILLA WAR

MAO'S WRITINGS

After 1938 Mao produced **1. Problems of Strategy in Guerrilla War against Japan** and **2. On Protracted war.** In 1940 he wrote one of his most famous books **On New Democracy** which summarized his theories of warfare, revolution and land reform. Between 1939 and 1942 the CCP accepted his ideas as official Communist policy.

HIS GUERRILLA TACTICS

"THE ENEMY ATTACKS, WE RETREAT;

THE ENEMY CAMPS, WE HARASS;

THE ENEMY TIRES, WE ATTACK;

THE ENEMY RETREATS, WE PURSUE."

Further Reading
Theme 3—Nationalist China

Spread

18.	John Robottom	*Modern China* (Ch. 5: 'Yuan Shih-kai and the Warlords')	Longmans, 1967
19.	George Moseley	*China: Empire to People's Republic*	Batsford, 1973
20.	Franklin W. Houn	*A Short History of Chinese Communism*	Spectrum Books, 1973
21.	Christopher Thorne	*The Limits of Foreign Policy*	Macmillan, 1972
22.	Dick Wilson	*The Long March, 1935*	Hamish Hamilton, 1971
23.	Emily Hahn	*China Only Yesterday*	Weidenfeld and Nicolson, 1963
24.	Martin Brice	*The Royal Navy and the Sino–Japanese Incident, 1937–41*	Ian Allen, 1973
25.	Mme. Chiang Kai-shek	*China Shall Rise Again*	Hurst and Blackett, 1940
	Stuart Gelder	*The Chinese Communists*	Gollancz, 1946
	Richard Storry	*A Short History of Modern Japan*	Pelican, 1960
26.	Michael Lindsay	*The Unknown War: North China, 1937–1945*	Bergstrom and Boyle, 1975

A lingering death for a river pirate: imprisoned in this roughly built wooden cage with his neck supported on wooden planks, he stands on six flat stones. Each day one stone is removed—until he strangles.

THEME 4

China and the Second World War

When Japan sent her fleet of aircraft carriers to raid Pearl Harbor in 1941 she was obviously confident of her ability to contain any localized attacks by Chinese armies. In fact, she had withdrawn some of her best troops from the China theatre to spearhead her blitzkrieg in the Pacific.

By 1941 Chiang Kai-shek was holed up in his battered headquarters in Chungking. From here the Generalissimo prosecuted the war against Japan by bribing and cajoling a motley band of war-lords to fight on his behalf. His supplies of arms and ammunition came via the Burma Road—until the Japanese cut it in 1942—and then by means of U.S. transport planes flying over the 'Hump'. As for Mao Tse-tung, he was carefully consolidating his position in Yenan. Though he master-minded a complex guerrilla war against the Japanese he spent most of his energy in disseminating Communist propaganda among the peasants of north China—and was highly successful in the process. Only when the Americans built up a strategic bomber force in western China did the Japanese go back on the offensive and during 1944 they overran a great deal of Chinese territory in their efforts to destroy the U.S. air bases.

Meanwhile, the Americans were working hard to bring Mao and Chiang together in a common cause—the creation of a peaceful, united China. They sent missions to Yenan and advisers to Chungking. Ambassador Hurley even managed to set up a meeting between Mao and Chiang during August 1945. But it was all in vain. For the Chinese people, the Second World War was simply an interruption in their protracted civil war.

27 'The Helping Hand'—Anglo-American aid to China

On 7 December 1941 Japanese dive-bombers plunged out of the skies above Pearl Harbor to begin an attack which destroyed America's battleship fleet in the Pacific. A few hours later, Japanese assault troops poured ashore at Kota Baru while their Taiwan-based bombers pounded U.S. positions in the Philippines.

China's new allies

Japan's attacks drew China into alliance with America and Britain. She had already been at war for more than four years and during most of that time had depended upon Soviet military aid. However, Hitler's invasion of Russia in June 1941 meant that the U.S.S.R. could not spare material for China. President Roosevelt saw immediately how serious the situation was: the Nationalists were tying up 1·2 million enemy troops and, if Free China surrendered, these Japanese soldiers would be able to reinforce their comrades in the Pacific.* So every effort must be made to funnel Anglo-American aid into China. The problem was how to get this aid to the Nationalists.

The Burma Road

The most obvious route was the Burma Road, a highway built by China during 1937–8. It began at Lashio and coiled its way across some of the toughest terrain in the world. Trucks began driving the 650-mile journey to Kunming in December 1939 and by the time of Pearl Harbor they were bringing in 15,000 tons a month. Foreign drivers using the Burma Road marvelled at the skill of the original 160,000 Chinese who had built the highway with hand-tools and a few sticks of dynamite. Thousands were still at work, repairing a road surface constantly churned up by lorry tyres, monsoon rains and landslides. Then, in 1942, a new threat appeared. Japanese soldiers invaded Burma and overwhelmed the British, Indian and Burmese forces that tried to stop them. Chiang Kai-shek sent some of his best divisions into Burma to help the British—but to no effect. On 29 April 1942 Japanese soldiers captured Lashio and cut the Burma Road.

The effect on China

It was a catastrophe for China. Apart from the loss of men and materials, the effect upon Chinese morale was highly significant. Many Chinese civilians panicked, hoarded goods and began to trade on the black market. This led to inflation which persisted throughout the war

and helped to cause the downfall of Chiang Kai-shek seven years later.

How to help China?

President Roosevelt appointed General Stilwell to command U.S. forces in the China–Burma–India (C.B.I.) war theatre. Stilwell was an expert on Chinese affairs. He spoke the language and had a great respect for the fighting qualities of Chinese soldiers who, in his view, simply needed good training, good equipment and good leadership. He collected the survivors of the Burma débâcle at Ramgarh and began retraining them. Stilwell intended to commit these troops and the British Fourteenth Army to a land campaign that would force the Japanese back and enable him to build a new road link with China. This road would save China and help win the war. That was his plan—but few people sympathized with him. There was far more support for the idea of an airlift into China.

The Hump

Roosevelt favoured flying supplies into China and March 1942 saw the first cargo planes take off from Dinjan and fly across the 'Hump'—the towering mountain ranges east of the Brahmaputra. Unarmed C-47 Skytrains risked freak weather conditions and prowling enemy fighters for a flight of three or four hours before landing at Kunming where Chinese coolies had built an airstrip more than a mile long. Between 1942 and 1945 Kunming handled about 75 per cent of the tonnage coming over the Hump. But though the airlift may have been 'one of the war's miracles'† it made little difference to the Chinese people, civilians and soldiers alike. Most of the supplies went straight to U.S. air bases under construction in China. Quite a lot found its way on to the black market. So, as far as China was concerned, the aid coming in over the Hump was essentially a morale booster for Chiang Kai-shek, visible evidence that he was being helped by the two most powerful industrial democracies in the world. And another boost to the Generalissimo's prestige came from the main American effort in the C.B.I. theatre—the establishment of a China-based Air Force to harry Japanese forces on the mainland and, eventually, to bomb enemy targets in Japan itself.

---

*Japan needed a mere 500,000 men to carry out her extraordinary conquests in the Pacific, December 1941–March 1942.
†Arthur N. Young, *China: the Helping Hand 1937–1945* (Harvard University Press, 1963) p. 245.

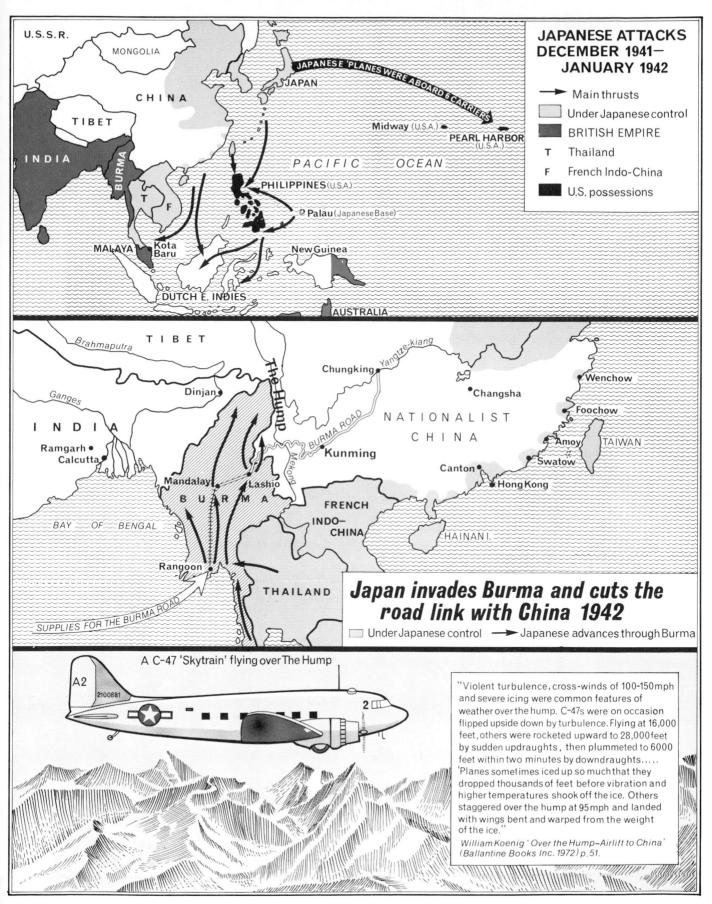

JAPANESE ATTACKS DECEMBER 1941— JANUARY 1942

→ Main thrusts
Under Japanese control
BRITISH EMPIRE
T Thailand
F French Indo-China
U.S. possessions

U.S.S.R.

MONGOLIA

CHINA

TIBET

JAPAN

JAPANESE 'PLANES WERE ABOARD 6 CARRIERS

Midway (U.S.A.)

PEARL HARBOR
(U.S.A.)

INDIA

BURMA

PACIFIC OCEAN

T

F

PHILIPPINES (U.S.A.)

Palau (Japanese Base)

MALAYA

Kota Baru

New Guinea

DUTCH E. INDIES

AUSTRALIA

TIBET

Brahmaputra

Ganges

Dinjan

The Hump

Chungking

Yangtze-kiang

Changsha

Wenchow

Foochow

NATIONALIST CHINA

Ramgarh

Calcutta

INDIA

BURMA ROAD

Mekong

Kunming

Amoy

TAIWAN

Mandalay

Lashio

B U R M A

Canton

Swatow

Hong Kong

BAY OF BENGAL

FRENCH INDO-CHINA

HAINAN I.

Rangoon

THAILAND

SUPPLIES FOR THE BURMA ROAD

Japan invades Burma and cuts the road link with China 1942

Under Japanese control ➡ Japanese advances through Burma

A C-47 'Skytrain' flying over The Hump

A2

2100881

2

"Violent turbulence, cross-winds of 100-150mph and severe icing were common features of weather over the hump. C-47s were on occasion flipped upside down by turbulence. Flying at 16,000 feet, others were rocketed upward to 28,000 feet by sudden updraughts, then plummeted to 6000 feet within two minutes by downdraughts..... 'Planes sometimes iced up so much that they dropped thousands of feet before vibration and higher temperatures shook off the ice. Others staggered over the hump at 95mph and landed with wings bent and warped from the weight of the ice."

William Koenig 'Over the Hump—Airlift to China' (Ballantine Books Inc. 1972) p.51.

28 China: U.S. air base

The Flying Tigers

The Flying Tigers were an air group created by Colonel Claire Chennault, a retired U.S. Army Air Force officer who worked for Chiang Kai-shek. The Generalissimo was so plagued by enemy air raids on Chungking that he asked Chennault to form an American Volunteer Group (A.V.G.) to combat them. Chennault bought some surplus American P-40 fighters and hired mercenaries to fly them.* They assembled at Kyedaw airfield and, by the time of Pearl Harbor, Chennault had fifty-five fighters ready for action. These performed heroic deeds in the defence of Burma, but failed to stop the Japanese from cutting the Burma Road. Eventually, they had to evacuate Burma and take refuge in Yunnan. Nevertheless, the Generalissimo was impressed by their achievements and dubbed the A.V.G. his 'Flying Tigers'.

The Doolittle raid, 1942

On 18 April 1942 the U.S. carrier *Hornet* launched sixteen B-25 Mitchell bombers in the first air strike against Tokyo. Led by Colonel Doolittle, the planes roared low over Tokyo, dropped their bombs and headed out for Free China where most of them crash-landed just beyond the main occupied zone. Chasing after them came the infuriated Japanese ground troops who killed anybody suspected of lending a hand to the downed American fliers. The raid was essentially a morale booster for the American people—their revenge for Pearl Harbor.†

China Air Task Force, 1942

Meanwhile, Chennault was busily incorporating the Flying Tigers into the China Air Task Force (C.A.T.F.). He managed to scrounge eight B-25 Mitchell bombers and with his P-40s flying as escorts he began harrying Japanese targets all over China. Soon a bitter struggle developed between C.A.T.F. and the small but efficient Japanese Air Force stationed in China. Try as they might, the Japanese could never wipe out Chennault's bases by bombing them—thanks to his remarkable early warning system. Chennault trained scores of Chinese in aircraft recognition, equipped them with radio sets and then stationed them around the forward air bases. He was usually ready for any Japanese surprise attack. Chennault was a fanatic about air power and was sure that, if he had some long-range heavy bombers, he could bomb Japan into surrender. Chiang Kai-shek found the idea attractive and recommended it to President Roosevelt. The Generalissimo certainly preferred it to the tough and unreward-

ing war being fought out in Burma where Stilwell's Chinese troops and their British allies were slogging through jungles and over mountains to build a new highway which would link up with the northern half of the now defunct Burma Road.

Operation Ichi-go, 1944

Stilwell had little time for either Chennault or the Generalissimo. He foresaw a violent Japanese reaction to a strong U.S. bombing force stationed in China. And he had no faith in the ability of Chiang's troops to contain a determined enemy drive on the eastern air bases. He knew that Chiang had failed to equip his armies in the east—he was husbanding his strength for the inevitable clash with the Communists. So Stilwell warned Roosevelt to build the new heavy bomber bases as far away from the Japanese as possible—around Chengtu. Stilwell's premonitions were correct. In May the Japanese began their biggest offensive of the war—*Operation Ichi-go*. Commanded by General Hada the *Ichi-go* armies overran the eastern bases, captured vast areas of Chinese territory and brought fresh misery to millions of Chinese. However, Hada failed in his main objective—the prevention of bomber attacks upon the Japanese homeland.

The value of the air war

Long-range bombing of Japan by unescorted B-29 Superfortresses began in 1944. It was dangerous work. For example, ten of the huge bombers crashed during one mission and follow-up raids had to endure suicide attacks from Japanese pilots who rammed their fighters into the American planes. In the meantime, the Americans' atoll-hopping tactics‡ brought them to the Marianas—superb island bases for the B-29s. So the Chengtu bases soon became redundant and by January 1945 the last B-29s had left China. Neither they nor Chennault's C.A.T.F. had made much impact upon the successful prosecution of the war, though their operations had certainly highlighted the selfishness of Chiang Kai-shek and the disagreements between the top American commanders. Stilwell and Chennault both lost their jobs before the end of the war, a war which would be decided by U.S. forces based in the Pacific, not in China.

*They received $500 for each Japanese plane they shot down.
†Chinese villagers saved 59 of the airmen. Japanese troops captured 8 Americans—and beheaded 3 of them.
‡See *A Map History of the United States*, 35: Assault from the air: the defeat of Japan, 1945.

SYMBOLS OF FREE CHINA'S AIR POWER

① The FLYING TIGERS —painted on aircraft and worn as a badge on flying jackets.

② Chinese Air Force markings

Territory controlled by Japan before Ichi-go.

Territory captured by Japan during 1944.

⟶ Main Japanese thrusts.

⟶ Chinese operations in Burma.

⤍ British operations in Burma.

★ Air bases captured by Japanese.

CHENGTU B29 Bases

CHUNGKING

LAOHOKOW

Yangtze-kiang

Wenchow

HENGYANG

SUICHUAN

Foochow

LINGLING

LEDO

KWEILIN

AMOY

LIUCHOW

SWATOW

TAIWAN

Burma Road

KUNMING

YUNNAN

CANTON

LASHIO

MANDALAY

KYEDAW ⊛ —original base of the Flying Tigers

FRENCH INDO-CHINA

THE ICHI—GO OFFENSIVE 1944

BURMA

THAILAND

SIGNIFICANCE OF THE AMERICAN ADVANCE IN THE PACIFIC FROM 1944

✳ Chengtu B29s attacking Japan had to fly over occupied China.

JAPAN

Tokyo

KYUSHU

First bombed by Marianas–based B.29s on 24 November 1944

Taiwan and Kyushu were heavily attacked by China-based B.29s

JAPANESE OCCUPIED ZONE

Okinawa captured 1945

BURMA

FRENCH

TAIWAN

Iwojima captured 1945

With the capture of Iwojima, the Americans had a base for their P.51 escort fighters—these now accompanied the B.29s to Japan.

THAILAND

INDO-CHINA

PHILIPPINES

Marianas captured 1944

US FORCES

Three B.29 bases established on **Saipan**, **Tinian**, and **Guam**. Distance from Tokyo just under 1600 miles.

29 The Nationalist war effort, 1941–5

The armed forces

During the Second World War the British and American people were quite willing to believe that Chiang Kai-shek's armies were bearing the brunt of a hard-fought struggle in China. They did not realize that they had been largely taken in by the Generalissimo's propaganda experts who presented the outside world with a picture of Nationalist soldiers gallantly stemming attacks by hordes of Japanese along a front line which stretched from the Great Wall down to Canton. In fact, the Japanese had already slowed down their offensive operations in China. They had captured the most productive parts and did not want to encourage guerrilla activities by over-extending their own lines of communication. Of course, the Japanese did launch offensives after 1941 but these were always for limited purposes such as, for example, their occupation of Chihkiang Province in retaliation for the 1942 Doolittle raid on Tokyo. These offensives met with some Nationalist opposition: one division fought an epic last stand at the *Battle of Changteh* (1943–4) while other divisions fought the *Battle of Heng-yang* and held up the *Ichi-go* offensive for eight weeks during 1944. But neither these defensive battles nor the hundreds of Nationalist-inspired guerrilla raids were of any significance in the long run—simply because the Generalissimo refused to commit his main armies to a full-scale war against Japan. Proof of this was in the fact that, throughout this period, he stationed his best troops in the north-west in order to maintain a blockade of Communist positions in Yenan.

The Cairo Conference, 1943

Of course, President Roosevelt and Prime Minister Churchill were aware of the Generalissimo's reluctance to fight. Nevertheless, they badly needed his assistance for the reconquest of Burma and that was why they invited him to the 1943 Cairo Conference. They had already guaranteed that foreign nations would relinquish their extra-territorial rights in China; now they promised that Nationalist China would regain Manchuria, Taiwan and the Pescadores as soon as Japan surrendered. In the meantime the Allies would do everything they could to help Free China. Reluctantly, Chiang agreed to commit a few of his divisions to help the Allies in their most pressing task—running the Japanese out of Burma.

Burma: the Ledo Road, 1944–5

Chinese troops played an important role in Burma. Many flew in from Yunnan to reinforce their comrades stationed in India and together they fought in the campaigns that helped to liberate northern Burma. In addition, they assisted in building the Ledo Road which in 1945 linked up with the Burma Road and reopened land communications with China. This new road meant that American aid could now flood into China; moreover, the Nationalist divisions that had fought in Burma could now literally drive home. So, in 1945, thousands of Chinese troops returned to Nationalist China with U.S. trucks, tanks and heavy artillery. This was how the Generalissimo acquired a brand-new, well-equipped fighting force which could be salted away for the coming struggle against the Communists.

The armaments industry

Chiang's propaganda machine churned out endless statistics about the achievements of Free China's war production. In fact, until November 1944 most factories were working at half capacity, dogged by the ever-inflating cost of raw materials. It was this inflation, together with the corruption that characterized most officials working for Chiang, that turned out to be Free China's most dangerous enemy.

Chiang Kai-shek, Roosevelt, Churchill and Mme Chiang Kai-shek at the Cairo Conference, 1943.

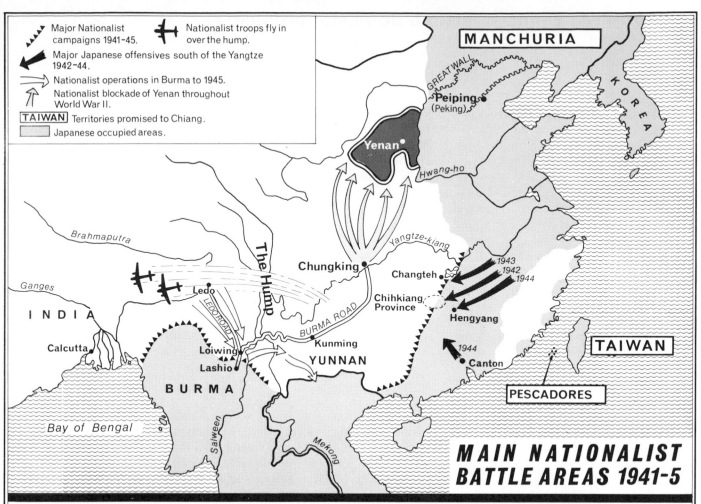

Legend:

- Major Nationalist campaigns 1941–45.
- Nationalist troops fly in over the hump.
- Major Japanese offensives south of the Yangtze 1942–44.
- Nationalist operations in Burma to 1945.
- Nationalist blockade of Yenan throughout World War II.
- TAIWAN Territories promised to Chiang.
- Japanese occupied areas.

MANCHURIA

GREAT WALL

Peiping (Peking)

KOREA

Yenan

Hwang-ho

Brahmaputra

Ganges

INDIA

Calcutta

The Hump

Ledo

LEDO ROAD

Chungking

Yangtze-kiang

Changteh

Chihkiang Province

1943
1942
1944

Hengyang

TAIWAN

BURMA ROAD

Loiwing

Lashio

BURMA

Kunming

YUNNAN

1944

Canton

PESCADORES

Salween

Bay of Bengal

Mekong

MAIN NATIONALIST BATTLE AREAS 1941-5

LIGHT-WEIGHT TANKS USED IN THE C-B-I WAR THEATRE

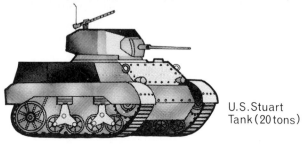

U.S. Stuart Tank (20 tons)

Japanese type 95 Tank (10 tons)

Light-weight tanks were more use than medium and heavy tanks in the difficult terrain of the China–Burma–India war theatre. The Stuart, used by many Chinese armoured units, carried a 37mm gun and two machine-guns; the Type 95, though much lighter, carried the same armament.

PRODUCTION ACHIEVEMENTS

Manufacture of small arms   1941–5

RIFLES	263,735
MACHINE GUNS	44,718
MORTARS	10,392
HAND GRENADES	16,000,000

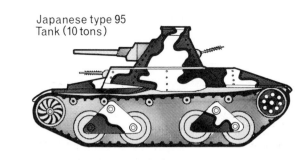

AND AFTER NOV. 1944

PIG IRON	up by 46%
STEEL	up by 52%
COAL	up by 35%
ALCOHOL (FOR MAKING MOTOR FUEL)	up by 30%
ELECTRIC POWER	up by 8%

30 Free China: wartime domestic problems

Inflation

When the war against Japan began in 1937 a peasant with 50 Chinese dollars could just afford to buy a cow; had he saved the money until the time of Pearl Harbor (7 December 1941) the 50 dollars would have just covered the cost of a chicken; and when the war ended in August 1945 the 50 dollars represented the selling price of one egg. Inflation was China's biggest single problem during the Second World War. Everything was in short supply and the prices of consumer goods simply rocketed. And when the workers clamoured for wage increases the government merely issued more banknotes until these were not worth much more than the paper they were printed on. Moreover, it was a matter of public scandal that Chiang Kai-shek was flying these banknotes (printed in the U.S.A.) over the Hump, thus wasting valuable plane space with loads of inflationary money.

The black market

Equally scandalous was the fact that Chinese truck drivers were smuggling in luxury goods from India for sale on the black market. Precious medicines, petrol and canned foodstuffs also found their way on to the black market—about 30 per cent of foreign aid was misused in this manner. Thousands of Chinese suffered as a result of these unpatriotic activities. Stuart Gelder, a journalist assigned to China during the war, reported in 1944 that Nationalist soldiers were dying from dysentery because they could not get any of the sulpha drugs shipped in from the United States. Yet these same sulpha drugs were on sale at highly inflated prices in a Kunming chemist's shop.

Corruption

This sort of problem could never be solved because of the corruption of Nationalist officials. Gelder complained to one Chungking official about the sulpha drug racket and the official promised to have the chemist shot: 'He would indeed. "Face" would have been saved by his execution and four or five hundred others would have continued to do flourishing business.'* Government officials profited from inflation by taking a 'rake-off' from the smugglers; some even managed to organize a mail order business between merchants in the occupied zone and the cities of Free China! Several of China's best-known families made fortunes during this period and probably deserved the Communist accusation that the 'Kuomintang-controlled areas had become an abyss of degeneracy and corruption'.†

The problem of law and order

In the face of inflation, black market deals and government corruption it was inevitable that there would be plenty of public protest. Riots in Kwangtung, demonstrations in Szechwan and a spate of bandit attacks upon government centres in Kansu forced Chiang Kai-shek to employ terror tactics against his own people. He used a mysterious but powerful figure named Tai Li to direct the secret police. Tai Li was Chiang's most trusted henchman—it was said that he was the only officer allowed to wear his sword in the presence of the Generalissimo—and he set up a rule of terror rivalled only by the Gestapo in Nazi Germany. Tai Li established so-called *thought correction camps* outside Chungking and those detainees lucky enough to survive a spell inside these concentration camps were, according to the U.S. ambassador to China, 'usually broken both in body and in mind'.‡

True friends of China

During the war hundreds of missionaries had moved westwards to join their more adventurous colleagues of the China Inland Mission who had been working in the interior for several decades. By 1942 the missionaries were everywhere, providing shelter for travellers, medical care for the sick and wounded, schooling for the peasant children. They were of many nationalities—German, French, British, Italian, Canadian, American, Irish—and between them they brought the Chinese people a great deal of comfort. One remarkable Quaker group formed the Friends' Ambulance Unit (F.A.U.). Their big Sentinel and Chevrolet trucks transported medical supplies all over China. When the Japanese cut the Burma Road in 1942 and the F.A.U. ran out of petrol supplies they converted their lorries to charcoal burning—much to the delight of Chinese children who called these strange vehicles *ma ma hu hu* (*horse horse tiger tiger*), neither one thing nor the other! Stuart Gelder gave the F.A.U. proper credit for their labours: 'Only when the American army and the Friends' Ambulance Unit were handling drugs could they be certain of reaching their proper destination. Thousands of Chinese are alive today who but for the Quakers would be dead.'§

*Stuart Gelder, *The Chinese Communists* (Gollancz, 1945) p. xvi.
†Contained in a Chinese Communist history book published in 1964.
‡Quoted in Richard Alstyne's *The United States and East Asia* (Thames and Hudson, 1973) pp. 156–7.
§Gelder, p. xvi.

CORRUPTION AND DISORDER IN FREE CHINA 1941–44

The over-taxed, under-fed peasantry followed the traditional path of protest – they became bandits and terrorized government officials in Kansu. Many peasants escaped the clutches of the secret police by taking refuge in the Communist headquarters in Yenan.

U. S. S. R.

MONGOLIA

SINKIANG
(Under Russian influence for most of the war)

TIBET

Yenan

Hwang-ho

KANSU

SZECHWAN

Yangtze kiang

• Chungking

BURMA

• Kunming

YUNNAN

KWANG-TUNG

Korea

JAPAN

Shanghai–
captured by Japanese in 1937

Both ports were centres of trade between the occupied zone and Chungking.

Hong Kong–
captured by Japanese in 1942

★ Yenan – communist headquarters.

↗ Black market goods smuggled in over the Burma Road (until 1942).

◖ Postal services maintained for much of the war period.

▭▭ Limit of Japanese advance 1943.

There was serious famine in Kwangtung during 1943. This, plus the heavy taxes levied by the Kuomintang government, made the peasants almost welcome the 1944 Japanese offensives which led to the occupation of most of the province.

FRIENDS' AMBULANCE UNIT

The F.A.U. symbol – painted on the side of a lorry, it was much more valuable than a passport in wartime China.

The hopper: the fire had to be poked down before adding the charcoal.

33

The conversion unit (weighing half a ton) to enable the lorry to run on charcoal gas.

"Briefly, this consisted of a large tin box capable of holding up to 400 lbs of crushed charcoal, at the bottom of which was the fire, brought up to white heat by a crank handle geared to a fan. In the fire the gas was generated, and then made its way through a grid at the back of the fire and along the pipes which ran round the back of the lorry to the engine. Three filters removed impurities from the gas before it reached the manifold. Pipes, filter and charcoal container were all supposedly air-tight. The supply of air to be mixed with the gas was regulated by a hand-control on the dashboard."

Bernard Llewellyn 'I left my roots in China' (Allen & Unwin 1953) p.42.

Llewellyn drove a charcoal burner in China during the war and his book contains many fascinating accounts of everyday life.

A CHARCOAL BURNER :

Conversions began in the Spring of 1942. The technical ideas were based upon 5 **Sentinel** lorries (all designed as charcoal burners) exported by Britain to China in 1940.

31 The Communist war effort, 1941–5

The price of guerrilla activity

While there were no cancers such as corruption and inflation to eat out the heart of the Communist armies, neither was there any keenness to engage the Japanese invader in open combat. Ever since their victory at Pinghsinkuan back in 1937 the Communists had refused to commit their troops to set-piece battles. Instead, Mao Tse-tung had developed a military strategy based entirely upon guerrilla operations. It didn't always work. For example, his guerrillas successfully disrupted Japanese communications in Shansi, Hupeh and Honan during the *Hundred Regiments Offensive*, 1940–41. But when the infuriated Japanese retaliated with a series of anti-guerrilla sweeps the Communists lost about 100,000 men in the years 1941–3.

Other setbacks

In fact, the Communists were badly mauled by a variety of foes during this period. In January 1941 Chiang Kai-shek treacherously attacked units of the New Fourth Army at their headquarters in Anhwei. This was the notorious *Anhwei Incident* which not only cost the Communists another 10,000 men but also wrecked any hopes of future co-operation between the Communist and Nationalist armies. Shortly after this the Japanese began raiding Communist bases in central China and made extensive use of puppet troops conscripted in the coastal regions. These puppet soldiers owed allegiance to a man who was, in effect, China's Quisling* during the Second World War. He was Wang Ching-wei, a former henchman of Chiang Kai-shek. In 1940 the Japanese proclaimed Wang to be 'ruler' of China—and used his troops against the Communists for the rest of the war.

The extent of guerrilla operations

A fog of propaganda obscures the history of Communist guerrilla operations. There are many accounts of *sparrow warfare* in which the guerrillas scattered 'like sparrows over wide areas, appearing and disappearing unexpectedly to surprise the enemy forces'.† Mao's guerrillas used *land-mines* to destroy railway lines and resorted to *tunnel warfare* by attacking enemy patrols from village strongpoints cunningly linked together by means of underground tunnels. However, the Japanese took effective counter-measures and protected their main bases and vital communication links with barbed-wire entanglements, trenches, armoured trains and aircraft. Gradually, they came to accept a situation in which the Communists could be safely left in control of the rural

areas so long as they didn't interfere with Japanese military operations. This arrangement delighted Mao because it enabled his guerrillas to win the hearts and minds of the peasants with a long-overdue programme of land and currency reform. By mid-1944, when the Japanese Ichi-go offensive was in full swing against the U.S. air bases, the Americans were naturally suspicious that Communist inactivity in the north might be due to some sort of understanding between Mao and the Japanese.

The Yenan Mission, 1944

Though they had never bothered to send Mao any military aid, the Americans now hoped to integrate the Communist war effort into the struggle against Japan. They sent a U.S. Army Observer Group to Yenan in 1944 to persuade Mao to liven up the war in the north. The Americans arrived in July and were amazed to see how active and enthusiastic Mao's supporters were. John Service, a member of the mission, had the run of Yenan and could see with his own eyes the extent of Communist land reform, the absence of corruption and the enormous potential for guerrilla warfare against the Japanese. When he and other members of the mission heard that President Roosevelt's personal representative, Ambassador Patrick Hurley, was coming to Yenan in November, they hoped that he might be able to forge an alliance with the Communists.

Failure of a mission, 1944–5

Ambassador Hurley arrived in Chungking via Moscow, met Chiang Kai-shek—with whom he was greatly impressed—and then flew on to meet Mao in Yenan. Part Indian, Hurley greatly alarmed the reception committee on Yenan air strip by letting out a Choctaw war whoop! He then tried to convince Mao that, at a time of national emergency, Chinese Communists and Chinese Nationalists should sink their political differences and learn to work together—just as American Democrats and American Republicans did in the U.S.A. Hurley made no headway whatsoever in his self-imposed task of uniting Mao and Chiang and America's attempt to influence the Communist war effort bore very little fruit.

*Quisling was the name of a Norwegian politician who helped govern Norway on behalf of the Nazi invaders during the Second World War.
†Quoted by Fitzgerald and Roper, *China: A World So Changed* (Heinemann Educational Books, 1972) p. 108.

WARFARE IN NORTH CHINA

Between 1941 and 1945 guerrilla warfare in North China took the form of a gigantic game of hide-and-seek played out between the Communists and Japanese occupation forces. Below is an account (quoted in *CHINA RECONSTRUCTS 1970*) of 'tunnel warfare' fought out in the village of Jan, Hopei province, towards the end of the war.

"We worked during the day and dug tunnels at night. By the beginning of 1945 we had completed four main tunnels with 24 branches radiating out from them. We also dug more than 15 kilometres of tunnels to connect us with neighbouring villages. Our tunnels not only had direction signs and oil lamps at the turns, but we had rest-places, food storage, kitchens and latrines. The entrances were usually at the base of a wall under brick beds or in dry wells. Inside the entrance we made the tunnel dip down and up again.... If the enemy pumped in poison gas we blocked the concaves with earth so the gas couldn't get in.... As the sun came up on 20 June 1945, the Japanese and puppet troops attacked.... We were ready for them. Suddenly, from every direction above and below ground we poured our revenge into the enemy...."

Nationalist blockade of Yenan.

Hurley's flight to Yenan 1944.

Scene of the Battle of PINGHSINKUAN 1937

Scene of the ANHWEI INCIDENT 1941
(Each side accused the other of firing first.)

Communist 'liberated areas', 1944.

Japanese occupied areas (1944–5).

Rail links vital to Japanese military operations.

The expansion of Communist power in the rural areas of North China 1943–1945

32 1945: the unexpected victory over Japan

War-weary Japan

By the summer of 1945 the Japanese people were steeling themselves for a fight to the death. Already their cities and industrial centres lay in ruins, victims of the B.29 firestorm raids. In Burma their armies suffered total defeat. Okinawa, a mere 350 miles from the Japanese homeland, was in American hands. And they were well aware that the Anglo-Americans were planning invasions of Kyushu and Honshu which could easily cause the death of millions of Japanese civilians. Yet their most terrifying and decisive experience of the entire war was still to come: attack by atomic bomb. It began on the morning of 6 August 1945, just as the people of Hiroshima were setting out for work. A solitary B.29 flew over their city and with a single nuclear bomb turned it into an atomic desert.

The Russians declare war

Hiroshima galvanized the Communists into action. On 8 August Stalin sent his troops into China, Manchuria and Korea. And on the same day that another B.29 dropped its atomic bomb on Nagasaki (9 August) Mao Tse-tung began a general offensive against the Japanese in north China. With 130,000 civilians lying dead in Hiroshima and Nagasaki and thousands more dying from radiation burns and neutron bombardment, Emperor Hirohito commanded his armed forces to lay down their arms—an order which the Kwantung Army found difficult to swallow. Consequently, there were some fierce clashes between Soviet and Japanese troops as the Russians swept across East Asia in their bid to occupy as much territory as possible.*

The surrender problem

Stalin had already agreed with Chiang Kai-shek that Japanese troops in China should surrender to the Nationalists. Unfortunately, there were no Nationalist units operating in north China at the time—a situation quickly exploited by the Chinese Communists who accepted not only the surrender of the Japanese soldiers but also their arms, ammunition and well-stocked supply dumps. This naturally enraged Chiang Kai-shek and he pestered the Americans to ferry Nationalist troops to key cities, rail centres and ports in the north. Even though this was bound to lead to renewed hostilities between the Communists and Nationalists, the Americans felt obliged to render this service to their ally. But to minimize the danger the Americans decided to station some of their own marines along the Chinese coast.

Mao meets Chiang, August 1945

Ambassador Hurley was still working to bring the Communists and Nationalists together—and he scored a minor triumph by persuading Mao to meet the Generalissimo in Chungking. Mao didn't stay long as he preferred Chou En-lai to do the talking. And while the talking went on, a Communist general named Lin Piao was leading the guerrilla armies into the richest prize of all—the Manchurian provinces that had been lost to the Japanese in 1931. Control of the Manchurian industrial centres was Mao's immediate aim; for Manchuria could be the base from which he could overthrow the Generalissimo and establish Communist rule throughout China.

Chiang chases Lin Piao

Chiang had no illusions about Mao's intentions. He assembled his crack divisions—troops originally trained by Stilwell for the Burma campaign—and persuaded the Americans to transport them to Manchuria. However, the Russians refused to let them disembark and so the U.S. landing craft took them across to Chinwangtao. From here the Nationalists began their pursuit of Lin Piao, catching up with him in late October. They immediately attacked and thus resumed the civil war which had been in abeyance—officially, at least—since 1937.

Hurley resigns

In Chungking, Chou En-lai condemned the Nationalist attack. He stated that further discussion was futile and flew back to Yenan on 25 November. Hurley, who was in Washington for talks with President Truman,† refused to return to Chungking and resigned as ambassador. These events led Truman to change America's policy towards China. He proposed to force the Generalissimo to form a government which included representatives of the C.C.P. If the Generalissimo resisted, then America would cut off military aid to the Nationalists. It would not be said of America that she spent the taxpayers' money supporting *one* side in a civil war. Truman needed an ambassador capable of carrying out the task and he chose General George C. Marshall. But he had given Marshall an impossible assignment. No American could expect to bring the Chinese civil war to a conclusion that would be satisfactory from an *American* point of view. Nevertheless, Marshall intended to do his utmost to unravel the 'China tangle'.

*According to the Russians, they killed 84,000 Japanese and took 594,000 prisoner at a cost to themselves of 30,000 dead and wounded.
†Harry S. Truman, Vice President, became President of the U.S.A. on the death of Roosevelt in April 1945.

1945: WORLD WAR II ENDS

U.S.S.R.

SAKHALIN

MONGOLIA

MANCHURIA

Legend:
- ★⟹ Russian attacks.
- ⟹ Mao's general offensive.
- ✈--- Mao's flight to Chungking.

Kalgan

Peking

Chinwangtao

Vladivostok

Tientsin
Taku

Pyongyang

Dairen

38th Parallel

KOREA

Tokyo

HONSHU

Japanese surrender 14 August 1945.

SHANTUNG

Yenan

Tsinan

Hiroshima

Atomic attack 6 August 1945.

C H I N A

Suchow

Nagasaki

KYUSHU

Atomic attack 9 August 1945.

U.S. planes fly Nationalist troops to key cities

Shanghai

Hangchow

Chungking

U.S. troop movements after the Japanese surrender.

OKINAWA

1945: CHINESE CIVIL WAR RESUMES

Mukden ■
An important rail and industrial centre.

Lin Piao and the Eighth Route Army take up their positions behind the Great Wall

RUSSIAN OCCUPATION TROOPS

R. Yalu

■ Peking

Shanhaikuan
Chinwangtao

Tientsin ✪

Taku ✪

Russians in Dairen turned back the U.S. transports.

Chefoo ✪

Legend:
- ✪ 53,000 U.S. marines based in these ports.
- ⟹ Nationalist attack across the wall led to the Communist withdrawal from Shanhaikuan.
- ⟵ U.S. transports carrying Nationalist troops.

Tsingtao ✪

Ambassador Hurley with Mao Tse-tung.

Further Reading

Theme 4—China and the Second World War

Spread

27.	William Koenig	*Over the Hump: Airlift to China*	Ballantine Books, 1972
	Arthur N. Young	*China and the Helping Hand, 1937–45*	Harvard University Press, 1963
28.	Ron Heiferman	*Flying Tigers—Chennault in China*	Ballantine Books, 1972
	Carl Berger	*B.29—The Superfortress*	Macdonald, 1971
29.	D. D. Rooney	*Stilwell*	Pan/Ballantine, 1973
30.	Stuart Gelder	*The Chinese Communists*	Gollancz, 1946
	R. Deacon	*A History of the Chinese Secret Service*	Frederick Muller Ltd., 1974
31.	C. P. Fitzgerald and Myra Roper	*China: A World So Changed* (Ch. 9)	Thomas Nelson and Heinemann Educational Books, 1971
32.	Anthony Kubek	*How the Far East Was Lost History of the Second World War*, Vol. 6	Intercontex, 1971 Purnell

THEME 5

The Communist Victory

In Manchuria, the Japanese had created one of Asia's most important centres of heavy industry and both Mao Tse-tung and Chiang Kai-shek were prepared to fight for its possession. This was why the Generalissimo chased north in 1946 to meet the Communists on their own ground. It was a fatal decision for at this moment in Chinese history the Americans decided to cut off aid to Chiang so that they could not be accused of helping one side in particular in the civil war.

While the fighting went on in the north, inflation was making life a misery in the south. The high cost of living and the constant threat of conscription wrecked morale among the civilians. Their despair spread to the troops and the will to resist Communism on the battlefield diminished every day. In April 1949 the Communists were crossing the Yangtze-kiang and pressing on through the chaos of a crumbling Nationalist defence. Literally millions of Chiang's troops defected to the Red Army, taking their arms and equipment with them. By September 1949 the civil war was virtually over and Mao decided that the time was ripe to proclaim a new Republic of China. Speaking to the Chinese people from Peking's Gate of Heavenly Peace, he said, 'Our work shall be written down in the history of mankind, and it will clearly demonstrate the fact that the Chinese, who comprise one quarter of mankind, have from now on stood up ... We have united ourselves and defeated both foreign and domestic enemies by means of the People's War of Liberation and the People's Great Revolution and we announce the establishment of the People's Republic of China ...'

Although Chiang Kai-shek had to concede that the Communists had beaten him on the mainland, he decided to transfer the rump of the Nationalist government to the off-shore island of Taiwan. He arrived in December 1949 and remained there as President until his death in 1975.

33　The Marshall Mission to China, December 1945–January 1947

A brief truce

General Marshall's mission was to stop the civil war and get the Communist and Nationalist leaders to sit round the conference table. He did not waste much time. He invited Chou En-lai to fly down from Yenan to attend a *Political Consultative Conference* in Chungking. At first, the Communist and Nationalist delegates seemed to get on well together. Chou En-lai soon agreed to a truce, approved a proposal for drafting a new constitution and accepted the idea of placing Communist guerrilla forces and Nationalist soldiers under a single military commander. On 10 January 1946 Marshall announced that a cease-fire was operating throughout China. And when the Russians finally evacuated Mukden in March 1946 the General was delighted to see Nationalist troops move into the city without any interference from the Communists. It seemed a good omen as, on 12 March, he flew back to America to confer with President Truman.

A broken truce

Five days after he left, civil war flared up in Manchuria. Lin Piao blocked the Nationalist advance northwards by winning the *First Battle of Szepingkai*. Chiang Kai-shek promptly leap-frogged the Communist defence lines by airlifting troops into Changchun. And while fighting raged around this city another Nationalist force—the New First Army—completely defeated the Communists at the *Second Battle of Szepingkai*. Marshall hastily returned to China and managed to patch up the broken truce—a move which probably saved the Communists from further defeat at the hands of the New First Army. These crack troops not only outnumbered the Communists but also enjoyed the rare advantage of first-class field commanders and the latest American equipment.

No more aid for the Nationalists

But this was the stage when General Marshall had to reconcile his desire to see Chiang Kai-shek emerge as the leader of a united China with his own role as an impartial mediator in a civil war. Mao Tse-tung was currently taking the Americans to task for selling arms to the Nationalists but denying all aid to the Communists. It was an embarrassing moment for the General as America had already promised to dump in Nationalist China all her surplus Second World War materials (vast quantities were still scattered around the battle-scarred islands of the Pacific). So Marshall had to make a difficult decision: there would be no more aid for the Nationalists. So at

the very moment (July 1946)* when the New First Army had the advantage in Manchuria, Marshall was giving the Communists a chance to regroup and rearm their battered formations. Inevitably, it was not long before some Nationalist units ran out of the vital ·30 calibre ammunition. Chiang Kai-shek had to disband several divisions—and some of these immediately went over to the Communist side. General Marshall was paying a dangerously high price for his impartiality.

America's fears

By 1946 America's Cold War with Russia had already begun and a crisis was looming up in divided Germany. President Truman had set his face against further extension of Soviet power—Russia must be contained. He was convinced that it was Stalin who was masterminding the Communists in Manchuria and he regarded Mao Tse-tung as Stalin's political tool. Yet he still believed that there was a slim chance that America could wean the Communists away from their 'allegiance' to Moscow and persuade them to co-operate with the Nationalists. After all, there was some precedent for this; in France the Communists had agreed to join a coalition government.† Truman knew he was running a serious risk in cutting off aid to the Nationalists but it seemed worth taking if it encouraged Mao to throw in his lot with Chiang Kai-shek.

The collapse of America's policies

As far as China was concerned, the American President was living in a dream world. Mao Tse-tung was never Stalin's political tool. And he never intended—despite what he might say to American mediators such as General Marshall—to collaborate with Chiang Kai-shek. Mao regarded the Generalissimo as the last of a long line of war-lords; Chiang was equally intolerant of Mao. By the beginning of 1947 it was clear to Marshall that his mission had turned into a fiasco. He asked the President to recall him and totally frustrated by the deep distrust that existed between Mao and Chiang he left China just as the Generalissimo was about to launch an attack upon the Communist headquarters in Yenan.

---

*It also coincided with the evacuation of U.S. marines from north China. Part of the U.S. 1st Marines did, however, remain in Tientsin until 1947.

†They were not in office for long. The French Prime Minister dismissed his Communist ministers in May 1947.

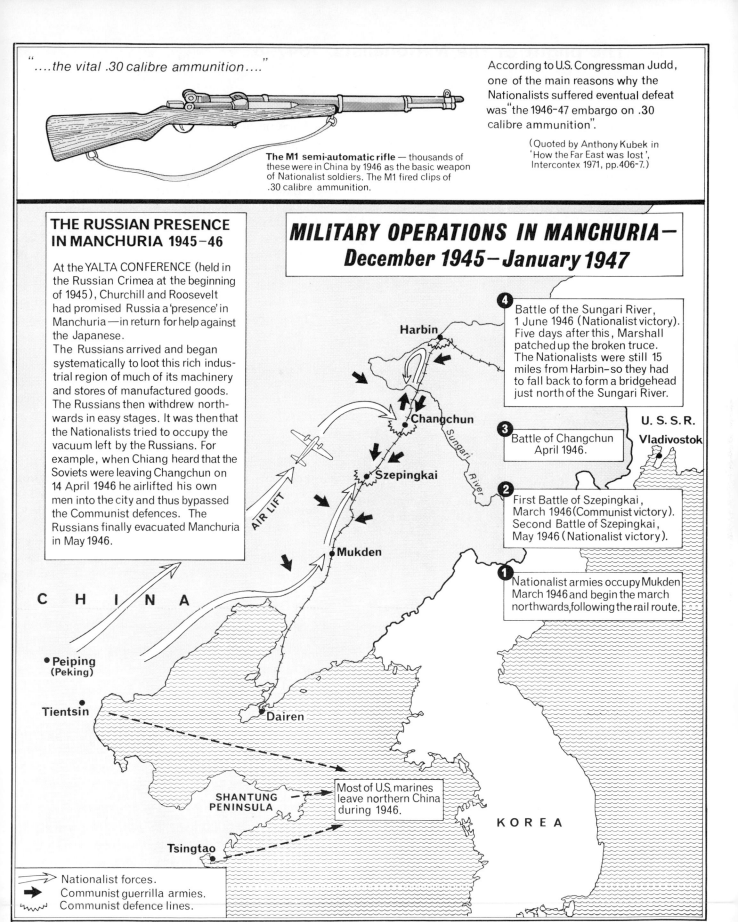

The **M1 semi-automatic rifle** — thousands of these were in China by 1946 as the basic weapon of Nationalist soldiers. The M1 fired clips of .30 calibre ammunition.

According to U.S. Congressman Judd, one of the main reasons why the Nationalists suffered eventual defeat was "the 1946-47 embargo on .30 calibre ammunition".

(Quoted by Anthony Kubek in 'How the Far East was lost', Intercontex 1971, pp.406-7.)

THE RUSSIAN PRESENCE IN MANCHURIA 1945–46

At the YALTA CONFERENCE (held in the Russian Crimea at the beginning of 1945), Churchill and Roosevelt had promised Russia a 'presence' in Manchuria—in return for help against the Japanese.

The Russians arrived and began systematically to loot this rich industrial region of much of its machinery and stores of manufactured goods. The Russians then withdrew northwards in easy stages. It was then that the Nationalists tried to occupy the vacuum left by the Russians. For example, when Chiang heard that the Soviets were leaving Changchun on 14 April 1946 he airlifted his own men into the city and thus bypassed the Communist defences. The Russians finally evacuated Manchuria in May 1946.

MILITARY OPERATIONS IN MANCHURIA— December 1945 – January 1947

Harbin

Changchun

Szepingkai

Mukden

AIR LIFT

Sungari River

U.S.S.R.

Vladivostok

4 Battle of the Sungari River, 1 June 1946 (Nationalist victory). Five days after this, Marshall patched up the broken truce. The Nationalists were still 15 miles from Harbin–so they had to fall back to form a bridgehead just north of the Sungari River.

3 Battle of Changchun April 1946.

2 First Battle of Szepingkai, March 1946 (Communist victory). Second Battle of Szepingkai, May 1946 (Nationalist victory).

1 Nationalist armies occupy Mukden March 1946 and begin the march northwards, following the rail route.

C H I N A

• **Peiping** (Peking)

Tientsin •

Dairen

SHANTUNG PENINSULA

Most of U.S. marines leave northern China during 1946.

K O R E A

Tsingtao •

⟹ Nationalist forces.
➤ Communist guerrilla armies.
⌇➤ Communist defence lines.

75

34 The plight of the Nationalists, 1947–8

A hollow victory

In March 1947 Chiang Kai-shek tried to boost Nationalist morale by announcing the capture of Mao's headquarters in Yenan. In fact, Mao had deliberately abandoned Yenan as a base in order to avoid an unnecessary pitched battle with the Nationalist armies advancing across Shensi. He withdrew northwards, but ordered his guerrillas to harass the Nationalists—and it was not long before the invaders of Yenan found themselves under siege. Chiang Kai-shek's capture of Yenan proved to be a hollow—and short-lived—victory.*

On the defensive in Manchuria

Exactly the same fate overtook the Nationalists in Manchuria. Though they had occupied various important cities such as Mukden, Szepingkai, Changchun and Kirin, they had not gained control of the countryside where Communists roamed at will, blowing up railway lines and generally intercepting supplies en route to the cities. However, Chiang still had one advantage: command of the air. Scores of wartime transports and B.24 Liberator bombers remained in China and though these big aircraft were of little value in anti-guerrilla operations they were useful for dropping supplies to Nationalist troops pinned down in the cities.

Defeat in Manchuria, 1948

In 1948 the Nationalists found they were fighting a new kind of war. Brand-new Communist formations confronted them. Mao had summoned together his guerrilla bands and ordered his generals to fashion them into conventional armies. They had an amazing array of weapons: ex-Japanese tanks and mortars given to them by the Russians; pre-war Czech machine-guns captured from the Nationalists; and every day that passed saw an increasing stock of American jeeps, howitzers and bazookas as more and more Nationalist soldiers came over to the Communist side. Chiang decided to abandon Manchuria and ordered his armies to break out from the garrison towns. But to his horror Lin Piao's armies swept down to straddle the escape route from Manchuria into north China. In the valleys between Mukden and Chinchow, Communist and Nationalist soldiers fought a series of desperate battles at the end of October 1948. When the fighting ended Lin Piao had killed, wounded or captured 400,000 men. Chiang Kai-shek had lost the cream of his front-line armies.

Conditions in the south

Meanwhile, inflation continued to make most people's lives a misery. During 1947–8 it reached the sort of proportions experienced in Germany after the First World War. Bank notes had very little meaning; one Western couple, having dinner in a smart Shanghai hotel during 1947, found that the bill came to 250 million yuan! People had to resort to barter—though most peasants had very little in the way of food surpluses to exchange. A lot would have starved had it not been for the efforts of missionaries, American Red Cross workers and members of the *United Nations Relief and Rehabilitation Administration* working in China. For a time factory workers managed to peg their wages to prices but people on fixed incomes—teachers, soldiers, local government officials—were soon on the poverty line. Savings were utterly worthless; unemployment became the scourge of the cities, first as small firms went under, and then as thousands of refugees swarmed in from the countryside.

The breakdown of government

Government had no answer to inflation. It was alienating the people by ruthlessly conscripting men and boys to fight in the civil war. Soldiers started to live off the land; academics turned Communist; 'the squeeze'—or bribe—tempted many a government official. Press-gangs roaming the countryside sparked off more than one peasant revolt; student demonstrations broke out in Nanking† and Shanghai. On Taiwan the rioting was so serious that Chiang had to send in an infantry division to restore order. Travellers took their lives into their hands and soon every train had its soldiers on board to keep off bandit attacks while even the river steamers festooned their superstructure with iron spikes to deter the pirates. Law and order had broken down.

Belated aid from America

For some time the U.S. Congress had been worried about the Communist advance. Mao now seemed to be as big a threat as Stalin—the President must change his China policy and send help to Chiang. In April 1948 Truman signed the *China Aid Bill*. But by the time the first ammunition ship sailed to China (November 1948) it was a case of 'too little, too late'. The Communists had begun the offensives that would drive Chiang from the mainland for ever.

*He lost it to the Communists in 1948.
†Chiang moved his capital from Chungking to Nanking during 1946.

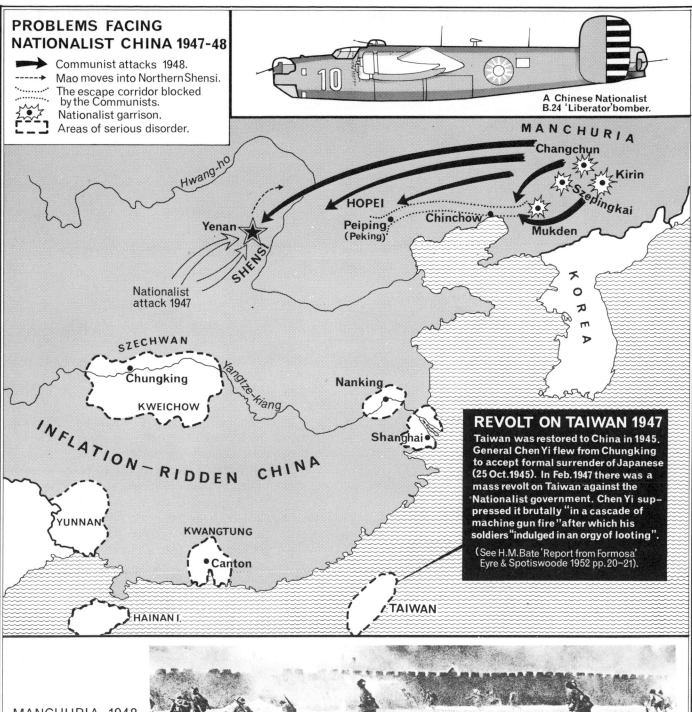

PROBLEMS FACING NATIONALIST CHINA 1947-48

➡ Communist attacks 1948.
⇢ Mao moves into Northern Shensi.
⋯> The escape corridor blocked by the Communists.
✳ Nationalist garrison.
⬚ Areas of serious disorder.

A Chinese Nationalist B.24 'Liberator' bomber.

MANCHURIA

Hwang-ho

Changchun

Kirin

Szepingkai

HOPEI

Peiping (Peking)

Chinchow

Mukden

Yenan

SHENSI

Nationalist attack 1947

KOREA

SZECHWAN

Chungking

Yangtze-kiang

KWEICHOW

Nanking

Shanghai

REVOLT ON TAIWAN 1947

Taiwan was restored to China in 1945. General Chen Yi flew from Chungking to accept formal surrender of Japanese (25 Oct.1945). In Feb.1947 there was a mass revolt on Taiwan against the Nationalist government. Chen Yi suppressed it brutally "in a cascade of machine gun fire" after which his soldiers "indulged in an orgy of looting".

(See H.M.Bate 'Report from Formosa' Eyre & Spotiswoode 1952 pp.20–21).

INFLATION–RIDDEN CHINA

YUNNAN

KWANGTUNG

Canton

HAINAN I.

TAIWAN

MANCHURIA, 1948

Communist infantry charge the walls of a town held by Nationalist soldiers.

35 The Communist offensives: to the crossing of the Yangtze, 1949

The Chinese Red Army

Unlike Chiang, Mao did not attempt to control military operations at this critical stage of the civil war. He left such matters to Chu Teh and his generals. Mao was principally interested in the social and political conduct of his troops and the relationships they fostered with the ordinary people. He had always maintained that China's present misery was caused by the 'carpet-bagging' tactics of the Nationalists after 1945. According to Mao, as soon as the Nationalists entered the 'liberated areas' (zones controlled by the Communists in 1945), 'the peasants' land was confiscated, Fascist secret police terrorized the populace, traitors and local tyrants came back and were made officials by Chiang Kai-shek's government'.* Mao therefore insisted that his troops would come as friends of the people, as members of a 'People's Liberation Army'.

The capture of Peiping (Peking), 1949

The Chinese Red Army began its general advance towards the Yangtze-kiang in October 1949. On 7 November it encountered fierce resistance from the Nationalists and for the next two months the decisive battle of the civil war was fought out to the east of Hsuchow. With the Nationalist defeat, the way to the Yangtze lay open. This great victory at the *Battle of Hsuchow* now encouraged the Nationalist general defending Peiping to surrender the city. Here was a chance for the Communists to make a good impression upon the citizens of China's ancient capital. People were amazed that the Communist soldiers paid for everything they needed—and, moreover, paid in the 'Great Wall' Communist currency that wasn't subject to inflation. The people liked the way the soldiers tidied up their billets, put right any damage they caused, and treated the civilians with politeness and respect. As one commentator remarked, the city 'had known many armies through the past fifty years, but never one like this'.† Mao put the final touch by coming down from his headquarters near Pingshan to restore the name of Peking to the ancient capital.

Crossing the Yangtze, April 1949

Chiang Kai-shek now stepped down as President to let his successor, Acting-President Li, negotiate peace terms. But Mao refused to negotiate—he was interested only in unconditional surrender. So the civil war dragged on with neither side ready to resume full-scale fighting. South of the Yangtze, the Nationalists rather desultorily built earthworks and trenches. On the other side of the river, the Communists regrouped and prepared for the big attack. On 20 April they began to move across, and met little opposition. They were in Nanking within three days and their main problem was coping with thousands of defecting Nationalist troops who wanted to join the Red Army. Then there suddenly occurred an incident which made headlines in the Western world.

The Amethyst incident, 1949

When the Japanese surrendered in 1945 the British had returned to their colony in Hong Kong. But, because of an agreement signed in 1943, they waived their right to patrol the Yangtze-kiang. However, they had permission from the Nationalists to send warships up-river from Shanghai to rescue any British citizens caught up in the civil war. The frigate H.M.S. *Amethyst* was doing precisely this in April 1949 just as the Communists were crossing the Yangtze. Communist gunners opened fire and badly damaged the *Amethyst*. She was beached near Chinkiang where the Communist troops swarmed around her and refused to let her proceed until she either helped ferry the Red Army across the Yangtze or admitted firing first and causing Communist casualties. Lt.-Commander Kerans, the frigate's captain, refused to co-operate and laid plans for the ship's escape. On the night of 30 July *Amethyst* slipped her moorings and sailed down-river in the wake of a passing steamer. She ran the gauntlet of Chinese shore batteries; she smashed her way through a river boom; and she ran down several junks that got in her way. Eventually, a very battered *Amethyst* made the open sea and came home to a tumultuous welcome from the British press. Her heroic dash down the Yangtze undoubtedly left many British people with a feeling of hostility towards the Chinese Communists. For Mao, the incident was of useful propaganda value. He had demonstrated to the Chinese people that 'imperialist gun-boats' could no longer sail down their rivers with impunity.

*From a C.C.P. statement issued in 1947 and quoted in *The China White Paper*, Vol. 2, pp. 699–700.

†R. and N. Lapwood, *Through the Chinese Revolution* (Spalding and Levy, 1954) p. 44.

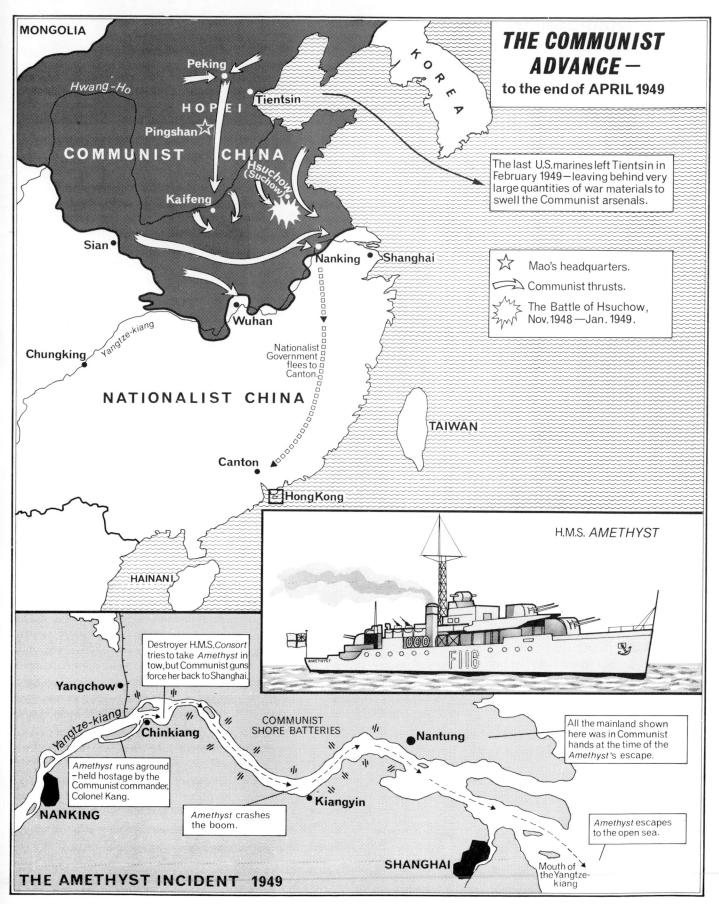

MONGOLIA

Hwang-Ho

Peking

Tientsin

H O P E I

Pingshan ☆

COMMUNIST   CHINA

Hsuchow
(Suchow)

Kaifeng

Sian

Nanking   Shanghai

Wuhan

Chungking   *Yangtze-kiang*

NATIONALIST CHINA

Nationalist
Government
flees to
Canton.

TAIWAN

Canton

☐ Hong Kong

HAINANI

THE COMMUNIST ADVANCE –
to the end of APRIL 1949

The last U.S. marines left Tientsin in
February 1949 – leaving behind very
large quantities of war materials to
swell the Communist arsenals.

☆   Mao's headquarters.

➤   Communist thrusts.

✦   The Battle of Hsuchow,
Nov. 1948 – Jan. 1949.

H.M.S. *AMETHYST*

AMETHYST   F116

Destroyer H.M.S. *Consort*
tries to take *Amethyst* in
tow, but Communist guns
force her back to Shanghai.

Yangchow

COMMUNIST
SHORE BATTERIES

Nantung

All the mainland shown
here was in Communist
hands at the time of the
Amethyst's escape.

Yangtze-kiang

Chinkiang

Amethyst runs aground
– held hostage by the
Communist commander,
Colonel Kang.

NANKING

Amethyst crashes
the boom.

Kiangyin

Amethyst escapes
to the open sea.

SHANGHAI

Mouth of
the Yangtze-
kiang

THE AMETHYST INCIDENT 1949

36 Red Star triumphant

The people's support

Once the Communists were across the Yangtze, the Nationalist soldiers began to surrender in droves. So there were not many battles fought after April 1949 and for most of the Red Army units the next six months turned into a triumphant 'long march' from the cities along the Yangtze down to the South China Sea. On the way they linked up with the peasant resistance movements that were sprouting everywhere. In some villages, the peasants had already lynched the landlords. In others they had been more merciful. But as soon as the old passions were dead the Red Army sent in land reform teams to begin distributing land to the people—even though the civil war was still going on. This was a masterly stroke. Land reform absorbed the attention of all the peasants and guaranteed their support for the agent of change—the Red Army. Although very few peasants were Communists in 1949 they all recognized the hopelessness of the Nationalist government and understood that its removal was essential if they were to improve their own standards of living.

The People's Republic of China (P.R.C.)

By September 1949 Mao felt strong enough to summon a *People's Political Consultative Conference* in Peking. Within a week it had produced the preamble to a new constitution—the Organic Law of the Central People's Government. This defined Communist China as 'a State of the People's Dictatorship, led by the working class, based on the alliance of workers and peasants, and rallying all democratic classes and various nationalities within the country'. China's government would· henceforth be run on the principle of *democratic centralism*, as in the U.S.S.R.* It was on 1 October 1949 that Mao announced the creation of the P.R.C. with himself as Chairman of the Central Government. Among his Vice-Chairmen were Chu Teh and the widow of Sun Yat-sen, Soong Ching-ling. Chou En-lai was Premier and Minister of Foreign Affairs.

Driving out the Nationalists

Meanwhile, the P.R.C. still had a civil war on its hands. Red Army units reached Canton on 14 October and forced President Li and the Nationalists to flee to Chungking—where he decided he had had enough. Li quit China and went to live in America. Chiang Kai-shek promptly resumed the leadership and shifted his government to Chengtu. Here he decided to abandon the mainland and to transform the island of Taiwan into 'Nationalist China'. Ever since 1947 Nationalist troops had found refuge there and as Chiang still had the Nationalist Navy and Air Force under his command he was able to ferry his supporters to the island. Chiang Kai-shek arrived in Taipeh on 10 December—the same day that the Communists took Chengtu.

The final military operations

The Red Army still had to winkle out several Nationalist strongholds—and in the process suffered one permanent setback. In October the Nationalist garrison on Amoy had evacuated to the island of *Quemoy*. When the Communists attacked the island they came off worst. So they took great care not to suffer the same fate when attacking *Hainan Island*. Assault troops underwent rigorous training in special bases on the Luichow Peninsula; experienced guerrilla fighters infiltrated the island by night and linked up with the native resistance movement. By April 1950 the Communists were ready to go in—but their first two assault waves suffered defeat. Then they gained a foothold and Chiang Kai-shek realized he was about to lose another important garrison of some 100,000 men. He therefore mounted a major rescue operation and ferried his troops all the way to Taiwan.

Recognition of Communist China

Apart from the offshore islands of Taiwan, Quemoy and Matsu, China was now under Red Army control. Mao secured the nation's defences by dividing the P.R.C. into six regions, each controlled by a *Military and Political Committee* (M.P.C.). These he placed in the hands of his most trusted commanders. Central government remained in direct control of the provinces surrounding Peking. China was ready to face the world. And most countries were ready to recognize her new government: Russia and her satellites in Eastern Europe did so on 1 October 1949; Britain followed suit on 5 January 1950. But America remained hostile—quite sure that Mao's visit to Moscow (December 1949) was the prelude to another round of Communist conquests in Europe and Asia. Because of America's distrust and the influence she exercised in the United Nations, the People's Republic of China could not join the U.N. So, on 9 January 1950, Chou En-lai began the herculean task of ejecting *Nationalist China* (the island of Taiwan) from the U.N. Security Council and substituting the P.R.C. in her place. It was to take him twenty-two years.

*Briefly, this meant that all bodies in government (from grass roots level to the top committees) were elected to form a pyramid of power in which the decisions of the higher bodies were binding on the tower. For a view of the Russian system see Brian Catchpole, *A Map History of Russia*, pp. 110–11, 116–17.

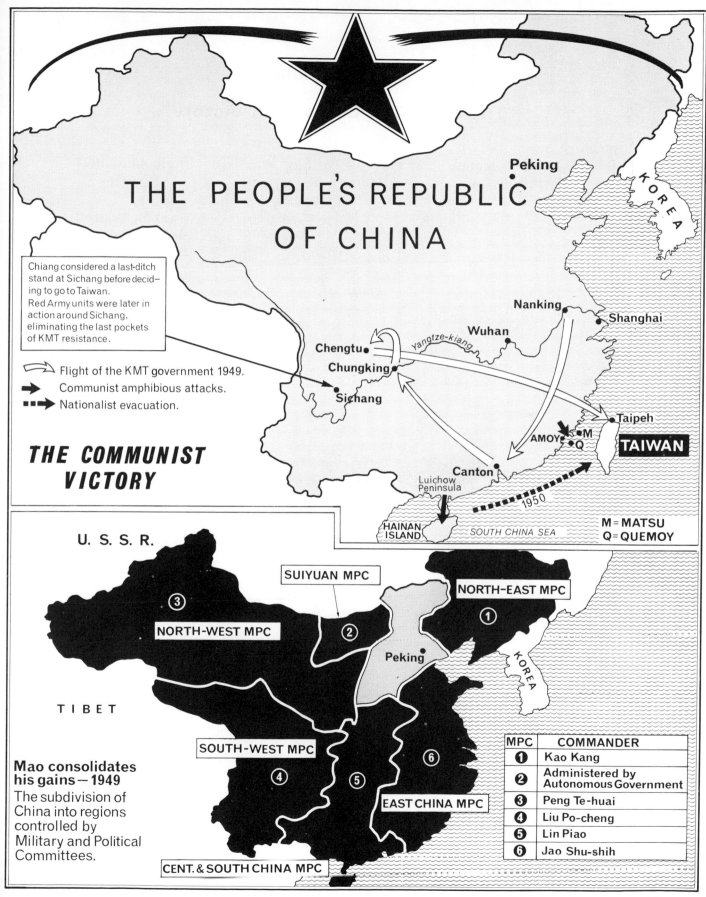

THE PEOPLE'S REPUBLIC OF CHINA

Peking

KOREA

Chiang considered a last-ditch stand at Sichang before decid–ing to go to Taiwan.
Red Army units were later in action around Sichang, eliminating the last pockets of KMT resistance.

⇗ Flight of the KMT government 1949.

➡ Communist amphibious attacks.

▪▪▪➡ Nationalist evacuation.

THE COMMUNIST VICTORY

Nanking

Shanghai

Wuhan

Yangtze-kiang

Chengtu

Chungking

Sichang

Taipeh

AMOY · **M** Q

TAIWAN

Canton

Luichow Peninsula

HAINAN ISLAND

SOUTH CHINA SEA

1950

M = MATSU
Q = QUEMOY

U. S. S. R.

SUIYUAN MPC

NORTH-EAST MPC

③

NORTH-WEST MPC

②

①

Peking

KOREA

TIBET

SOUTH-WEST MPC

Mao consolidates his gains — 1949
The subdivision of China into regions controlled by Military and Political Committees.

④

⑤

⑥

EAST CHINA MPC

CENT. & SOUTH CHINA MPC

MPC	COMMANDER
❶	Kao Kang
❷	Administered by Autonomous Government
❸	Peng Te-huai
❹	Liu Po-cheng
❺	Lin Piao
❻	Jao Shu-shih

Further Reading

Theme 5—The Communist victory

Spread

33.	Anthony Kubek	*How the Far East Was Lost*	Intercontex, 1971
34.	F. F. Liu	*A Military History of Modern China*	O.U.P., 1956
35.	Trevor Nevitt Dupuy	*The Chinese Civil War*	Franklin Watts Inc., 1969
36.	Chien Po-tsan	*Concise History of China*	Foreign Languages Press, 1964
	Franklin Houn	*A Short History of Chinese Communism*	Prentice-Hall, 1973

P.L.A. troops in Nanking, 1949.

THEME 6

The People's Republic of China

China's new society enjoys a life style based upon Marxist-Leninist principles interpreted through the thought of Mao Tse-tung. To the outside world, China presents a picture of unity, determination, prosperity and happiness—characteristics to be seen in most of her propaganda photographs. Visitors to China are generally impressed by the apparent truth of this propaganda, though they comment on the intense security that surrounds most kinds of communal life.

Mao Tse-tung has taught his people to prepare for the future. A determined, united people can drown any invader in 'the vast ocean of a People's War'. A determined, united people can prevent natural disasters from dominating their lives—a determined, united people can always cope with plagues, floods and famines. Everyone must work for the increasing happiness of the people—and there is no room for the slacker. As the Constitution puts it:* 'He who does not work, neither shall he eat' and 'from each according to his ability, to each according to his work'.

The People's Republic has emancipated women. In 1950 it banned the use of 'matchmakers' and child betrothal; divorce became possible and once the state provided communal canteens and children's nurseries women had the same chance as men to follow their chosen careers. A major problem remains: keeping China's population in check. Since the Communists came to power in 1949 the population increase has zoomed by 40 per cent to around 800 million people. At first the Communists were hostile to birth control but by the beginning of the 1970s the Health Ministry, the factory and commune committees and the rural medical teams—the so-called 'barefoot doctors'—had devised a massive educational programme to encourage late marriages and small families. China's aim is to achieve Z.P.G. (Zero Population Growth)—a formidable task.

*1975 Constitution, Article 8.

37 Making China Communist: unifying the people, 1949–50

Mao's leadership

When Mao announced the creation of the People's Republic of China in October 1949, he was demonstrating the truth of one of his best-known sayings: that political power grew out of the barrel of a gun. Now he had to convince the vast majority of Chinese who were not members of the C.C.P. that his government, with its new-found political power, really meant to put right all the ills and injustices which Mao had always blamed on the Nationalists. Mao's leadership was therefore crucial to the making of Communist China. And because of the strong bond that united him with his senior political comrades—all veterans of the Long March, the war with Japan and the struggle against the Kuomintang—it went unchallenged for the next ten years.

'Fanshen'

Mao at least had the sympathy of the people. It was largely he who had spread the spirit of *fanshen* across China since 1945. Literally, *fanshen* means 'to turn over' and it had become an everyday greeting for many people: 'Comrade, have you fanshened?'* When a Chinese said this he was really uttering the hope that China was on the brink of a brave new world where there were no tyrannical landlords, no individual enslavement because of ignorance and social inferiority. Years before, the Kuomintang had had the chance to put things right. They had failed—and the Chinese people disowned them. Now it was the turn of the Communists. How would they win the people's trust? Would China really 'turn over'?

The political cadres

Mao understood the challenge and hit on the idea of sending political cadres among the people to convince them of the worth of C.C.P. rule. These cadres were teams of young, enthusiastic C.C.P. members—mainly peasants, factory workers, demobbed P.L.A. soldiers and university students. During 1949–50 they took over the 'grass-roots' government of China and began the gigantic task of conveying the thoughts of Mao Tse-tung to 600 million people. They had plenty of difficulties to contend with—some of them inadvertently caused by the central government in Peking. For example, one instruction issued from the capital at the end of 1949 called in all the gold bars and silver coin—the most popular forms of the new currency—and ordered the substitution of banknotes. This was a blunder. The memory of inflation was so vivid in people's minds that everyone wondered if the same old story of government incompetence was about to be repeated. There was certainly a feeling of despair in the town of 'Duliang'. One American teacher, William Sewell, was still working there and he recorded: 'The shopkeepers put up their shutters. The smiles faded away. Joy had gone out of life; we returned once again to the old anxious days.' Even the P.L.A. soldiers, until now popular with everyone, became objects of distrust. '"Liberated!" spat out a rickshaw puller to a soldier who had been arguing with him. "Liberated! Liberated for what?"' But it was a brief moment of anxiety. It was soon obvious that the cadres were on the side of the people. Black markets disappeared; prices kept going *down*; taxes did *not* go up. So at least the government was not going to make excessive financial demands. Of course, serious food shortages still plagued the country—that could not be put right overnight. But for the first time in living memory the soldiers did not raid the people and steal their meagre supplies. Instead the P.L.A. men shared their own scanty rations with 'old hundred names',† an outward and visible sign that government, cadres, army and people were all united as one.‡

The Sino–Soviet Treaty, 1950

Back in 1945, when Stalin had little faith in Mao Tse-tung's chances, the Russian leader had signed a *Treaty of Friendship and Alliance* with the Nationalists. Now he was ready to admit he had backed the wrong horse. In December 1949 he welcomed Mao to Moscow and in February 1950 the two leaders signed a new *Sino–Soviet Treaty of Friendship and Alliance*. It guaranteed military protection against a resurgent Japan and, through a series of trade agreements, promised Soviet economic aid to China. With this in his pocket, Mao returned to Peking where he could tell the people that they were now allied to one of the world's two super-powers. No longer need they feel isolated and deprived of allies. Mao rammed home the message with every possible propaganda device—by radio, street posters, the *People's Daily*, postage stamps and school text books. The Chinese people were now members of a great international Communist brotherhood.

*Traditionally, it was 'Brother, have you eaten?'.

†Again, traditionally, this was the expression used to describe all the descendents of the Han people—the Chinese.

‡The quotations in this paragraph are taken from p. 73 of William Sewell's book *I Stayed in China* (Allen and Unwin, 1966). He prefers not to identify 'Duliang' precisely: 'Duliang,' he says, 'is not to be found on any map of China, and yet it is real enough ...'

THE CADRES MOVE IN (1949-1950)

"There was no doubt that China had been united under the People's Red Flag much more quickly than anyone expected."

THE FLAG OF THE PEOPLE'S REPUBLIC OF CHINA:-
THE LARGE STAR STANDS FOR THE COMMUNIST PARTY.
THE OTHER FOUR STARS REPRESENT THE PEASANTS,
THE FACTORY WORKERS, THE 'SMALL' BUSINESSMEN
AND THE 'MEDIUM' BUSINESSMEN. THE LANDLORDS
AND THE CAPITALISTS (bankers and big industrialists)
WERE NOT INCLUDED IN THE PRC.

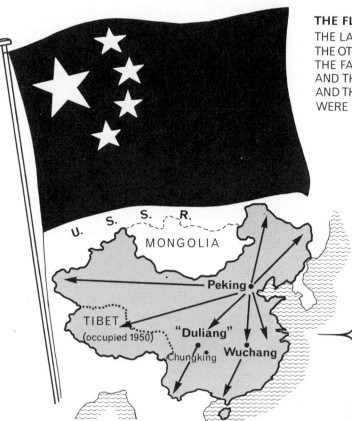

→ The cadres move into the furthermost regions of China. Sewell located "Duliang" three days' travel by road from Chungking.

Statements made by Englishmen who were working in China at the time of the communist victory :—

1. **WILLIAM SEWELL** on the subject of the cadres who took over the government of 'Duliang' city.
   "....We in 'Duliang' suffered from the administration of well-meaning but not very knowledgeable leadership, whose experience was largely acquired in other parts of China, and so lacked understanding of local conditions........it might have ended in disaster except for the sheer good will and desire to help the people which motivated even the most inexperienced and exasperating of cadres."

   (From Sewell's "I stayed in China" p.72)

2. **TOM RICHARDSON** on the subject of relations with the Soviet Union.
   Tom Richardson was a missionary teacher at the Wesley Middle School in Wuchang. He helped to translate the writings of Mao Tse-tung (in this case 'Concerning the People's Dictatorship') into English for use in the more advanced foreign language courses.

   "......the Soviet Communist Party has won its victory; under the leadership of Lenin and Stalin they have shown that, not only are they capable of revolution, but of reconstruction too. They have already built up a great and glorious Socialist State. The Communist Party of the Soviet Union is our best teacher; we must learn of the Communist Party of the Soviet Union.

   (p.22)

This stamp depicts the friendship between Stalin and Mao on the occasion of the Sino-Soviet Treaty, February 1950.

CHINESE POSTAGE STAMP — 1950

38   The fate of the merchants and missionaries

Xenophobia (the hatred of foreigners)

Foreigners had never been popular in China and it was therefore easy for the Communists to whip up hatred against selected nationalities whenever they wished. And it was in their interest to do this during the Korean War (1950–3) when P.L.A. 'volunteers' fought U.N. forces—mainly composed of American and British Commonwealth troops. In 1950 this hatred fell upon the two most prominent groups of foreigners in China—the businessmen and the missionary workers.

The businessman's stake in China

British and American merchants had dominated the China trade since the beginning of the twentieth century, though it was the British who were especially vulnerable to the Communist takeover. Before the Second World War British merchants had owned 35 per cent of all foreign investments and controlled 50 per cent of the entire Chinese coastal trade. The Second World War had damaged their interests, and the struggle between the Kuomintang and the Communists had hampered their post-war commercial activities. Nevertheless, their tangible possessions remained enormous, for the merchants had spent millions of pounds on factories, warehouses, port facilities, roads, housing and sports clubs. Shanghai's Bund—the rows of impressive commercial buildings—was the most obvious example, especially when one realizes that it was the merchants who had built up Shanghai from a miserable collection of mud-flats to the third busiest seaport in the world.

Their decline and fall

For most of the foreign firms the Communist victory meant the end of a highly profitable era. Companies that tried to survive found themselves operating in what was virtually an enemy country where they had to endure insults and cope with hosts of petty regulations. They found it hard to get staff, and so firms had to accept the inevitable. Most of the big banking houses in Peking, Tientsin and Swatow closed down during 1952, though Sassoons, one of the biggest property companies in China, held out until 1958. Another British firm, an important textile manufacturer in Shanghai, held out until 1959. By then it was all over. Shareholders continued, in theory, to draw dividends on businesses nationalized by the Communists. In fact, these dividends were lodged in the Chinese state banks which then refused to transfer any accounts abroad. There was some consolation in the fact that the end of the China trade would not last for ever.

The plight of the missionaries

No such consolation existed for the 10,000 missionaries working in China at the time of the Communist victory. They had been striving since 1927 to create a truly Chinese church in their adopted homeland and hoped to have Chinese priests and bishops in charge of all the parishes and diocesan centres. It was a hard struggle, for most Chinese distrusted Christianity with its strong colonial and commercial associations. And it had not been helped by the war against Japan—a war which had seen many a missionary wind up in a Japanese internment camp. So by the time the Communists came to power in 1949, the missionaries were still years away from creating a unified Chinese church.

An abrupt end to their influence

At first the Communists seemed to tolerate the missionaries. But once their troops intervened in the Korean War (October 1950) their attitude hardened. The C.C.P. ordered all Chinese Christians to adopt the 'Three-Self' Movement, that is, they had to sever all connection with missionaries. Understandably, not many missionaries accepted the idea and stubbornly stayed at their posts. So the Communists retaliated by closing down the Roman Catholic University in Peking—run by the American Fathers of the Divine Word—and arresting the American Bishop of Suchow. In 1951 the Communists shut down the Catholic headquarters in Shanghai and Chou En-lai completed the attack upon U.S.-sponsored missions by ordering the Chinese Christians to have no further contact with any missionaries supported by American funds. Chinese hostility towards the Roman Catholics in particular was partly caused by the Pope's denunciation of Communism; the C.C.P. regarded all Catholic priests and nuns as potential counter-revolutionaries and trumped up some incredible charges against them. At the same time, the Communists had no further interest in Protestant missionaries—not even the fellow-traveller type of missionary (such as Tom Richardson)* who worked directly under Communist control. So the missionaries made their undignified exit from China. Apart from invaluable services rendered in the fields of education and medicine, they had not made much impact upon China's religious beliefs.

*See the previous spread.

One missionary summed up his opinion of the Chinese intervention in the War in Korea in the following terms:

"This proved to be one of the most advantageous opportunities for the Communist Government to rally and unify the people of China, for Communist propaganda needs a 'hate point' as the focus for its mass decisions and its mass actions—and what better than the 'invasion' by a capitalist, imperialist power of its immediate neighbour."

His last point was, of course, a reference to the fact that UN forces crossed the 38th Parallel after defeating the North Koreans (who had invaded the south) in an effort to unite the two Koreas into one country.

MANCHURIA

Peking ☆

Tientsin

There were about 3000 students attending the Roman Catholic Fujen University in Peking when the Communists ordered it to close down.

Yalu R.

NORTH KOREA

------ 38th Parallel

SOUTH KOREA

Hwang-ho

PEOPLE'S REPUBLIC OF CHINA

Suchow

Yangtze-kiang

Nanking

Shanghai

The Communists regarded missionaries as 'spies' or 'special agents'. When they closed down the Roman Catholic HQ in Shanghai they accused the missionaries of working against the interests of the Chinese people, of blackening the reputation of the Peking government and of deliberately preventing the Chinese from creating their own independent church in China.

The Communists accused two Roman Catholic nuns at the Sacred Heart Orphanage in Nanking of maltreating Chinese children — both were sentenced to ten years in jail.

Canton **Swatow**

TAIWAN (NATIONALIST CHINA)

☒ **HONG KONG**

THE FLIGHT OF THE MISSIONARIES

THE MISSIONARIES LEAVE CHINA - 1951

The Communists accused the nuns who ran the Roman Catholic orphanage in Canton of murdering scores of Chinese children. The Communists even tried to press charges of cannibalism. However, the Communists eventually allowed most of the jailed missionaries to leave China--though they usually had to undergo the humiliation of being paraded through the streets. Most left China via Hong Kong.

UN troops, counter-attacking after the original invasion of South Korea by North Korea, advance almost to the Yalu River.

PLA volunteers intervene to drive them back.

Said the Vatican: "the year 1951 would go down in history as one of the worst for the Roman Catholic Church in China".

39 The Chinese Communist Party and the Thought of Mao Tse-tung

Mental and physical control

When the Communists came to power in 1949 they were determined to create a government so strong that it could influence the lives of everybody living within the People's Republic. Between 1949 and 1954 they deliberately set out to control not only what people were doing but also what people were thinking. They doubled the size of the C.C.P. by recruiting members from among the urban population (this made a total of 6 million Communists in China) and used them to develop a variety of mass organizations which were under the direct control of Party headquarters. It was not long before Communist-guided *Peasant Associations* replaced the last of the clans and secret societies that still lingered on in the country-side; while *co-operative* and *trade union federations* sprang up in the towns to control the thoughts and actions of the factory workers.

The 1954 Constitution

The C.C.P. arranged for the entire adult population to participate in the election of representatives to attend the various Congresses which met to discuss local and national issues. Government business, however, re-mained firmly in the hands of the C.C.P. which used the pyramid of Congresses to transmit Party instructions to the mass of the people. Party instructions originated in the Politburo—a small group of Communist leaders who formed the powerhouse of China's new government. These men made the decisions which were binding on the whole population—no deviation from the Party line would be permitted. Such in essence was the constitution of 1954, a constitution which has been much modified over the years.

The thought of Mao Tse-tung

To make this sort of dictatorship palatable to the mass of the people, the C.C.P. put maximum effort into glorify-ing the thought of Mao Tse-tung. This is not simply a matter of blind adulation of the leader. It is part of a care-fully planned and implemented policy—as it has to be in all totalitarian states. Quite justifiably, the C.C.P. has given Mao credit for developing the political philosophy of Karl Marx and for illustrating in a practical fashion some of the theoretical ideas of Lenin and Stalin.* Con-sequently, Mao's thought comes across as contem-porary, relevant and sinified. He is thinking in terms of the needs of the Chinese. Two examples show how his thought is applied (*a*) to an immediate crisis situation and (*b*) to a long-term, highly desirable aim:

(*a*) *The famine of 1949–50*   One legacy the Communists

did not want to inherit was China's age-old problem of persistent famine. Famine was already raging in 1949 and one of the new Vice-Premiers, Tung Pi-wu, blamed it on 'an unprecedented series of natural disasters' and reported that the worst-hit area was in the traditional 'famine-belt' between the Hwang-ho and the Yangtze-kiang. By 1950, however, the famine had spread to many other provinces. Mao therefore guided the thinking of the people so that all could understand why they must lend a hand. Those lucky enough to be in provinces untouched by famine would make a contribution by joining the 'single bowl of rice movement'; every P.L.A. soldier would donate something to the 'ounce of rice movement'. Though this was good propaganda it did not really help the 8 million famine refugees crowding into the cities. To cope with this, the Party workers moved food surpluses from remote parts of China into the famine-belt so that it was the grain from Szechwan, Manchuria and Inner Mongolia which probably brought the greatest relief—a tribute to the organizational skill of the C.C.P. in those difficult years following a civil war in which most of the railway links had been severed.

(*b*) '*Learn from Tachai!*'   The government of the P.R.C. has to respond, as does any other government, to the long-term needs of its people. Above all, Mao needed to improve food production and reduce the risk of famine. He was able to draw inspiration from the example of a team of cadres working in the village of Tachai, Shansi Province. The Communists had liberated Tachai in 1945 and the cadres had been working on land reform ever since. Led by the local C.C.P. secretary, Cheng Yung-kuei, the villagers had formed themselves into *mutual aid teams*, which meant that they pooled their resources and worked as a village team rather than as individual farmers. Very rapidly, they increased their annual output so that in 1952 Cheng proposed to transform Tachai into a co-operative farm. However, officials at county (*chou*) level refused to give their permission and delayed Cheng's plans for a year—red tape abounds in Communist countries as much as in others! Despite official opposition, the villagers used their initiative and formed their co-operative in 1953. Within twelve months they had doubled their grain pro-duction. They then went on to collectivize all of their land and possessions to become the nucleus of one of China's first *communes*. Tachai was ahead of its time and in the years to come the thought of Mao Tse-tung would con-tain the exhortation: 'In agriculture, learn from Tachai!'†

---

*For example, he demonstrated that revolution could be carried out by the peasants as well as by the urban proletariat.

†There is an interesting survey of Tachai's post-1945 history in *China Reconstructs*, November 1974.

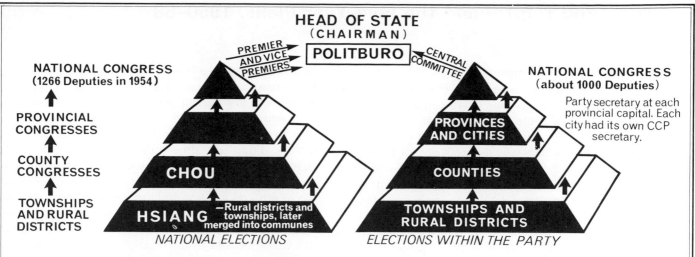

HEAD OF STATE
(CHAIRMAN)

POLITBURO

PREMIER AND VICE PREMIERS → ← CENTRAL COMMITTEE

NATIONAL CONGRESS (1266 Deputies in 1954)

↑ PROVINCIAL CONGRESSES

↑ COUNTY CONGRESSES

↑ TOWNSHIPS AND RURAL DISTRICTS

CHOU

HSIANG — Rural districts and townships, later merged into communes

NATIONAL ELECTIONS

NATIONAL CONGRESS (about 1000 Deputies)

Party secretary at each provincial capital. Each city had its own CCP secretary.

PROVINCES AND CITIES

COUNTIES

TOWNSHIPS AND RURAL DISTRICTS

ELECTIONS WITHIN THE PARTY

The relationship between people and party under the 1954 CONSTITUTION.

"The aspects of Mao's thought..........that have been particularly useful to China's nation—building efforts are the extolment of **HARD WORK, PLAIN LIVING, SELF— RELIANCE, INVENTIVENESS** and **FEARLESSNESS BEFORE DIFFICULTIES AND DANGER.**" *(The view of Franklin W. Houn in his 'Short History of Chinese Communism', Prentice-Hall 1973, p.83.)*

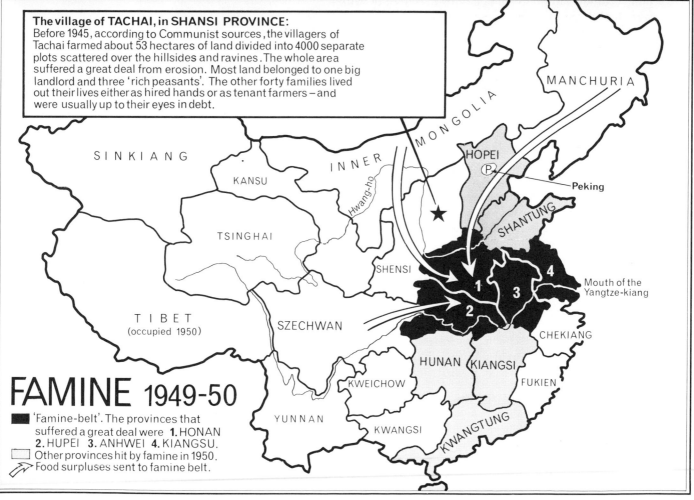

The village of TACHAI, in SHANSI PROVINCE:
Before 1945, according to Communist sources, the villagers of Tachai farmed about 53 hectares of land divided into 4000 separate plots scattered over the hillsides and ravines. The whole area suffered a great deal from erosion. Most land belonged to one big landlord and three 'rich peasants'. The other forty families lived out their lives either as hired hands or as tenant farmers – and were usually up to their eyes in debt.

MANCHURIA

SINKIANG

KANSU

INNER MONGOLIA

HOPEI (P)

Peking

Hwang-ho

TSINGHAI

SHANTUNG

SHENSI

1

3

4

Mouth of the Yangtze-kiang

2

TIBET (occupied 1950)

SZECHWAN

CHEKIANG

HUNAN   KIANGSI

FUKIEN

FAMINE 1949-50

KWEICHOW

KWANGSI

KWANGTUNG

YUNNAN

■ 'Famine-belt'. The provinces that suffered a great deal were **1.** HONAN **2.** HUPEI **3.** ANHWEI **4.** KIANGSU.
☐ Other provinces hit by famine in 1950.
⇗ Food surpluses sent to famine belt.

40 Land reform and the Five-Year Plans, 1950–58

A feudal agricultural heritage

Land reform began in earnest with the *Agrarian Reform Law* (*June 1950*). It was long overdue. Landowners and rich peasants had controlled 75 per cent of China's best land for centuries. They had either hired people as day labourers or divided the fields into strips for renting out to the peasants. Rent usually took the form of payment in kind—often half the annual crop. It was a system reminiscent of medieval England: oppressive, cumbersome and uneconomic. But it was so firmly entrenched that any attempt to change it overnight might have caused it to fail entirely. That was why Mao ordered the cadres to redistribute land wherever possible but not to be afraid of allowing rich and poor peasants to co-exist if this would guarantee continued agricultural production. So about 3 million peasants benefited from land reform and for the first time emerged with smallholdings of their own to cultivate. As for the landlords, about 2 million were murdered or executed in what was a violent and bloodthirsty programme of land redistribution. By 1952 China had become a nation of small landowners, half of whom were mobilized into mutual aid teams.

Fears for the future

By 1955 it was obvious to Mao that land reform had not worked out as well as he had expected. Some farmers were salting away their profits; others were displaying distinct capitalist tendencies by offering poor peasants good prices for their smallholdings and then employing the landless families as hired hands. Mao decided it was time to hold up the shining example of the peasants of Tachai. Co-operative farming had worked there; now it must work for the rest of China. Mao published his ideas in *On the question of agricultural co-operation* (1955) and warned the people that unless they made 'a leap from small-scale farming' to bigger, co-operative enterprises, China would never see her dreams for the future come true. Co-operatives would enable the people to begin large-scale afforestation and irrigation schemes; they would provide banks to look after people's savings and build up cash reserves for investment in industrial projects; they would have schemes for looking after the sick and needy; and they would unite the fragmented fields and strips into easily worked, monster farms.

Mass human effort

Mao was preaching that 'big means better'. The response was overwhelming. Within two years 800,000 co-operatives were in action. Each one employed about 1,000 people organized on strict military lines. Each *hsiang*

(township) became a *production brigade*. Nearby villages formed *production teams*. These new co-operatives transformed China's agriculture by bringing millions more acres under the plough. Peasants meticulously carved out new terraced fields or constructed elaborate irrigation ditches. Effort on this scale absorbed most of the peasants' energy—though they kept enough strength in reserve to tend their private plots in the evenings. Visually, it was very exciting and there was no doubt that the extra crops helped to banish the spectre of recurring famine. A co-operative would produce a food surplus; this would be sold to the state so that, after deduction of tax, the remaining profit could be invested in a co-operative bank. It was a simple arrangement and it seemed to work. Certainly, for the next twenty years this use of mass human effort was typical of China's agricultural revolution. By 1975, however, there were signs that the Chinese leaders were thinking in terms of farm mechanization and the abolition of private plots.

Industry

While the peasants were engrossed in changing their farming methods the factory workers were taking part in their own industrial revolution. Up to 1949 the major industrial centres—especially Wuhan, Hengyang, Tientsin, Shanghai, Shenyang and Harbin—had been the victims of a great deal of war damage, especially as a result of U.S. bombing during 1944–5. So the Communists had first to mount a rehabilitation programme in these areas before they were able to imitate the Soviet example of a series of *Five-Year Plans* for heavy industry. The first Five-Year Plan began in 1953. Russia lent a hand and Chou En-lai paid tribute to China's new friend who was 'giving our country large long-term credits and sending over large numbers of technicians and experts to help our construction work'. Results were good: the steel, electricity and coal industries more than doubled their output. Nevertheless, China still depended upon her agriculture to finance industrial expansion. It was the home-grown food surpluses that paid for the imports of machine-tools; it was the home-grown cotton that provided the raw materials for the all-important textile consumer goods. But it took time to secure any sort of balance between industry and agriculture. For example, there was a serious shortage of cotton goods in 1954 and China had to introduce clothes rationing. What was needed was an increase in food surpluses; these would give a spur to light industry so that more consumer goods could come on the market. This was why Mao came up with a fresh challenge in 1958—the *Great Leap Forward*.

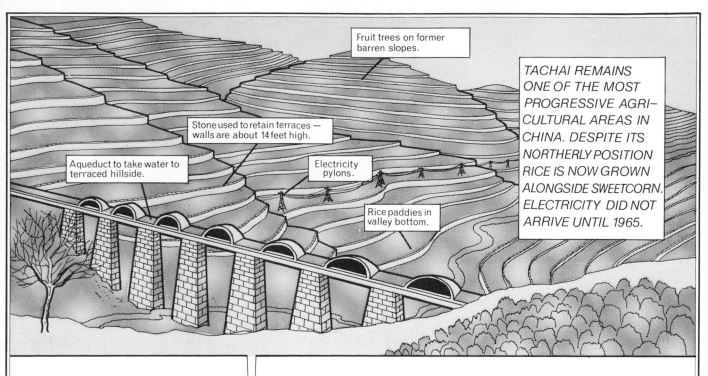

Fruit trees on former barren slopes.

Stone used to retain terraces — walls are about 14 feet high.

Aqueduct to take water to terraced hillside.

Electricity pylons.

Rice paddies in valley bottom.

TACHAI REMAINS ONE OF THE MOST PROGRESSIVE AGRI- CULTURAL AREAS IN CHINA. DESPITE ITS NORTHERLY POSITION RICE IS NOW GROWN ALONGSIDE SWEETCORN. ELECTRICITY DID NOT ARRIVE UNTIL 1965.

Harbin

Shenyang

Tachai

HONAN

CHINA

Shanghai

Wuhan

Hengyang

Writing in 'THE TIMES' (26 July 1975), David Bonavia commented on agriculture in Honan Province with these words:

"....... the famous terracing method, using only manual labour, creates giant green staircases which soar out of the valleys. Sometimes the obsession with terracing seems almost a mania as when a miniature stone platform is built to grow only a few blades of wheat."

PRODUCTION ACHIEVEMENTS DURING THE FIRST FIVE YEAR PLAN

1953 – 1957

COAL	1953	66,500,000 TONS
	1957	130,700,000 TONS
STEEL	1953	1,300,000 TONS
	1957	5,350,000 TONS
ELECTRICITY	1953	7 BILLION KILOWATT HOURS
	1957	19 BILLION KILOWATT HOURS
PETROL	1953	50,000 TONS
	1957	1,500,000 TONS

Industrial and Agricultural Progress 1950–1958

41 The Great Leap Forward, 1958–60

Mao assesses the situation

Dissatisfied with the earlier Five-Year Plans for agriculture and industry, Mao travelled the countryside in September 1958 to assess the economic situation for himself. 'During this trip,' he said, 'I have witnessed the tremendous energy of the people. On this foundation it is possible to accomplish any task ...' And to make his point clear, Mao urged the people to read his version of the Fable of the Foolish Old Man.

The Fable of the Foolish Old Man

An old man lived in northern China and was known as the Foolish Old Man of North Mountain. His house faced south and beyond his doorway stood two great peaks, obstructing his way. He called his sons and they began to dig up these mountains with determination. Another greybeard, known as the Wise Old Man, said derisively, 'How silly of you to do this! It is quite impossible for you to dig up these mountains.' The Foolish Old Man replied, 'When I die my sons will carry on; when they die, there will be my grandsons and then their sons and grandsons, and so on to infinity. High as they are, the mountains can't grow any higher and every bit we dig they will be that much lower.' Having refuted the Wise Old Man, he went on digging every day, unshaken in his conviction. God was moved by this and he sent down two angels who carried the mountains away on their backs. Today (*said Mao*) two big mountains lie like a dead weight on the Chinese people. One is imperialism, the other is feudalism. The C.C.P. has long made up its mind to dig them up. We must persevere and work unceasingly and we too will touch God's heart. Our God is none other than the masses of the Chinese people. If they stand up and dig together with us, why can't these two mountains be cleared away?*

The Great Leap Forward, 1958–60

Mao decided that there must be radical changes in the way people lived and worked. He abolished the regional system of government and replaced it with the *communes*. These communes were to take over all industry, agriculture, education, commerce, welfare and defence. This meant the merging of the co-operatives and the abolition of the private plots and was to be a leap forward to the establishment of a pure Communist society: 'differences between workers and peasants, town and country, mental and manual labour ... will gradually disappear'. Perhaps the most publicized feature of the Great Leap Forward was the sudden obsession with manufacturing processes. According to early Communist reports, molten steel was flowing from furnaces in people's backyards, barbers' shops, laundries and grocery stores. Children built their own kilns at school. Millions of peasants trooped off to the hills to look for iron ore deposits. And while these amateur prospectors neglected their agricultural duties, millions of city workers arrived to take their place in an extraordinary *hsia-fang* (back to the farm) movement.

The enterprise founders

At first all went well. Harvests were good in 1958. Some big projects got under way, notably the reservoir and hydro-electric schemes on the Sinan River and the steel-rolling mills in Dairen and Shenyang. Mao himself lent a hand in building a reservoir outside Peking. But the Communists were expecting too much. It was naïve to think that rapid industrialization and huge harvests could be guaranteed in the space of a few years. Bad weather began to hamper everything. 'Unprecedented floods' wrecked Manchuria's soya bean harvest. North-East China reeled under a succession of typhoons. Yet in Shantung the Hwang-ho actually dried up! About half of China suffered crop failures during the Great Leap Forward.

'Too much haste means waste'

China discovered this harsh economic fact the hard way and in 1961 the C.C.P. formally abandoned the Great Leap Forward. Peasants regained their private plots. Rice from Burma and Ceylon, wheat from Canada and Australia helped to save the day. China rapidly recovered from her over-hasty attempt at economic expansion and in fact gained some distinct advantages from her experience.† In many respects the communes were a success. They provided a centre for small-scale industry in the countryside and were thus able to mop up surplus population from the crowded cities. Small chemical factories such as the forty sulphuric acid plants established on Kiangsi's communes during 1959 proved invaluable for future industrial expansion. But above all the planners learnt to exercise restraint and to become more selective in developing new industries and improving agricultural methods. It was this new sophistication that enabled China, over the next six years, to feed her 700 million people and to establish a number of technologically advanced industries.

*The story dates back to the 4th century B.C. Mao added the ending in 1945.

†Many Western accounts of the Great Leap Forward are highly critical. For a balanced and detailed description see Wheelwright and McFarlane, *The Chinese Road to Socialism* (Pelican, 1973) Chapter 2.

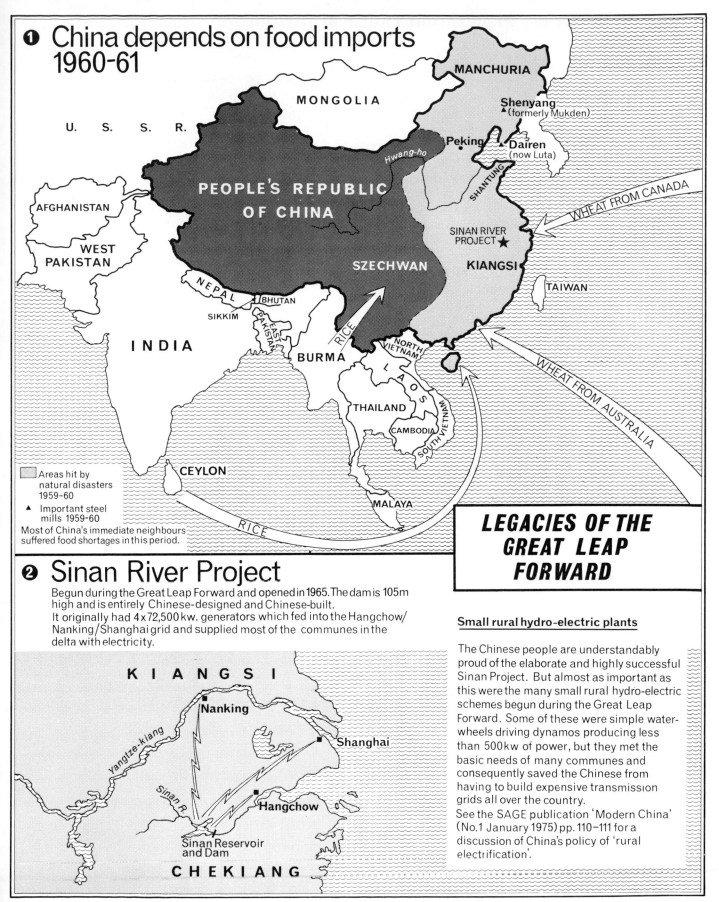

❶ China depends on food imports 1960-61

MANCHURIA

U. S. S. R.

MONGOLIA

Shenyang
▲ (formerly Mukden)

Peking ● ▲ Dairen
(now Luta)

Hwang-ho

SHANTUNG

PEOPLE'S REPUBLIC OF CHINA

WHEAT FROM CANADA

AFGHANISTAN

WEST PAKISTAN

NEPAL

BHUTAN

SIKKIM

EAST PAKISTAN

INDIA

SZECHWAN

SINAN RIVER PROJECT ★

KIANGSI

TAIWAN

BURMA

NORTH VIETNAM

LAOS

THAILAND

CAMBODIA

SOUTH VIETNAM

RICE

WHEAT FROM AUSTRALIA

CEYLON

MALAYA

RICE

▨ Areas hit by natural disasters 1959-60

▲ Important steel mills 1959-60

Most of China's immediate neighbours suffered food shortages in this period.

❷ Sinan River Project

Begun during the Great Leap Forward and opened in 1965. The dam is 105m high and is entirely Chinese-designed and Chinese-built.
It originally had 4 x 72,500 kw. generators which fed into the Hangchow/Nanking/Shanghai grid and supplied most of the communes in the delta with electricity.

KIANGSI

■ Nanking

Yangtze-kiang

■ Shanghai

Sinan R.

■ Hangchow

Sinan Reservoir and Dam

CHEKIANG

LEGACIES OF THE GREAT LEAP FORWARD

Small rural hydro-electric plants

The Chinese people are understandably proud of the elaborate and highly successful Sinan Project. But almost as important as this were the many small rural hydro-electric schemes begun during the Great Leap Forward. Some of these were simple water-wheels driving dynamos producing less than 500kw of power, but they met the basic needs of many communes and consequently saved the Chinese from having to build expensive transmission grids all over the country.
See the SAGE publication 'Modern China' (No.1 January 1975) pp. 110–111 for a discussion of China's policy of 'rural electrification'.

42 The Great Proletarian Cultural Revolution

The 'Hundred Flowers'

In a speech made during May 1956, Mao Tse-tung invited all the intellectuals to make a contribution to the Communist Revolution. He chose symbolic words: 'To the artists and writers we say: Let a hundred flowers blossom, let a hundred schools of thought compete.' Mao picked up this theme again in 1957 when he warned the intellectuals that while they were having their debates they would have to learn to discriminate between 'fragrant blossoms and poisonous weeds'. He was really hinting that some 'poisonous weeds' were already growing inside the C.C.P. and that the revolution was in danger—as was his own position. This was particularly so after 1958, when Mao resigned as Chairman of the People's Republic* in order to concentrate upon the Great Leap Forward.

The ideological split in the C.C.P.

One major issue was whether or not China should model herself on the Soviet example. The new Chairman of the Republic, Liu Shao-chi, admired some of the features of Soviet society—especially the new privileged class of scientists, engineers, managers and economists who had done so much to develop Russian industry. Mao totally disagreed with the growth of an élite—but his own power was on the wane during 1961–5. Not until 25 July 1966 did he bounce back into the news after reports that he had swum nine miles down the Yangtze-kiang in sixty-five minutes. Despite his age—he was seventy-two—he was fit and a force to be reckoned with inside China.

Mao's Cultural Revolution

Obviously, a power struggle was going on inside the C.C.P. Yet Mao refused to win it by resorting to Stalin-type terror tactics, by rounding up and killing off all his political opponents. Mao wanted to teach the people to abandon selfishness, to abhor the idea of a 'rat-race' and to dedicate themselves to a classless society in which they, and not a privileged élite of bourgeois bureaucrats, would rule. Of course, Mao would need bands of disciples to preach this new Maoism and to act as the agency of change inside China. This is why he chose to unleash the Red Guards of the Cultural Revolution.

The Red Guards

Literally millions of young people, mainly schoolchildren and university students, received from Mao Tse-tung the sacred 'right to rebel' against anyone in authority who showed signs of 'bourgeois thinking'. Mme Mao became the leader of this mass movement which first flexed its muscles on 18 August 1966. One million Red Guards marched past Mao in a monster rally in Peking.† Mao was sporting a Red Guard armband while next to him Defence Minister Lin Piao made rousing speeches in support of the role of the Red Guards in the forthcoming Cultural Revolution. Two days later the Red Guards moved into action. They went into the communes to work in the fields with the peasants; they took their places next to workers on the factory floor. They forced their teachers to recant 'bourgeois beliefs'. Some urged lorry drivers to stop when traffic lights turned green and to move forwards when they turned red! Others insisted that anyone who hailed a pedicab—rickshaws had been abolished in the early sixties—should pedal the vehicle himself while the driver lounged in the passenger seat! Usually, the Red Guards were peaceable and well-behaved—until 1967. Then they turned into a law and order problem.

A year of chaos, 1967–8

The worst example of violence in China during 1967 was at Wuhan where Red Guards clashed with large numbers of disaffected P.L.A. soldiers. And continuous trouble came from the hordes of Red Guards wandering through the countryside on mini 'Long Marches'. They often fell out with railway workers when they were waiting for trains and caused many a protest strike by infuriated railwaymen. Law and order broke down completely in some of the remote provinces and Mao had to suspend provincial governments and substitute 'Revolutionary Committees'. A few provinces, notably Sinkiang, Tibet, Kwangsi, Yunnan and Fukien, refused to come to heel until August 1968.

The aftermath

At the 1969 Party Congress Lin Piao stated that 'We have won a great victory. However, the defeated class will still struggle...Therefore we cannot speak of a final victory—not even for decades.' But to all intents and purposes the Great Proletarian Cultural Revolution was over. Mao Tse-tung and Chou En-lai emerged as the two most powerful men in China. Liu fell into disgrace. Lin did not last long. He was supposed to have staged an abortive plot against Mao in 1971 and fled for his life in a commandeered Trident jet. En route to Russia, the Trident crashed into the wastelands of Mongolia, killing everyone on board. But just how far Mao's Cultural Revolution succeeded must be gauged by seeing how people have been educated and governed since 1968.

*But not as Chairman of the C.C.P. and Head of State.
†Altogether, Mao reviewed 11 million Red Guards in a series of rallies held in Peking.

The Great Proletarian Cultural Revolution

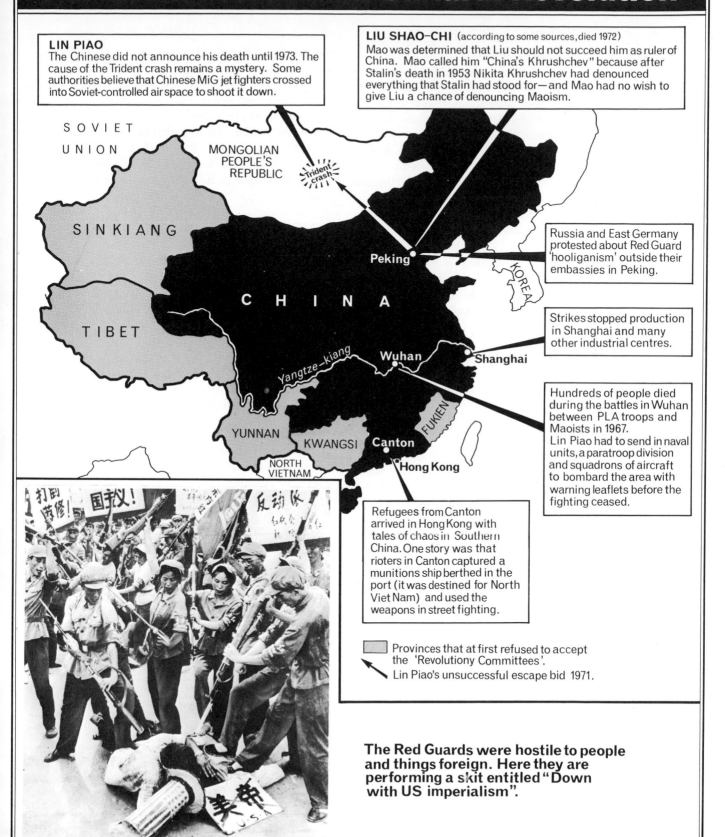

LIN PIAO
The Chinese did not announce his death until 1973. The cause of the Trident crash remains a mystery. Some authorities believe that Chinese MiG jet fighters crossed into Soviet-controlled air space to shoot it down.

LIU SHAO–CHI (according to some sources, died 1972)
Mao was determined that Liu should not succeed him as ruler of China. Mao called him "China's Khrushchev" because after Stalin's death in 1953 Nikita Khrushchev had denounced everything that Stalin had stood for—and Mao had no wish to give Liu a chance of denouncing Maoism.

SOVIET UNION

MONGOLIAN PEOPLE'S REPUBLIC

SINKIANG

TIBET

CHINA

Trident crash

Peking

KOREA

Yangtze-kiang

Wuhan

Shanghai

YUNNAN

KWANGSI

FUKIEN

Canton

Hong Kong

NORTH VIETNAM

Russia and East Germany protested about Red Guard 'hooliganism' outside their embassies in Peking.

Strikes stopped production in Shanghai and many other industrial centres.

Hundreds of people died during the battles in Wuhan between PLA troops and Maoists in 1967. Lin Piao had to send in naval units, a paratroop division and squadrons of aircraft to bombard the area with warning leaflets before the fighting ceased.

Refugees from Canton arrived in Hong Kong with tales of chaos in Southern China. One story was that rioters in Canton captured a munitions ship berthed in the port (it was destined for North Viet Nam) and used the weapons in street fighting.

Provinces that at first refused to accept the 'Revolutiony Committees'.
Lin Piao's unsuccessful escape bid 1971.

The Red Guards were hostile to people and things foreign. Here they are performing a skit entitled "Down with US imperialism".

43 The educational revolution

Mass literacy campaigns, 1949–66

China's biggest educational problem in 1949 had been the almost total illiteracy of the peasant population. The Communist answer had been a crash programme of remedial teaching. It had simple, limited aims: to teach the peasants to recognize simplified characters standing for everyday words—horse, plough, field, cadre. Villages had their own reading groups and wherever there were schools literate children taught illiterate adults. Peasants bringing goods to market had to pass through 'literacy check-points' manned by enthusiastic cadres. Workers on big industrial projects devoted sixty minutes every day to reading and writing. By 1958 illiteracy had fallen to about 20 per cent of the population under forty-five; by 1966 it was down to 10 per cent. Of course, 'literacy' did not imply a very high order of skills. It meant that an adult had mastered a limited number of the new simplified characters—enough for him to participate in the political activities of the Cultural Revolution 1966–9. During those years the widespread use of Mao's *Little Red Book* of quotations and 'big character posters' was evidence of the success of the mass literacy campaigns.

Education during the Cultural Revolution, 1966–9

Chinese education became the subject of world interest when Mao closed down all schools and universities 'to effect a thorough reform of the educational system'. In fact, the mass closure of schools in 1966 meant that Mao could recruit the schoolchildren into the Red Guards. But though there was little formal education going on, the school and university premises acted as the forum of political debate and as the headquarters of many unusual educational activities. For example, there was an upsurge in archaeological interest. Red Guards and P.L.A. soldiers made all sorts of remarkable finds, the most outstanding of which was the discovery of the tombs of the western Han dynasty, near Mancheng. When the archaeologists opened the tombs in 1968 they found the unique jade funerary suits belonging to Prince Liu Sheng and his wife.

After the Cultural Revolution

When the schools and universities reopened (1969–70) the central government did not impose any standard educational programme on the teachers and students. Instead, it provided a new educational philosophy—the thought of Mao Tse-tung—and it was this that transformed Chinese education into a process which prepared the individual to serve his country. Knowledge for its own sake had no more value. Lesson content must be decided according to the current needs of the people. Children must spend less time in school and study fewer subjects. They must learn that education is always linked with service to the people. An educated student must always be prepared to go back to the people for re-education—for what use is a degree in agriculture if you don't know how to plough a field, plant rice or manure a vegetable plot?

The educational revolution in practice

In 1969 a Revolutionary Committee working in Manchuria devised a completely new school curriculum. This became known as the Kirin programme* and many Chinese schools adopted modified versions of it over the next three or four years. Consequently, Chinese children now embarked upon or were slotted into a programme of full-time education which might last between six and ten years, depending on the region in which they went to school. Revolutionary Committees arbitrarily divided this period into 'primary school' and 'middle school'. After kindergarten (nursery education is particularly well-developed in China), children followed a basic syllabus designed to give them a fair degree of literacy, mathematical competence and political understanding before they moved into the middle school.† Mao Tse-tung's thought dominated: all children studied *The Foolish Old Man of North Mountain*, *In Memory of Norman Bethune* and *Serve the People*. Local peasants often wrote text books and supplied the schools with problems relating to agriculture—and frequently acted as temporary teachers. Students who wished to go up to university after middle school entered compulsory national service first—two years on a commune, in a factory or in the P.L.A. About 90 per cent of town children were attending middle school during 1970–75; children in the remote rural areas had less opportunity—about 60 per cent were in the middle school. But, as far as Mao was concerned, time spent in school was not the crucial factor. For him education in the People's Republic of China was to be a life-long process.

*The Kirin programme—'A Draft Programme for Primary and Middle Schools in the Chinese Countryside'—is printed in *Education in China*, pp. 77–81 (Anglo-Chinese Educational Institute, 1974).

†According to Professor G. N. Brown, writing in *The Times Educational Supplement*, 14 November 1975, illiteracy has been virtually eliminated in those aged forty-five and under.

THE KIRIN PROGRAMME:
drafted by the Revolutionary Committee of Lishu County, Kirin Province, and first published in the 'People's Daily' on 12 May 1969.

PRIMARY SCHOOL

Five main courses for boys and girls
1. Politics and Language
2. Arithmetic
3. Revolutionary Literature and Art
4. Military Training and Physical Culture
5. Productive Labour in Industry and Agriculture

MIDDLE SCHOOL

Five main courses for boys and girls
1. Education in the Thought of Mao Tse-tung (including modern Chinese history with special reference to the Cultural Revolution)
2. Agriculture: including Mathematics and Science
3. Revolutionary Literature and Art
4. Military Training and Physical Culture
5. Productive Labour in Industry and Agriculture

EDUCATION IN CHINA

People living in areas shaded black do not speak Chinese. Elsewere in China there are distinct dialects of which Northern Mandarin, Southern Mandarin and Cantonese are the most important. Peking is trying to spread the use of Mandarin through the use of simplified characters and (this is unpopular) a Romanized script.

MANCHURIA

Kirin

The Uighurs of Sinkiang speak a Turkic language

MONGOLS

Peking ★

Mancheng

NORTHERN MANDARIN

Shanghai

People here speak Tibetan

SOUTHERN MANDARIN

Thai people and mountain tribes

CANTONESE

VIET NAM

KIRIN Province

The 'minority' people of modern China.

Discovery of jade funerary suits at Mancheng 1968. Reported by PLA men to Chinese Institute of Archaeology. Site excavated by PLA, Red Guards and local peasants.

Middle schools in the Shanghai region reflect the industrial emphasis of the area. Children tend to stay at school for 10 years. Subjects are biased towards technology. English is the main foreign language studied.

Professor Brown on the subject of the Chinese people and the Thought of Mao Tse-tung:
"....they receive a life-long education in the subject at kindergarten, proceeding throughout their schooling and working lives and for some, ending in old people's homes (two sessions of political education a week)."

Literacy poster: The girl is writing "Everyone must learn the new annotating alphabet of Chinese language".

Two middle school girls assemble car components during productive labour in a school factory.

44   Life in the countryside

The communes

By 1970 China had settled on the commune as the basis of rural life—a crucial decision for the Chinese people as about 85 per cent of them live in the countryside. By the mid-seventies about 75,000 communes existed, some relatively small (2,000 people) and others enormous (60,000 people). But they all had one thing in common: they emphasized the role of the people in governing the commune's affairs. An elected Revolutionary Committee organizes the commune and negotiates with other committees at county or city level the annual targets that the commune has to meet—how much grain, how many ducks, goats, pigs and vegetables to send to market. In return the county or city committee will supply the commune's needs—truckloads of fertilizer or one of the new Red Star combine harvesters. It also keeps back a percentage of the value of the commune's produce to pass on to central government as 'tax'. As there is no personal income tax in China, this is the government's main source of revenue.

Prices and incomes

Central government decides the cost of living for the Chinese people. It fixes prices and incomes with two factors uppermost in its mind: the need to protect the people against inflation; and the need to ensure that the full range of goods produced is available to the entire community at a fair price. Of course, in a country so vast as China transport costs are bound to cause price variations. The government therefore fixes maximum prices for consumer goods and essentials such as salt and medicines and then assumes that regional adjustments can be made below the maximum price. And because it can fix prices, the government can ensure that wages remain stable. In many communes, the revolutionary committees pay the workers on a points system. A normal day's work is given a points value—an average allocation would be 9 points—so that over a $5\frac{1}{2}$ day week (assuming Saturday afternoon and all Sunday to be free) the rural worker can earn about 50 points. This is then translated into yuan (1 yuan = 15 new pence) so that the average weekly wage worked out at 12 yuan. This may seem very low by Western standards—yet a family bringing in 30 yuan per week can enjoy a reasonable standard of living—in the rural areas, that is. Most families can achieve the usual ambition of owning 'three wheels and a carry'—a bicycle, a wristwatch, a sewing machine and a transistor radio. And as rent is very low—4 or 5 yuan monthly—a family can expect to put aside 100–150 yuan every year. In 1977 most families received a substantial wage increase.

Leisure

For day-to-day leisure and recreation the average family on a commune will turn to the transistor radio. Chess is popular; spirits and tobacco are cheap. However, there is very little drunkenness in China though smoking has been on the increase since 1966. People tend to prefer the theatre to the cinema and the numerous theatre troupes, story-tellers, jugglers, dancers and acrobats plus cheap ticket prices mean that communes can enjoy shows regularly. Children living near the commune headquarters will have good basket-ball, swimming and table-tennis facilities, though those in the outlying brigades will enjoy relatively little sports provision. *Tai Chi Chuan*, symbolic 'fist-fighting' using thirty-seven basic actions slowly and rhythmically, is increasingly popular among children and adults.

A sample brigade

Two Swedish sociologists, Jan Myrdal and Gun Kessle, have produced a detailed study of the Liu Ling Brigade.* located in a dry and, at times, bitterly cold part of China. They spent some time with the brigade during 1969 and noted the prices being charged in the local store, called 'Seven Mile Village Shop'. Bicycles were 145 yuan; alarm clocks were 7.10 yuan; cotton cloth was 0.28 yuan per chi. Everybody had joined the brigade health scheme (cost was 1.50 yuan per annum) and had the services of a qualified doctor who provided various treatments including antibiotics, vaccinations and acupuncture† for rheumatism, ear, nose and throat problems and for illnesses caused by stress. He sent serious cases off for treatment at the commune hospital. Liu Ling Brigade had erected its own noodle factory and apples were a staple crop. New terracing techniques and plenty of fertilizer guaranteed better harvests of maize, cabbages, beans, kaoliang and potatoes. The brigade's latest scheme was to feed waste from the noodle factory to pigs and rear enough to sell meat in bulk to the cities and thus increase brigade income. Perhaps Liu Ling was not typical in all respects but it is an example of how a progressive brigade undertook successful planning in one part of China where farming conditions are none too easy.

*Their book is called *China: the Revolution Continued* (Penguin, 1973). Jan Myrdal had visited Liu Ling before, in 1962, and his account of this trip is also published by Penguin—*Report from a Chinese Village* (1963).

†An ancient Chinese treatment accomplished by inserting fine needles into certain points in the body. Myrdal notes that 'Nowadays the needles are sterilized each time'.

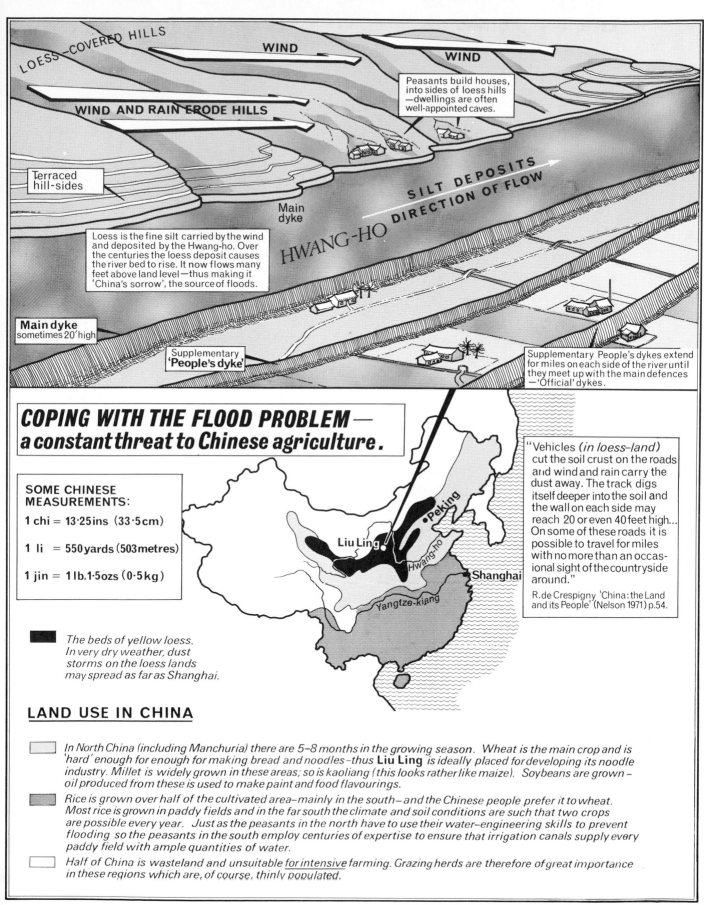

LOESS-COVERED HILLS

WIND

WIND

WIND AND RAIN ERODE HILLS

Peasants build houses into sides of loess hills —dwellings are often well-appointed caves.

Terraced hill-sides

SILT DEPOSITS

HWANG-HO DIRECTION OF FLOW

Main dyke

Loess is the fine silt carried by the wind and deposited by the Hwang-ho. Over the centuries the loess deposit causes the river bed to rise. It now flows many feet above land level—thus making it 'China's sorrow', the source of floods.

Main dyke sometimes 20' high

Supplementary **'People's dyke'**

Supplementary People's dykes extend for miles on each side of the river until they meet up with the main defences —'Official' dykes.

COPING WITH THE FLOOD PROBLEM — a constant threat to Chinese agriculture.

SOME CHINESE MEASUREMENTS:

1 chi = 13·25ins (33·5cm)

1 li = 550 yards (503 metres)

1 jin = 1 lb.1·5ozs (0·5kg)

Peking

Liu Ling

Hwang-ho

Shanghai

Yangtze-kiang

"Vehicles (*in loess–land*) cut the soil crust on the roads and wind and rain carry the dust away. The track digs itself deeper into the soil and the wall on each side may reach 20 or even 40 feet high... On some of these roads it is possible to travel for miles with no more than an occasional sight of the countryside around."

R. de Crespigny 'China: the Land and its People' (Nelson 1971) p.54.

The beds of yellow loess. In very dry weather, dust storms on the loess lands may spread as far as Shanghai.

LAND USE IN CHINA

In North China (including Manchuria) there are 5–8 months in the growing season. Wheat is the main crop and is 'hard' enough for making bread and noodles - thus **Liu Ling** is ideally placed for developing its noodle industry. Millet is widely grown in these areas; so is kaoliang (this looks rather like maize). Soybeans are grown - oil produced from these is used to make paint and food flavourings.

Rice is grown over half of the cultivated area–mainly in the south–and the Chinese people prefer it to wheat. Most rice is grown in paddy fields and in the far south the climate and soil conditions are such that two crops are possible every year. Just as the peasants in the north have to use their water–engineering skills to prevent flooding so the peasants in the south employ centuries of expertise to ensure that irrigation canals supply every paddy field with ample quantities of water.

Half of China is wasteland and unsuitable for intensive farming. Grazing herds are therefore of great importance in these regions which are, of course, thinly populated.

45 Life in the cities

Urban communes

The Chinese regard their big towns and cities as 'urban communes', members of which elect their Revolutionary Committees to run industry and the usual social services. Life is truly more communal in the urban environment, though this does not mean it is unreservedly popular with the people. Certainly, the abundance of nursery schools makes it easy for mothers of young children to go out to work; communal canteens solve the problem of midday meals; sports centres and television viewing centres offer a chance of communal leisure. But the Chinese also like their home life. They save up for bicycles partly to avoid queuing up for trolley-buses at the end of the factory shift. They like to be home in the evening to enjoy the family meal and—if they are one of the lucky families—some television. Even so, they can expect the local Communist Party to invade some of their precious leisure time simply because most urban families are subject to the will of 'courtyard committees' or their equivalent.

Courtyard committees

Peking is an example of one of China's older cities divided up into 'courtyard committees'. Each committee looks after the interests of the thirty or so families living in the traditional courtyard houses. An important duty is to keep a sharp eye open for subversives—people who display very little interest in applying the thought of Mao Tse-tung—for every city has its share of drop-outs. When they are caught they usually wind up in a local 're-indoctrination centre'. Another function is to whip up enthusiasm for a political rally or a 'hate' campaign against such arch-enemies of the state as Lin Piao. Families coming home from work may have to attend an hour or two of political study before taking advantage of other organized courtyard activities such as a table-tennis tournament or a trip to the theatre. If Peking is typical of other cities, then the C.C.P. has since 1969 developed a very successful system of 'thought control' as far as the urban population is concerned.

Law and order

Visitors to Chinese cities since the end of the Cultural Revolution usually comment to the cleanliness of the streets and the honesty of the people. Flies and vermin seem to have disappeared. Intensive D.D.T. campaigns apparently wiped them out—together with most of China's birds! And there is very little pilfering. In fact, visitors complain that they can't throw anything away because it is always returned by a smiling Chinese! Crime is not a serious problem in Chinese cities. Credit for this is partly due to the courtyard committees who have kept a firm grip on the children, occupying them in social work and street-cleaning. Juvenile delinquency is rare. Adults who have broken the law are fined or sent to prison labour camps where, through community work rather than by physical punishment, they are re-educated as far as possible to take their place in society.* Policemen are not greatly in evidence in Peking where they seem to be mainly engaged in traffic control and acting as escorts to visiting dignitaries. Sometimes, however, they have to cope with public disorder. For example, during 1975 factory workers demanding higher wages caused riots in several provinces; in Hangchow 'moderate' Communists clashed with 'radical' Communists. Here the riot was so serious that the police had to call out the local factory militia—all Chinese factories have squads of armed part-time soldiers available at a moment's notice. And in the same year there were riots among the Muslim Hui people in Kunming, protesting against Communist hostility to their religion in various parts of Yunnan province.

'The Big Red Steeltown'

This is China's name for the sprawling industrial complex growing up in the conurbation of Wuhan. It is a very different sort of city from Peking. Between 1958 and 1972 it grew rapidly to become China's second steel centre. Anshan No. 1 Works in Shenyang is bigger—but it was the Japanese who originally developed it. Wuhan's Iron and Steel Company is a Chinese Communist achievement. It provides its employees with housing, gas, electricity, transport, sewage facilities, health services and holidays. It pays higher wages than most of the rural communes, though most of its workers in the rolling mills and nearby coalmines are young apprentices who draw much less than the usual monthly wage of 58 yuan. Wage rates, hours of work and production targets are all decided by the elected Revolutionary Committees. It is they who provide the management so that the entire labour process is controlled from the shop floor. Nevertheless, the workers have to toe the Party line as far as low wages are concerned. Chinese factories are highly *labour intensive*—they employ far too many workers. High wages would mean that the factories would have to be *efficient*. Efficiency would cause mass *redundancy*—perhaps something that the C.C.P. dare not risk in China's overpopulated cities.

*Psychiatric offenders receive help from psychologists and mental health workers. For an account of 'Psychiatry in Shanghai' see *China Now*, June 1975. Since Mao died in 1976 reports of executions have increased, e.g. in Nanking during 1977.

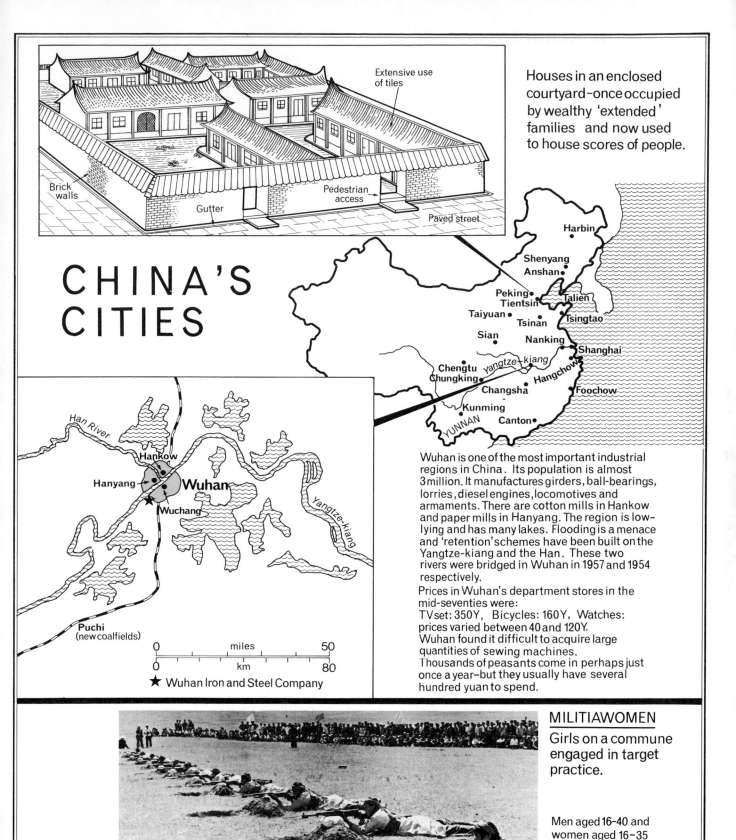

Houses in an enclosed courtyard–once occupied by wealthy 'extended' families and now used to house scores of people.

Extensive use of tiles

Brick walls

Gutter

Pedestrian access

Paved street

CHINA'S CITIES

Harbin

Shenyang
Anshan

Peking
Tientsin
Taiyuan
Talien

Tsinan
Tsingtao

Sian
Nanking
Shanghai

Chengtu
Chungking
Yangtze-kiang
Hangchow

Changsha
Foochow

Kunming
Canton

YUNNAN

Han River

Hankow

Hanyang
Wuhan

Wuchang

Yangtze-kiang

Puchi
(new coalfields)

| 0 | miles | 50 |
| 0 | km | 80 |

★ Wuhan Iron and Steel Company

Wuhan is one of the most important industrial regions in China. Its population is almost 3 million. It manufactures girders, ball-bearings, lorries, diesel engines, locomotives and armaments. There are cotton mills in Hankow and paper mills in Hanyang. The region is low-lying and has many lakes. Flooding is a menace and 'retention' schemes have been built on the Yangtze-kiang and the Han. These two rivers were bridged in Wuhan in 1957 and 1954 respectively.

Prices in Wuhan's department stores in the mid-seventies were:
TV set: 350Y, Bicycles: 160Y, Watches: prices varied between 40 and 120Y.
Wuhan found it difficult to acquire large quantities of sewing machines.
Thousands of peasants come in perhaps just once a year–but they usually have several hundred yuan to spend.

MILITIAWOMEN

Girls on a commune engaged in target practice.

Men aged 16–40 and women aged 16–35 spend part of each week training with the factory militia.

46 The minority peoples

A potential security risk

Scattered across China are millions of people belonging to fifty-one minority nationalities. Most of them live in the frontier regions which are vital to China's security. China needs to be sure of the loyalty and co-operation of these people and is anxious to integrate them fully into the People's Republic. This is why China fosters the growth of co-operatives and communes among people who until recently were primitive hunters, herdsmen or 'slash and burn' farmers, and why she strives to make them literate and capable of exploiting to the full the industrial and agricultural potential of their homelands. In her propaganda to the outside world China makes a rather extravagant claim to protect the culture of her national minorities as far as native languages, religious beliefs and domestic crafts are concerned. In fact, China carefully limits the degree of religious freedom she allows her minority peoples to enjoy. Total freedom might encourage them to question the thought of Mao Tse-tung. This is a delicate problem and more than once the C.C.P. has run into trouble over it. For example, the Muslim revolts in Yunnan during 1975 showed that the C.C.P. had not fully solved the problem of conflict between religious beliefs and Communist ideology.

The Autonomous Regions

Since 1949 the C.C.P. has systematically granted to minority areas the status of either Autonomous Region or Autonomous District. This label guarantees certain cultural rights—but little else. After all, Article 4 of the Constitution states that 'The People's Republic of China is a unified, multinational state. All nationalities are equal.' This is a revolutionary definition of Chinese society and is in complete contrast to the views expressed by ancient emperors and, in more recent times, by leaders such as Sun Yat-sen and Chiang Kai-shek. They had always clung to the totally incorrect belief that 'pure' Chinese were the descendants of the Han people; the implication was that those who were not the 'sons of Han' were in some way inferior. The Communists rejected any hint of racial discrimination. They intended to assimilate—or *sinicize*—all the minority peoples within the frontiers of the P.R.C.* However, they have deliberately allowed the minorities to observe their own traditions and to make a study of their cultural origins. The C.C.P. fully understood the importance and reverence that Asian national groups attach to their past achievements.

Two examples

(*i*) *Inner Mongolia Autonomous Region* The Mongolians provide a good example of this sort of policy in action. They have a very strong historical tradition and hero-worship the memory of Genghis Khan. Conscious of the depth of this feeling, the C.C.P. took great pains in 1954 to arrange the ceremony of bringing home the ashes of Genghis Khan to their original resting place.† This won the respect of the Mongolian herdsmen and before long they allowed themselves to be absorbed into Chinese society. In the schools, Chinese became a compulsory subject; sheepfarmers' co-operatives and 200 rural communes soon eroded the nomadic way of life; motor roads and the Trans-Mongolian Railway brought new jobs and new settlers. Young Mongolians imitated the Chinese immigrants and took jobs as steelworkers and coalminers. They became labourers on the new irrigation projects designed to defeat the constant threat of drought which bedevils Inner Mongolia. Thus the Mongolians have abandoned their traditional way of life. They have managed to preserve their language and the memory of their customs but in the process they have lost all trace of economic independence.

(*ii*) *Sinkiang-Uighur Autonomous Region* The Uighurs have had a similar experience—though they have seen even more drastic change. Not only is Sinkiang one of China's newest oil-producing regions but it is also the nuclear test centre of the People's Liberation Army. And as the P.L.A. needs to turn this western outpost of the People's Republic into an area capable of sustaining itself through simultaneous agricultural and industrial expansion, the Uighurs are undergoing a particularly rapid social transformation. So while they take part in a miniature industrial revolution—there are new coalmines, oilfields, blast furnaces, textile factories and huge repair shops for the thousands of trucks that rumble across the new motor roads—they also retain the responsibility for maintaining the region's reputation as the most important sheep and cattle rearing area in China. The system seems to work. The C.C.P. has made the Uighur language the *official* language of the region; it has given some of the top administrative posts to Uighur officials; and it respects Uighur religious beliefs to the extent of allowing some teaching from the Koran to figure on school timetables. Sinkiang-Uighur Autonomous Region's recent history is a tribute to the assimilation policies of the C.C.P.

---

*In 1949 Tibet was not part of the P.R.C. Chinese troops occupied it during 1950. See Spread 48.

†The Kuomintang had taken the ashes to Chinghai in 1939—to prevent the Japanese from using them for propaganda purposes!

INNER MONGOLIA A.R. In 1969 the Chinese decided to reduce the size of the Inner Mongolia Autonomous Region. Its north-east areas went to the Manchurian provinces of Heilungkiang, Kirin and Liaoning; its western zones went to the Ningsia Hui A.R. and to the province of Kansu. No clear reason for this was ever given by the Chinese who in 1962 had settled the border with the Mongolian People's Republic in these regions. It was probably due to China's growing fear of Soviet military power in the Mongolian People's Republic — a disguised form of military reorganization.

The autonomous regions of the People's Republic of China

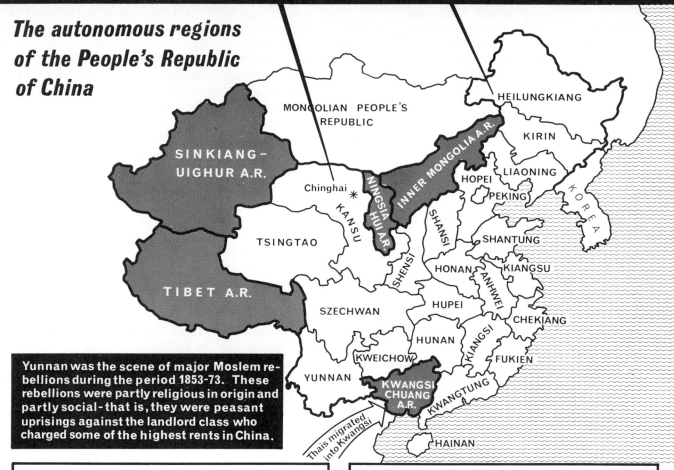

Yunnan was the scene of major Moslem rebellions during the period 1853-73. These rebellions were partly religious in origin and partly social - that is, they were peasant uprisings against the landlord class who charged some of the highest rents in China.

RELIGION IN THE PEOPLE'S REPUBLIC OF CHINA

Most Chinese over the age of 20 have a background of either Confucian or Buddhist training — or both. Islam and Christianity are regarded as foreign religions and those who follow either of these faiths run the risk of being identified with these foreign origins.

Today there are far more Moslems than Christians in the PRC. Most big Chinese cities have a mosque or two, although the main Moslem groups (called Hui or Dungans by the Chinese) live around the oases of the old trade routes with India, the Middle East and with Mongolia. The biggest group is located in Ningsia, notorious for its shifting sand dunes and fierce sandstorms. Kansu has almost as many Moslems as Ningsia (over half a million each) while Yunnan has about 250,000.

As the minority peoples become assimilated so will the different religions decline in importance: "Islam is .... declining in China; only the older people keep to its precepts".[*]

[*](Albert Kolb: East Asia, Methuen 1971 p.102.)

THE CHUANG PEOPLE OF THE KWANGSI A.R.

The Chuang people are a branch of the Thai and migrated from Thailand to occupy the area today known as the Kwangsi Chuang A.R. They are not in the majority–in fact they account for just over 50% of the non-Chinese population (which includes a variety of hill tribes such as the Tung, Miao and Yao).

The Chuang are interesting because they have already become almost completely assimilated in Chinese society. They tend to speak the Cantonese dialect and have adopted Chinese customs. According to Albert Kolb, "Many of them are now indistinguishable from the Chinese.....they have merged with the Chinese and lost all consciousness of their Thai connections". (East Asia p.259)

If this is so, it is a pointer towards the fate of the other minority peoples. In time they too will be completely merged with the Chinese.

47 The People's Liberation Army

According to Article 15 of the 1975 Constitution 'The Chinese People's Liberation Army and the People's Militia are the workers' and peasants' own armed forces led by the Chinese Communist Party; they are the armed forces of the people of all nationalities … The Chinese P.L.A. is at all times a fighting force and simultaneously a working force and a production force.'

The Production and Construction Corps

One of contemporary China's most interesting military organizations is the P.L.A.'s Production and Construction Corps (P.C.C.). It began modestly enough when the P.L.A. occupied Sinkiang during 1949–50. As it mopped up the last elements of KMT resistance, thousands of Nationalist soldiers flocked to surrender and rather than locking them up in prisoner-of-war camps the P.L.A. set them to work under the supervision of Communist commanders. In this way they formed the Sinkiang P.C.C. and began the task of transforming the province into a rich farming area. The Corps simply moved into a district, constructed irrigation works and then ploughed up the land to form manageable fields. When the job was over, the Corps handed the district over to Chinese immigrants who converted it into a 'state farm'. It was a highly successful device and many other parts of China—especially the Shenyang and Peking Military Regions—adopted the scheme. By 1970 the P.C.C. numbered literally millions of soldiers and began to take on more specialized duties. For example, over 300,000 P.C.C. men patrol the frontier with the Soviet Union and act as very efficient security guards.

The fighting forces

The term 'People's Liberation Army' includes all the armed services of the Republic, the army, air force and navy.

(*a*) *The army:* Chinese teenagers seem to have very little objection to conscription. Young men and women serve two years in the army where the slogan is 'Everyone a soldier!' Their tour of duty takes them to all parts of the vast Republic. Most join the infantry and there were about 125 operational divisions in the mid-seventies. Others choose the artillery or armoured units and there is keen rivalry for the more élite corps—such as the air-

borne division. China's conscripts have seen active service since 1950—in Tibet, Korea, in India and along the frontier with Russia where P.L.A. troops of the Sinkiang and Shenyang Military Regions have been in fire-fights with Soviet soldiers on several occasions.

(*b*) *The air force:* conscripts joining the Chinese Air Force have to serve a minimum of three years. The Air Force originally used captured KMT planes—such as the *P.51 Mustang*. But once China joined in the Korean War Stalin sent in his latest *MiG–15* jets. After the war ended in 1953, the Russians continued to supply China with improved versions of the MiG fighters and by 1960, when Russian aid ended, China had sufficient quantities of the aircraft to develop her own *Shenyang MiG–21* jet—which has proved to be a very efficient weapon. More than once it had defeated U.S. *Phantoms* in dogfights over the China–North Viet Nam border (before America withdrew from the war in 1973) and it has sufficiently impressed the Pakistanis to persuade them to buy some for their own air force.

(*c*) *The navy:* the Chinese Navy insists on four years' service from its conscripts, very few of whom spend much time at sea. The P.R.C. has no large naval vessels at its disposal and most of its units operate patrol craft such as those illustrated below. However, in view of China's rapid technological progress it is possible that she will develop a defence strategy in which nuclear submarines carrying M.R.B.Ms. will play an important part.

Units of the Chinese Navy on patrol off the South China coast.

An unexpected bonus in 1949–50: Captured KMT P.51D 'Mustang' fighters originally supplied by America.

A WEAPON OF THE FIFTIES

'Mustangs' were just a small part of the booty captured by the Communists 1949-50. Ironically, America desperately needed her own P.51 'planes during the Korean War (1950-53) because of their suitability for ground attack operations.

U. S. S. R.

U. S. S. R.

MONGOLIA – formerly a Chinese frontier state

Border clashes with Soviet troops

Border clashes with Soviet troops

SHENYANG

PLA involved in Korean War 1950-53

Peking ★

PEKING

AFGHANISTAN

PAKISTAN

KASHMIR

SINKIANG

LANCHOW

TSINAN

Chinese invasion of Tibet 1950

TIBET

1962 War between India and China

CHENGTU

WUHAN

NANKING

KOREA

JAPAN

INDIA

ASSAM

KUNMING

FUCHOW

CANTON

MATSU

QUEMOY

TAIWAN

Desultory warfare (shelling and air raids) with the Chinese Nationalists on Quemoy and Matsu.

VIET NAM

Chinese fighters, missiles and and anti-aircraft guns shot down a number of US 'planes which strayed off course during the American involvement in the War in Viet Nam.

CANTON The military regions into which China is divided.

THE P.L.A. IN ACTION ALONG – AND SOMETIMES ACROSS – CHINA'S FRONTIERS 1950-1975

A WEAPON OF THE SEVENTIES

Probably the best all-round mass-produced infantry weapon in the world, it was supplied by Russia up to 1960 - after which Sino-Soviet relations became distinctly chilly.

The Chinese version of the Soviet Kalashnikov AK–47 assault rifle.

105

Further Reading

Theme 6—The People's Republic of China

Spread

37.	William G. Sewell	*I Stayed in China*	Allen and Unwin, 1966
38.	Evan Luard	*Britain and China* (Chapters 6 and 7)	Chatto and Windus, 1962
39.	Victor Purcell	*China*	Ernest Benn, 1962
40.	E. L. Wheelwright and Bruce McFarlane	*The Chinese Road to Socialism*	Pelican, 1973
41.	T. R. Tregear	*The Chinese*	David and Charles, 1973
	John Gittings	*A Chinese View of China*	B.B.C., 1973
42.	T. R. Tregear	*The Chinese*	David and Charles, 1973
43.	Jack Belden	*China Shakes the World* (pp. 167–75)—deals with pre-1966 education.	Pelican, 1973
		Education in China—deals with post-1966 developments.	Anglo-Chinese Educational Institute, 1974
	Theodore Chen	*The Maoist Educational Revolution*	Praeger Publishers, 1974
44.	Jan Myrdal and Gun Kessle	*China: the Revolution Continued*	Penguin, 1973
	R. R. C. de Crespigny	*China: The Land and the People*	Nelson, 1971
45.	Harrison E. Salisbury	*To Peking and Beyond*	Hutchinson, 1973
46.	Albert Kolb	*East Asia*	Methuen, 1971
47.	Gerard H. Corr	*The Chinese Red Army*	Osprey, 1974

Andrew Watson's *Living in China* (Batsford, 1975) provides a good commentary on most aspects of Chinese life.

THEME 7

'China shakes the world'

China's attitude to world affairs has been a frequent source of anxiety to the West, and after 1960 it began to worry the Russians also. China's foreign policy objectives have often been misunderstood. America was quick to brand her as the aggressor when China occupied Tibet, intervened in Korea, fought India in the Himalayas and sent aid to the North Vietnamese. And when she supplied arms and instructors to nationalist guerrilla movements in, for example, Mozambique this was interpreted as a deliberate attempt to export Chinese Communism to Africa. Moreover, the Chinese have tended to oppose international moves to limit strategic weapons and to reduce world tension. They refused to sign the Partial Test Ban Treaty and roundly condemned the 1975 Helsinki talks between Russia and the West. According to the Chinese, the talks were about as useful as the Munich agreement had been before the Second World War.

It has always been difficult to pinpoint those members of the Chinese Politburo—apart from Mao Tse-tung and Chou En-lai—who make the key foreign policy decisions. Prominent Chinese have a habit of disappearing overnight. Sometimes they are reported as having died in mysterious circumstances—the fate of Liu Shao-chi and Lin Piao. Sometimes they manage to regain the political limelight. One politician who did this was Vice-Premier Teng Hsiao-ping who survived a period of disgrace as a traitor to the revolution. He succeeded Chou En-lai during the latter's protracted illness and many China experts tipped him as the man most likely to take the place of Chou. But when Chou died in 1976 a surprise announcement from Peking revealed that Hua Kuo-feng, another Vice-Premier, was to act as successor to Premier Chou. His first few months of office were filled with sadness. Throughout the summer of 1976 earthquakes caused heavy casualties in China and then in September came the news of the death of Mao Tse-Tung at the age of 82.

48 Fashioning new frontiers: the acquisition of Tibet

The invasion, 1950

Early in the morning of 7 October 1950 Chinese troops began crossing the frontier into Tibet. That day there was hardly any resistance as the Tibetans who lived on the border with China welcomed the P.L.A. men as liberators who would free them from the burdensome taxes levied by the Dalai Lama's government in the capital, Lhasa.* When the Tibetan Cabinet heard of the news of the Chinese invasion they immediately asked for assistance from Britain and the United States. But no help was ever forthcoming.

The motive for attack

Chinese soldiers had conquered Tibet during the eighteenth century when the Manchu emperors tried, without much success, to set up a protectorate over the country. When the 1911 Revolution toppled the Manchu Emperors, Tibet declared her independence—though the Chinese Nationalist governments never recognized this. When the Communist came to power they were determined to assert their control over Tibet because they genuinely believed it to be, on historical grounds, a part of China. They also had another reason: they knew that Nationalist troops had operated in Tibet during the Second World War so there was probably a chance that Chiang Kai-shek might try to set up bases in the area for a thrust into Yunnan. Mao Tse-tung decided to pre-empt such a move and the invasion of 1950, hastily planned and incompetently executed, was the result of this decision.

The campaign of 1950–51

The image of a remote, unworldly community of Tibetans, peacefully governed by kind lamas living in monasteries perched 16,000 feet above sea level, might have been true for some of the million or so people living in the southern part of the country. But it was certainly not the case as far as the Khamba people were concerned. These were fierce, nomadic tribesmen who lived not far from the border with China. Expert horsemen and armed with a motley collection of swords, pistols and rifles, they attacked anyone who dared to trespass into their mountain territory. And it was these 'Cossacks of the slopes' who stood directly in the path of the weary Communist troops making forced marches across some of the toughest terrain in the entire world. However, during the first week of the invasion the P.L.A. units were more worried by the Tibetan army that was supposed to be dug in around the town of Chamdo. However, they occupied Chamdo without a battle and pressed on to their main objective, Lhasa, still 700 miles away. It was at this point that they ran into the fearsome Khambas whose terrifying ambushes stopped the P.L.A. men in their tracks. For the next five months a terrible mountain war went on between the Khambas and the Communists—with the ill-equipped Chinese shivering in the Tibetan winter and losing about 5,000 men to fever and frostbite.

The deal with Peking, 1951

Meanwhile, the Dalai Lama began negotiating with Mao Tse-tung in the hope of saving part of Tibet from Chinese occupation. In May 1951 the Tibetan delegates in Peking signed the so-called *Seventeen Points Agreement*; in August the first P.L.A. representatives reached Lhasa; and in November five P.L.A. divisions marched into the capital. The Agreement allowed the Dalai Lama to remain ruler of part of Tibet—but he exercised very little political control. Between 1951 and 1954 the P.L.A. systematically searched the numerous monasteries for arms dumps and arrested the lamas or monks. At the same time the Construction Corps units built a series of military highways to link Tibet with Yunnan and Tsinghai.

Resistance grows, 1955–9

The Khambas never submitted to the Chinese occupation forces and in 1955 they began raiding P.L.A. outposts. By 1957 eastern Tibet was in a state of war,‡ a war which forced the P.L.A. to resort to air strikes, artillery bombardments and 'search and destroy' operations. Still they failed to winkle out the rebels and by March 1959 the revolt had spread to Lhasa to involve the Dalai Lama himself.

The Chinese victory, 1959

So serious was the situation that the Chinese moved in a quarter of a million troops to crush this nationalist revolt against Communist domination. This build-up of armed might dictated the Dalai Lama's next move—he decided to end his role as the spiritual and temporal leader of his people and escaped across the border to Tezpur in India. Behind him the Chinese exterminated the resistance fighters and began to assimilate the surviving Tibetans into the Chinese way of life. By the end of the year Mao Tse-tung had made good a statement he uttered in 1950: 'Tibet is a part of China.'

*The Dalai Lama is the spiritual and temporal leader of Tibet. His followers regard him as a divine being.
‡Technically a civil war: India and Nepal recognized Chinese jurisdiction over Tibet, 1954–6.

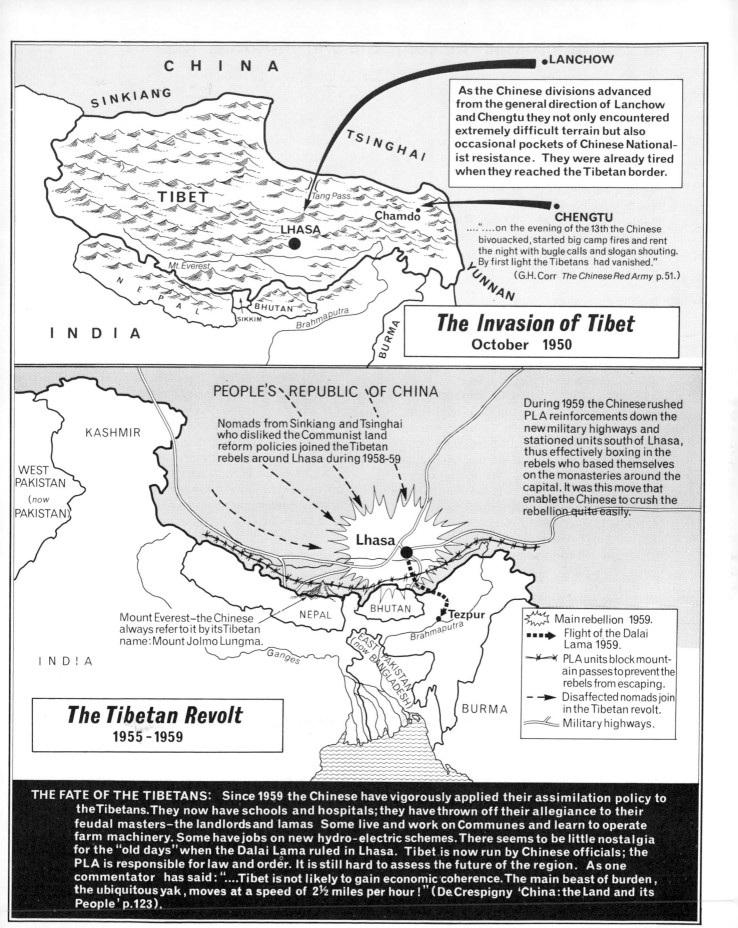

CHINA

SINKIANG

TSINGHAI

• LANCHOW

As the Chinese divisions advanced from the general direction of Lanchow and Chengtu they not only encountered extremely difficult terrain but also occasional pockets of Chinese National-ist resistance. They were already tired when they reached the Tibetan border.

TIBET

Tang Pass.

Chamdo

LHASA

CHENGTU

....".....on the evening of the 13th the Chinese bivouacked, started big camp fires and rent the night with bugle calls and slogan shouting. By first light the Tibetans had vanished."
(G.H. Corr *The Chinese Red Army* p. 51.)

Mt. Everest

N E P A L

BHUTAN

SIKKIM

Brahmaputra

I N D I A

YUNNAN

BURMA

The Invasion of Tibet
October 1950

PEOPLE'S REPUBLIC OF CHINA

KASHMIR

WEST PAKISTAN
(*now* PAKISTAN)

Nomads from Sinkiang and Tsinghai who disliked the Communist land reform policies joined the Tibetan rebels around Lhasa during 1958-59

During 1959 the Chinese rushed PLA reinforcements down the new military highways and stationed units south of Lhasa, thus effectively boxing in the rebels who based themselves on the monasteries around the capital. It was this move that enable the Chinese to crush the rebellion quite easily.

Lhasa

Mount Everest—the Chinese always refer to it by its Tibetan name: Mount Jolmo Lungma.

NEPAL

BHUTAN

• Tezpur

Brahmaputra

EAST PAKISTAN (now BANGLADESH)

Ganges

I N D I A

BURMA

$\mathcal{M}$ Main rebellion 1959.

➤ Flight of the Dalai Lama 1959.

⊣⊢➤ PLA units block mount-ain passes to prevent the rebels from escaping.

--➤ Disaffected nomads join in the Tibetan revolt.

∿ Military highways.

The Tibetan Revolt
1955 - 1959

THE FATE OF THE TIBETANS: Since 1959 the Chinese have vigorously applied their assimilation policy to the Tibetans. They now have schools and hospitals; they have thrown off their allegiance to their feudal masters—the landlords and lamas. Some live and work on Communes and learn to operate farm machinery. Some have jobs on new hydro-electric schemes. There seems to be little nostalgia for the "old days" when the Dalai Lama ruled in Lhasa. Tibet is now run by Chinese officials; the PLA is responsible for law and order. It is still hard to assess the future of the region. As one commentator has said: "....Tibet is not likely to gain economic coherence. The main beast of burden, the ubiquitous yak, moves at a speed of 2½ miles per hour!" (De Crespigny 'China: the Land and its People' p.123).

49 China crosses the Yalu: the war in Korea, 1950–51

The war

In June 1950 elements of the North Korean armed forces crossed the 38th Parallel dividing North from South Korea. U.N. forces, mainly American and Commonwealth troops, hurriedly arrived to bolster up the crumbling South Koreans engaged in battles around the Pusan perimeter. By October 1950 they had pushed the North Koreans beyond their original start line and begun a carefree advance towards the Yalu River. It was then that the Chinese intervened in the fighting.

China's motives

China had always regarded Korea as a client kingdom, a buffer state against invaders from Japan. When Japan removed Korea from Chinese control in 1895 the north-east frontier became highly vulnerable—as the events of 1931 proved. Now, in 1950, 'imperialist' armies were again invading the peninsula from their bases in Japan. This was why Chou En-lai meant it when he warned General MacArthur, the U.N. commander, that China would intervene if the advance continued to threaten the frontiers of the P.R.C. MacArthur chose to ignore Chou's warning, kept moving north and, on 9 October, called on North Korea to surrender. Ten days later, when his troops had occupied Pyongyang, rumours were flying around that Chinese troops had crossed the Yalu—though no one had actually seen them.

The People's Volunteers

In fact the P.L.A. had moved a quarter of a million soldiers into Manchuria. Lin Piao had the task of ferrying these 'People's Volunteers' across the Yalu to secret staging areas. There the 'phantom army' hid from the prying eyes of U.N. reconnaissance planes. This huge army moved only at night, quietly assembling its equipment and preparing for its assault on the unsuspecting U.N. soldiers. The main attack went in on 26 November as fourteen divisions of People's Volunteers fell on the U.N. troops, scattering them in all directions. By Christmas the Chinese had pushed the U.N. out of North Korea, crossed the 38th Parallel and, in the New Year, captured the South Korean capital, Seoul.

New commanders in Korea

Despite Lin Piao's remarkable victories, Peking recalled him in January 1951 and promoted General Peng Teh-huai to take command of the People's Volunteers. Peng had been serving in Tibet where he had won the reputation of being over-liberal with the lives of his fighting men. Then, in April, the U.N. command changed equally dramatically. U.S. President Harry Truman dismissed MacArthur because of the latter's eagerness to extend the war into China. Korea, said the President, was to be a limited war. There must be no escalation—there was too much risk of a nuclear holocaust. Consequently, MacArthur's replacement, General Ridgway, had to carry on with the war with conventional weapons.

The Chinese defeat

Peng had no such scruples. He would fight with anything he could lay his hands on. His first major campaign began on 22 April 1951 when, in a scene reminiscent of the set-piece battles of the First World War, thousands of Chinese troops began a general assault across the entire peninsula. Their tactics forced the U.N. to give ground and had the Gloucester Regiment not held a crucial gap in the line for three desperate days (the Battle of the Imjin), this orderly retreat might have turned into a rout. As it was, the U.N. managed to dig in and create a make-shift defence line across Korea. Undeterred, Peng ordered his Volunteers to adopt *human wave* tactics. Squad after squad rushed the U.N. positions, only to meet devastating machine-gun fire. Fresh units moved up only to wilt under napalm attacks and a hail of mortar and artillery fire. Brave as they were, the Volunteers could make little progress against this sort of opposition and the offensive petered out in June 1951. By then, some Volunteer units had lost over 50 per cent of their men killed and wounded.

Peace talks begin

Quite unexpectedly, the Russians suggested a cease-fire in Korea. General Ridgway promptly invited the Chinese to attend armistice talks and the two sides met first at Kaesong and then in the little village of Panmunjom. For the next two years, the talking went on while thousands of men met their death in the brown hills that flanked the Korean *No Man's Land*. Hand-to-hand combats and intense artillery duels became the order of the day. Communist *Bed Check Charlies* side-slipped through the hills at night to disturb the weary U.N. soldiers. Low-flying *Mustangs* skip-bombed their napalm tanks into the Chinese and North Korean bunkers. Such was the war in Korea by the end of 1951.

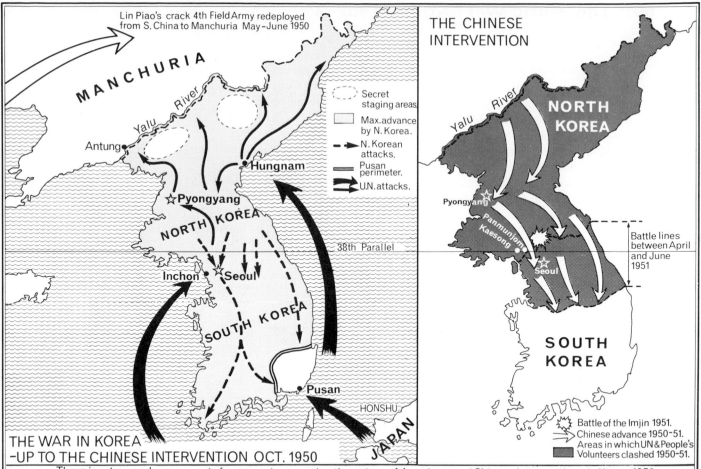

Lin Piao's crack 4th Field Army redeployed from S. China to Manchuria May–June 1950

MANCHURIA

Yalu River

Antung

Secret staging areas.

Max. advance by N. Korea.

N. Korean attacks.

Pusan perimeter.

U.N. attacks.

Hungnam

Pyongyang

NORTH KOREA

38th Parallel

Inchon

Seoul

SOUTH KOREA

Pusan

HONSHU

JAPAN

THE WAR IN KOREA
–UP TO THE CHINESE INTERVENTION OCT. 1950

THE CHINESE INTERVENTION

Yalu River

NORTH KOREA

Pyongyang

Panmunjom

Kaesong

Seoul

Battle lines between April and June 1951

SOUTH KOREA

Battle of the Imjin 1951.
Chinese advance 1950-51.
Areas in which UN & People's Volunteers clashed 1950-51.

There is a tremendous amount of argument concerning the nature of American and Chinese interventions in Korea 1950:

1. *The Communist view that America's intervention was a deliberately planned act of 'imperialist aggression': <u>there is no military evidence to support this</u>. In fact, the US Eighth Army (in Japan at the time of the outbreak of war) was in no way ready for combat. It was in particularly bad shape. According to Tim Carew its vehicles were in a 'deplorable condition.....no spare barrels for machine-guns.....shortages of trip flares, cleaning rods, grenades and and anti-tank mines. Illuminating flares did everything except illuminate.....' (Tim Carew, <u>The Korean War</u>, Pan Books, 1967, p. 28).*

2. *The view that China intervened because U.S. troops violated the Chinese border in 1950: this has been expressed by distinguished writers such as Denis Healey writing in The Times 1 December 1972. He said, 'Chinese intervention came only after a warning, because MacArthur CROSSED THE YALU and was trying to extend the war into China itself.....' In fact, no troops under MacArthur's command crossed the Yalu. However, US aircraft did strafe river craft and villages on the Chinese side of the border. The US agreed that on 7 August 1950 its 'planes did strafe accidently Antung airfield – and America offered to pay compensation to China. (See <u>China crosses the Yalu</u> by Allen S. Whiting, Macmillan 1960).*

'Bed Check Charlies' were in fact usually Polikarpov Po–2 biplane trainers supplied by Russia. Just one of these (flown by Lt. La Woon Yung) knocked out an entire flight of US Sabre jets parked on an airfield. They were very hard to intercept as they flew under the UN radar. Special US jet fighters had to be adapted to night operations–usually F7F Tigercats–but they never really eliminated the Bed Check raids. The most spectacular success (using Yak trainers as well as Po–2s) was over Inchon in 1953 when the Bed Check Charlies destroyed a UN dump containing 5 million gallons of fuel.

For details of Communist air power in the Korean War see 'Air War over Korea' by Robert Jackson (Ian Allan Ltd. 1973).

'Bed Check Charlie'

50 The static war: Korea, 1952–3

The nature of the war

(a) *The shooting war:* by the beginning of 1952 both sides had settled down to trench warfare. Both had become adept at transforming hillsides into elaborate defence systems. Between the main Chinese hill positions and the U.N. defence lines were damp paddy fields with lots of little hillocks which afforded good cover to the fighting patrols who ventured into this terrain. Most of the Chinese peaks and ridges featured deep, underground shelters which hid personnel, 75 mm. field guns and all the ammunition stores. Clever use of foxholes and *reverse slope* gun positions—all superbly camouflaged—made them virtually impregnable. Usually, when the Chinese decided to attack a U.N. hill position, they heralded their intention by means of a fearsome artillery barrage. For example, before attacking the Hook in May 1953, they fired their big guns continuously for eight days. Veteran British soldiers—who happened to be on the receiving end of this bombardment—described it as far worse than anything they had experienced during the Second World War. When the Chinese had pulverized everything in sight they then—as always—rushed the position, to the accompaniment of yells, high-pitched bugle calls and bursts of automatic fire from their highly effective 'burp-guns'.*

(b) *The psychological war:* the Chinese had an excellent intelligence service and always knew the names of regiments facing them in the line. It was likely that some of the South Korean porters who worked with the U.N. forces were Communist agents who simply slipped across No Man's Land with their latest information. Yet it was always disconcerting for U.N. relief battalions to find themselves welcomed by the Chinese loudspeakers and invited to send across their requests for a particular record. Occasionally, Chinese mortars sent over a shower of propaganda leaflets, warning the U.N. infantry that they were really fighting and dying for bloated American capitalists. The photograph opposite shows a banner found attached to the U.N. barbed wire on Christmas Eve 1952—the occasion on which cards arrived bearing the message 'Merry Christmas and Happy New Year from the Korean People's Army and the Chinese People's Volunteers'! But there was little evidence that this sort of activity had much effect on the morale of U.N. fighting men.

The armistice, 1953

One reason for prolonging this static campaign was the vexed question of prisoner-of-war repatriation. Some soldiers—especially Chinese—did not want to go home and so the issue was: did a soldier have the right to refuse repatriation? During the argument the Chinese hurled all sorts of accusations at the U.N., including charges of using poison gas and germ warfare in Korea—while the U.N. retorted by condemning the Communists for 'brainwashing' *their* prisoners. The Communist line was picked up by Chinese prisoners-of-war herded into Koje Island. In 1952 they organized a riot and actually captured the U.S. commandant, who was lucky to escape with his life. Eventually, the negotiators in Panmunjom signed an armistice and at 22.00 hours on 27 July 1953 all firing ceased. Next morning, when U.N. troops cautiously came into the open, the Chinese People's Volunteers were drawn up on their hillsides, their arms raised in the Communist salute. It was all over; the cease-fire line was roughly the same as the original 38th Parallel that had divided North from South Korea. China had successfully defended her border along the Yalu River; and North Korea, at least, seemed to have reverted to her pre-1895 role of being a tributary state of China. Since 1953 there have been no serious attempts to convert the armistice into a permanent peace. The U.N. still patrols the cease-fire line, though the last of the People's Volunteers left Korea in 1958. Korea remains a delicate international problem—and it is possible that her fate is tied up with other points of issue between America and China, especially the status of that 'other China', the Nationalist island of Taiwan.

*These were Chinese versions of the Soviet 'Pay-Pay-Shah' (PPSh-41) sub-machine gun.

A farewell salute from the Chinese People's Volunteers.

THE CHINESE SOLDIERS AND THEIR HILLSIDE STRONGPOINTS IN KOREA

Summers were warm–but winters were very cold indeed. The Chinese had uniforms of quilted cotton, well-padded against the cold. They were brown or blue–grey in colour and were very warm–though difficult to dry out after heavy rain. For extra warmth the Chinese wore their summer uniforms under their quilted outfits. They did not have steel helmets but favoured heavy fur or cotton caps with big ear flaps. They did not wear boots; instead they had rubber–soled lightweight laceless cotton shoes–very useful for silent patrol work.

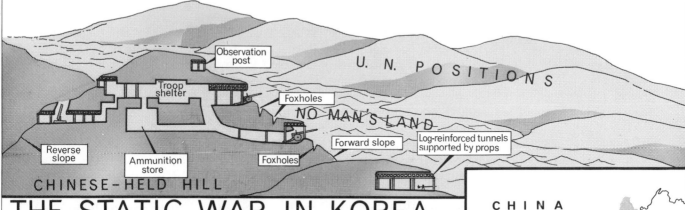

THE STATIC WAR IN KOREA

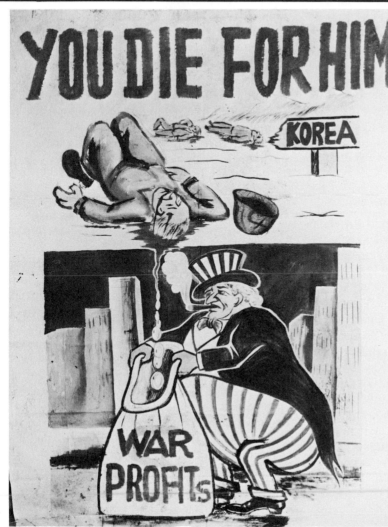

THE END OF THE AFFAIR

I captured the banner on Christmas Eve 1952. We had moved into a position north of Seoul. ...Although the manoeuvre had been carried out with the utmost secrecy we were, nevertheless, 'welcomed' by the Chinese forces over a loudspeaker.... I was called by one of my Section Posts who heard noises on the wire in front. I.....had more machine guns trained on the spot.....In the morning the wire was festooned with banners, Christmas cards, badges and miscellaneous propaganda.

(2/Lt. J.R.M. Keatley
Duke of Wellington's Regiment).

51　The 'Formosan Crisis'—the problem of Taiwan

Who owns 'Formosa'?

When the Second World War ended in 1945 everyone agreed that Taiwan belonged to China. But once the Communists had forced the Nationalist leader, Chiang Kai-shek, to flee to Taiwan, the question was: to which China? There was more than one answer and many politicians and statesmen rested their case on the island's extraordinary history. In 1895 the Chinese had ceded Taiwan to Japan; in 1943 the Cairo Conference agreed that it should be returned to China; in 1945 the Potsdam Conference decided it should be taken over by—but not ceded to—the armed forces of Nationalist China. Then in 1950 the U.S.A. arbitrarily decided to 'neutralize' the island by stationing the U.S. Seventh Fleet between the refugee Nationalists and the Communist-controlled mainland. When the U.N. tried to find a solution to the Taiwan problem it had become complicated by China's intervention in the Korean War. By December 1950 Chou En-lai was insisting on a package deal before he would agree to peace in Korea: '... all foreign troops must be withdrawn from Korea and Korea's domestic affairs must be settled by the Korean people themselves. *The American aggression forces must be withdrawn from Taiwan.* And the representatives of the P.R.C. must obtain legitimate status in the United Nations.' And to complicate matters even further, Japan finally signed her Peace Treaty with her old enemies in 1951. In it she agreed to relinquish all claims to Taiwan and the Pescadores—but did not actually cede them to anyone.

The P.R.C. employs force

Yet the P.R.C. had a powerful ally to support her claims to Taiwan. Russia had no doubts that the island belonged to China and her support gave the P.L.A. enough confidence to try to take what it wanted. P.L.A. gunners began shelling Quemoy and Matsu in 1954 while Communist aircraft bombed the Tachen Islands. Then, at the beginning of 1955, P.L.A. assault troops landed on the tiny island of Yikiangshan—and promptly escalated the risk of a new Pacific war. America sent reinforcements to Taiwan; Chiang Kai-shek increased the size of his garrisons on Quemoy and Matsu; while on the coastline facing Taiwan the P.L.A. assembled thousands of troops. The stage was set for a major war—but nothing happened. Suddenly, the Communists switched their tactics—possibly because Chou En-lai was due to speak at the Bandung Conference in April 1955. As this was the first great conference attended by 'Third World' nations, the Chinese wanted to make the right sort of impression.

It was their chance to win the support of the other twenty-eight nations present.* So the air strikes stopped, the shelling became intermittent and for the next three years peace reigned in the Taiwan Straits.

The 1958 crisis

It was August 1958 when the Communists sparked off the next and much more serious crisis. Their plan was to subject Quemoy† to constant bombardment, isolate it from Nationalist supply ships and force it to surrender. But President Eisenhower considered the preservation of this tiny Nationalist-held island so important that he assembled, in the words of the *New York Times*, 'the most powerful air and naval fighting force in history'. America's latest jet aircraft crowded the U.S. air bases in Japan, Okinawa and the Philippines; her biggest carriers, supported by a guided-missile cruiser, flocked to the Taiwan Straits; and there was no doubt that tactical nuclear weapons were on board some of those ships. Fortunately, America's strength was never put to the test. Quemoy survived—largely because the Communist gunners dared not fire on the Nationalist convoys once they were escorted by U.S. warships. In this way, the fighting became confined to the Chinese who clashed high above the Straits in foreign-built jet fighters: Communist *MiG-17s* (supplied by Russia) fought Nationalist *F-86 Sabres* (supplied by America)—though most of these actions were indecisive until the Sabres began using *Sidewinder* air-to-air missiles.

Non-involvement by the superpowers

In effect, both Russia and America had managed to restrain their protégés during these dangerous months. Admittedly, the Russian leader Khrushchev had warned Eisenhower that he would never tolerate 'atomic blackmail', implying that a U.S. attack on Communist China would be interpreted as an attack upon the U.S.S.R. But as America never launched any attack, the Chinese gained nothing from the crisis they had precipitated. They therefore had to content themselves with a re-definition of the Taiwan problem. Peng Teh-huai, now Defence Minister, stated categorically that the four areas of Taiwan, the Pescadores, Quemoy and Matsu were part of the People's Republic: '... they do not constitute another country. There is only one China, not two ...' But when the Nationalist leader, Chiang Kai-shek, died in 1975 he was still master of that 'other China'.

*See *A Map History of the Modern World*, Spread 51.
†Technically two islands: Quemoy and Little Quemoy.

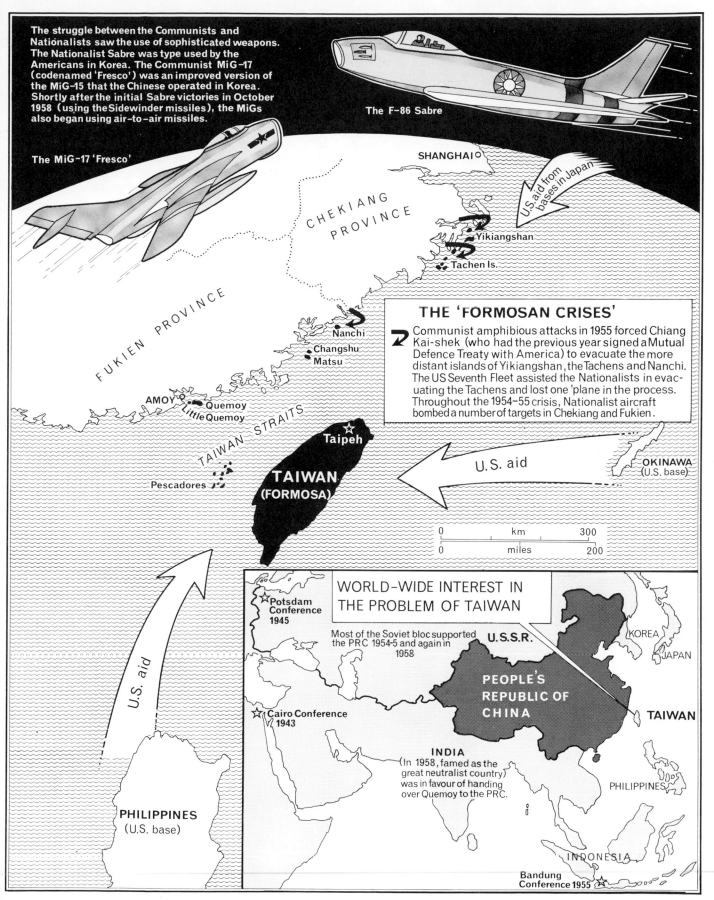

The struggle between the Communists and Nationalists saw the use of sophisticated weapons. The Nationalist Sabre was type used by the Americans in Korea. The Communist MiG-17 (codenamed 'Fresco') was an improved version of the MiG-15 that the Chinese operated in Korea. Shortly after the initial Sabre victories in October 1958 (using the Sidewinder missiles), the MiGs also began using air-to-air missiles.

The MiG-17 'Fresco'

The F-86 Sabre

SHANGHAI

CHEKIANG PROVINCE

U.S. aid from bases in Japan

Yikiangshan

Tachen Is.

FUKIEN PROVINCE

Nanchi

Changshu

Matsu

AMOY

Quemoy

Little Quemoy

TAIWAN STRAITS

Taipeh

Pescadores

TAIWAN (FORMOSA)

THE 'FORMOSAN CRISES'

Communist amphibious attacks in 1955 forced Chiang Kai-shek (who had the previous year signed a Mutual Defence Treaty with America) to evacuate the more distant islands of Yikiangshan, the Tachens and Nanchi. The US Seventh Fleet assisted the Nationalists in evacuating the Tachens and lost one 'plane in the process. Throughout the 1954–55 crisis, Nationalist aircraft bombed a number of targets in Chekiang and Fukien.

U.S. aid

OKINAWA (U.S. base)

| 0 | km | 300 |
| 0 | miles | 200 |

U.S. aid

WORLD-WIDE INTEREST IN THE PROBLEM OF TAIWAN

Potsdam Conference 1945

Most of the Soviet bloc supported the PRC 1954-5 and again in 1958

U.S.S.R.

KOREA

JAPAN

PEOPLE'S REPUBLIC OF CHINA

TAIWAN

Cairo Conference 1943

INDIA
(In 1958, famed as the great neutralist country) was in favour of handing over Quemoy to the PRC.

PHILIPPINES

PHILIPPINES
(U.S. base)

INDONESIA

Bandung Conference 1955

115

52   The war in the Himalayas

'Unprovoked Chinese aggression'?

By 1962 many people in the West saw the People's Republic as a country which wanted to expand its frontiers to the limits claimed by the Manchu emperors. Already, it seemed as though the Chinese Communists had a record as bad as any Western 'imperialist' nation: the invasion of Tibet, the intervention in Korea, the attempts to winkle the Nationalists out of their offshore islands. All seemed to be examples of Chinese Communist aggression. So when the news broke in October 1962 that Chinese infantry had attacked Indian soldiers stationed in the Himalayas it seemed to be proof—if any more were needed—that the P.R.C. was an aggressive, expansionist power. India's propaganda naturally reinforced this impression so that few people listened to the protestations of innocence that poured out of Peking. The fact that China is now seen as the aggrieved party in this dispute is largely due to the research carried out by an Australian historian, Neville Maxwell.

The problem in the Himalayas

The disagreement between China and India concerned the ownership of two stretches of land in the Himalayas: the Aksai Chin (or 'Desert of White Stones') and the North East Frontier Agency (N.E.F.A.). India claimed these lands on the grounds that in 1914 Britain—then the ruler of India—had negotiated these frontiers with Tibet, who had declared herself independent of China in 1912. However, successive Chinese governments refused to recognize these arrangements*—in fact, the Chinese Communists had built a military highway right through the middle of the Aksai Chin in order to link their Tibetan base at Gartok with Sinkiang Province. They naturally assumed that the Indians accepted both this and the Chinese occupation of N.E.F.A. to the north of the McMahon Line. Prime Minister Nehru had never raised serious objections and had always been friendly towards the People's Republic. Thus the Chinese were very surprised when Nehru ordered his troops to adopt a 'forward' policy in both sectors during 1962.

The Chinese blitzkrieg

(a) *The eastern sector*   By the autumn of 1962 the Indians had set up twenty-four military posts along the McMahon Line. They were under orders to take Thag La Ridge which was 16,000 feet above sea level. Compared with the Chinese troops who had been in the area for years, warmly dressed in quilted uniforms and snugly based in well-built bunkers, the Indians were totally unprepared for this sort of operation. They had no time to adapt to the oxygen shortage and many *jawans*† died from respiratory infections; their supplies depended on the few *Dakotas* capable of making air drops. Nevertheless, they struggled forward to occupy a deserted Chinese post at Dhola. But on 10 October the Chinese laid down a mortar barrage on the post and dispersed the Indians with a bayonet charge at battalion strength. Their full blitzkrieg began ten days later. They advanced down Thag La Ridge, pushed the Indians across the McMahon Line and pressed on until they were poised to invade the plains of Assam.

(b) *The western sector*   It was a similar story in the Aksai Chin. P.L.A. artillery barrages swamped the advancing Indians and cut off the *jawans* fighting their desperate actions in foxholes and command posts. It was soon over, though in this sector the Chinese blitzkrieg halted as soon as it reached its claim line.

The unexpected withdrawal

Then, to everyone's astonishment, the Chinese announced they would operate a cease fire from midnight, 21 November 1962. They withdrew their troops to a line 20 kilometres *behind* 'the lines of actual control which existed between China and India' in 1959—the year in which the Chinese had stated that 'it was impossible to entertain the absurd idea that our two friendly nations with a combined population of 1,000 million should start a war over such temporary and local disputes'. Yet although China had been *forced* to fight, she now gave up all the land she had taken by force of arms—and for which thousands of P.L.A. men had died. It was an extraordinary gesture. Perhaps it can be best explained in the words of Neville Maxwell: '... China had been engaged not on an invasion of India but on a giant punitive expedition'. The tragedy was that the matter could have been settled by negotiation in the first place: China wanted the Aksai Chin while India valued N.E.F.A. far more than she did the Desert of White Stones. This unnecessary war in the Himalayas influenced the international situation because it drove India into the arms of Russia whose hostility to China had been increasing since 1960. Thus the war robbed the Third World of its great self-appointed neutralist nation, the Republic of India.

*One of the few things on which the P.R.C. and the Nationalists were agreed. In 1962 Chiang Kai-shek said he had never accepted the 1914 arrangements with Tibet.
†Indian soldiers.

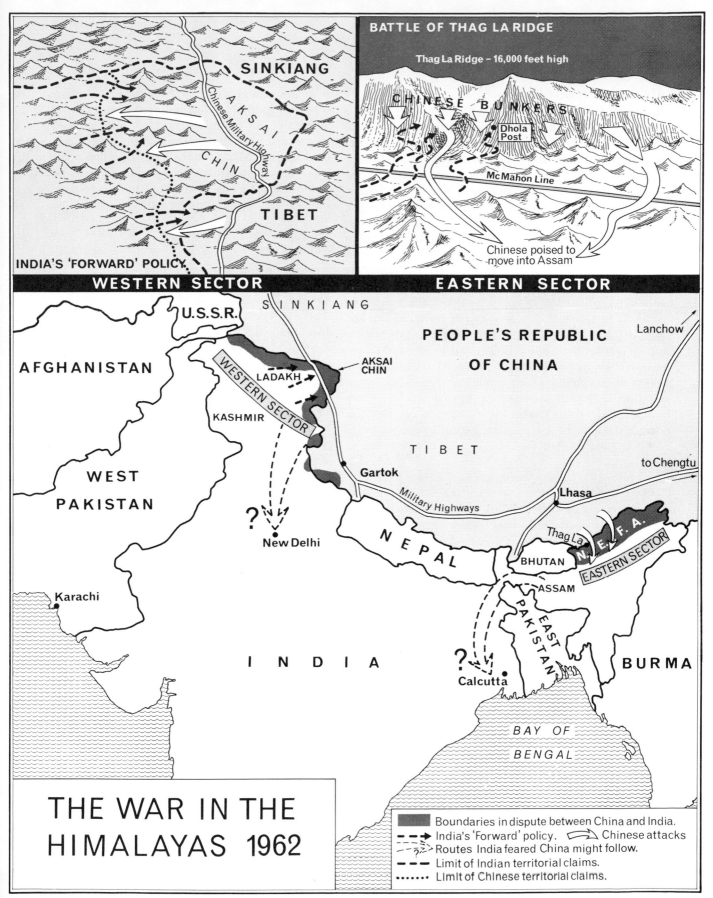

BATTLE OF THAG LA RIDGE

Thag La Ridge – 16,000 feet high

CHINESE BUNKERS

Dhola Post

McMahon Line

Chinese poised to move into Assam

INDIA'S 'FORWARD' POLICY

SINKIANG

A K S A I

Chinese Military Highway

C H I N

TIBET

WESTERN SECTOR

EASTERN SECTOR

U.S.S.R.

S I N K I A N G

Lanchow

PEOPLE'S REPUBLIC OF CHINA

AKSAI CHIN

AFGHANISTAN

WESTERN SECTOR

LADAKH

KASHMIR

WEST PAKISTAN

Gartok

T I B E T

Military Highways

to Chengtu

Lhasa

?

New Delhi

N E P A L

Thag La

N.E.F.A.

BHUTAN

EASTERN SECTOR

Karachi

ASSAM

EAST PAKISTAN

BURMA

I N D I A

?

Calcutta

BAY OF BENGAL

THE WAR IN THE HIMALAYAS 1962

Boundaries in dispute between China and India.

India's 'Forward' policy.   Chinese attacks

Routes India feared China might follow.

Limit of Indian territorial claims.

Limit of Chinese territorial claims.

53　The quarrel with Russia

Mao's initial respect for Russia

Although Stalin had never shown much interest in or understanding of the methods adopted by the Chinese Communists, Mao had always respected the Soviet dictator as the natural head of the *socialist bloc*—the term used for the group of countries ruled by Communist governments. Mao regarded socialist unity and strong leadership as crucial for the survival of Communism: 'The forces of imperialism have a head, which is America; our socialist bloc must have a head also, and that head is the Soviet Union. If we do not have a head, our forces are liable to disintegrate.' Though Mao was not especially impressed by Nikita Khrushchev, the man who eventually emerged as Russia's leader after Stalin's death in 1953, he was nevertheless ready to offer him advice and support. Khrushchev seemed to welcome this during the embarrassing affair of the Polish and Hungarian Uprisings in 1956. And in the following year Mao was delighted when Russia pulled off two remarkable 'firsts': an intercontinental rocket launched in August and the Earth satellite *Sputnik* in October. At last the socialist bloc had demonstrated that it was technologically superior to the United States of America.

The great dispute

Mao's joy was short-lived. Khrushchev obviously had no intention of asserting his new strength. Instead, he proposed to use it as the basis of a deal with the West. He brushed aside Mao's enthusiastic assertions that 'the East wind prevails over the West wind' and that all imperialists were now exposed for what they really were—'paper tigers'. Khrushchev reminded Mao that these paper tigers happened to have nuclear teeth; it was all very well for Mao to boast that he could sacrifice 300 million Chinese in a nuclear holocaust so that the other 300 million could inherit the Earth. But what sort of Earth? It was time for Mao to bring his Marxist–Leninism up to date. After all, not even Lenin could have foreseen that men would one day have hydrogen bombs capable of destroying the planet. Now this was a harsh fact of life—and Communists would have to face up to it. Khrushchev was brutally frank with the Chinese leader: 'Comrade Mao Tse-tung, if a war started now, how long do you think it would last? It wouldn't be like the last war. That was a war of air forces and tanks. Now there are missiles and atomic bombs. We'd probably have only a few days and after that there would be nothing left of us but a few tattered

remnants scratching along.'* So, for the Russians at least, wars—including wars of national liberation—were unacceptable. If Communists wanted to spread their gospel they would have to do it by peaceful means and not by force of arms. Mao soon realized that Khrushchev meant what he said; when the Taiwan Straits crisis boiled up in the following year (1958) the Russians refused to give him any additional military aid.

The split: 1960

The arguments were not simply over military matters. The two countries now had totally different approaches towards the Communist philosophy of world revolution. There was now a deep ideological gulf separating China from the U.S.S.R. Matters came to a head in 1960 when the outside world had its first glimpse of the extent of Sino–Soviet disagreement. There were bitter arguments between the Chinese and Russian delegates at the *Bucharest Conference* in June; then in August Khrushchev ordered the withdrawal from China of all financial and technical aid—including the small army of Soviet technicians busily building new factories and installing Russian-made equipment.† In December, when the world's Communist parties met for the *Moscow Conference*, the leader of the Chinese delegation‡ referred contemptuously to the Russians as 'revisionists' and accused Khrushchev of 'strengthening capitalism with his policy of world peace'.

Mao goes it alone

By 1961 the world was fully aware of the Sino–Soviet split; in 1962 it heard Mao's denunciation of Khrushchev's handling of the Cuban missile crisis; and in 1963, when Khrushchev signed the *Partial Test Ban Treaty*, it saw Mao make his bid for the leadership of the world revolutionary movement. For Mao had decided to act in opposition to Russia, to strengthen his frontiers against possible Soviet reprisal and to focus China's scientific efforts on the manufacture of nuclear weapons.

Khrushchev Remembers (B.C.A. Publications, 1971) p. 471.
†When they left they took with them not only their skills but also their blueprints, without which the Chinese could not proceed.' Edward Crankshaw, *The New Cold War*, (Pelican, 1965) p. 112.
‡Teng Hsiao-peng. He fell into disgrace during the Cultural Revolution and did not come back into favour until 1973. Then in 1976 he fell from power again, only to bounce back in 1977.

The Chinese Impact on the Soviet Bloc

NORWAY
FINLAND
SWEDEN
Oder-Neisse Line
Moscow
POLISH UPRISING 1956
EAST GERMANY
POLAND
Warsaw
THE WEST
CZECHOSLOVAKIA
HUNGARIAN UPRISING 1956
Budapest
HUNGARY
ROMANIA
Bucharest
YUGOSLAVIA (Communist, but outside 'Iron Curtain')
BULGARIA
ALBANIA
GREECE
TURKEY

Albania: anti-Russian and a strong supporter of China in the ideological quarrel.

When Khrushchev moved in warships and tanks to quell the Polish Uprising in June 1956, Mao sent Chou En-lai first to Moscow and then to Warsaw to counsel moderation. Because of her geographical position Poland could not possibly defect from the socialist bloc. Hungary (October 1956) was a different case. Her frontiers touched the West—she might contract out of the socialist bloc. Therefore Mao insisted that, in order to preserve unity, the revolt must be 'stopped by military action... regardless of bloodshed, regardless of appearances.' It was.

E.Crankshaw, *The New Cold War*, p.54

CHINA SUPPORTS WARS OF NATIONAL LIBERATION

Territory effectively controlled by the Soviet Union
CHINA
EGYPT (In the struggle against Israel)
Israel
CAMBODIA
NORTH VIET NAM
S.Viet Nam
Especially in Angola **A** and Mozambique **M** —two of the last areas to gain independence.
COLONIAL AFRICA

Mao passionately believed that war was the only way in which subject peoples could achieve liberation. He consistently supported nationalist movements in Asia and Africa until Russia (led by Brezhnev and Kosygin after 1964) had to concede that Mao's view of events was sound. The point was dramatically underlined during 1975 when North Vietnamese armies overthrew President Thieu's South Vietnamese government; and when, shortly afterwards, President LomNol fell from power in Cambodia. Both events were victories not only for Mao's political philosophy but also for Mao's methods of waging war.

54 China's policy of self-reliance, 1960–77

Defence priorities

Fear of attack from 'Soviet socialist imperialists'* was the main spur to Chinese self-reliance after 1960. Once the Russians had cut back their supplies of tanks, guns, aircraft and oil, China had no option but to build up her own armaments industry. However, 'home-made' defence programmes presuppose the existence of a well-organized iron and steel industry, advanced engineering capabilities, a nation-wide transport system and adequate supplies of fuel. As China did not possess all of these in 1960 she had to plan her industrial developments so that she could make up for her shortcomings as quickly as possible.

Importance of overseas trade

China decided to buy her most pressing needs abroad and pay for these by exporting coal, rice, tobacco and handicrafts. But she was very cautious: she did not hand out many contracts. Britain, for example, was lucky to win orders for 37 *Trident* aircraft. Moreover, though China was willing to import some ready-made products she did not seek the help of foreign experts—her memories of Soviet technicians were too vivid. So, as far as possible, China adapted the best foreign designs to her *own* needs and then mass-produced them in her *own* factories. This approach worked well with lorries, tractors and military aircraft though the best example of China's 'self-reliance' is probably the story of her remarkable petro-chemical industry.

China: oil producer

After the Russians cut back oil supplies during 1960–61 the Chinese worked flat out to exploit the experimental oil rigs sunk in the Taching area during the Great Leap Forward. By 1963 Taching had become 'China's most up-to-date oil base', so much so that Chou En-lai announced that 'China was basically self-sufficient in oil products'. After 1964 the Communists began extolling the Taching work force to the skies and Chairman Mao issued the call 'In industry, learn from Taching!' Over the next ten years production figures zoomed upwards as oil went on stream in Takang, Shengli and Karamai. In 1974 China occupied the Paracel Islands—another potentially rich source—and in 1975 opened a new field in Nanhai County. By the end of 1977 China was producing more than 65 million tons annually and, according to Japanese estimates, could be in the front rank of oil-producing nations by 1980 with an annual figure of 200 million tons.†

The problem of planning

Side by side with these rapid developments came China's

ambitious railway construction programme. Cross-country routes still had to be finished; rail spurs to the new oilfields were of top priority. Day-to-day running of such complex affairs gradually became too much for China's elderly leaders and in 1973 they chose Vice-Premier Teng Hsiao-ping as their new deputy. Tipped as Mao's eventual successor, Teng was essentially a planner, fully aware of the need to construct 'a sound technological and industrial runway for China's take-off into socialism'.‡ Teng and his economic experts spent most of 1975 preparing China's next Five-Year Plan. It was soon clear that the 'take-off' required even more economic growth than the 4 per cent which had been averaged during 1970–75. It was good by the standards of most developing nations but barely enough to keep up with the demands of a population expanding at the rate of 10 million annually. Teng therefore had to reconsider China's policies—particularly the impressive but highly expensive defence programme so recently completed.

*China's new term for the Russians.
†The quotations in this paragraph are from 'How China developed her oil industry', *China Reconstructs*, October 1974.
‡Dennis Bloodworth's phrase in *The Observer*, 28 December 1975.

A confident Teng Hsiao-ping steps out under the approving smile of Chou En-lai (left).

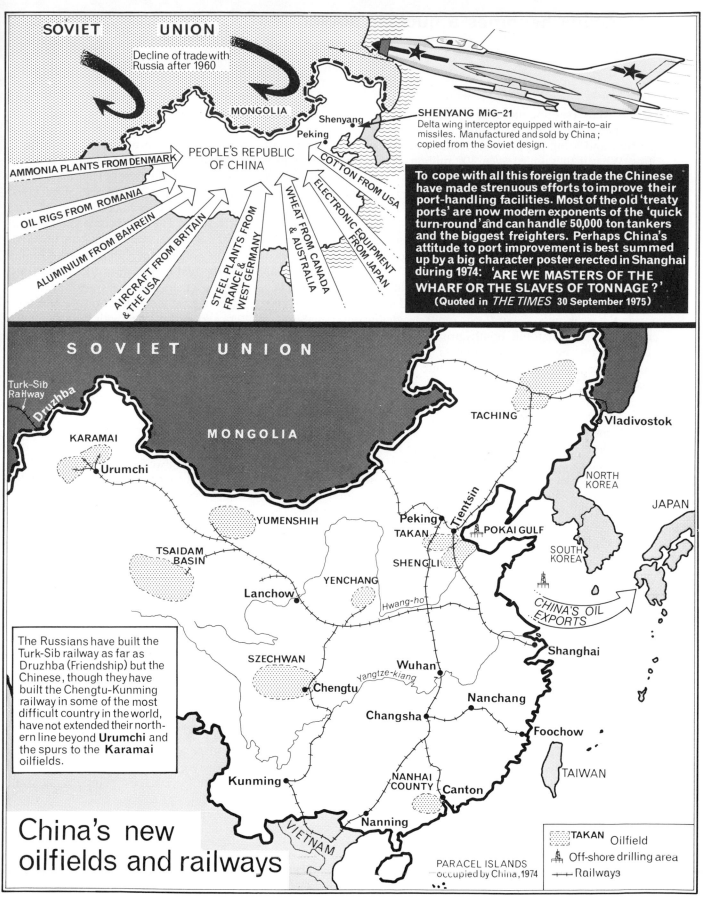

SOVIET UNION

Decline of trade with Russia after 1960

MONGOLIA

Shenyang

Peking

PEOPLE'S REPUBLIC OF CHINA

AMMONIA PLANTS FROM DENMARK

OIL RIGS FROM ROMANIA

ALUMINIUM FROM BAHREIN

AIRCRAFT FROM BRITAIN & THE USA

STEEL PLANTS FROM FRANCE & WEST GERMANY

WHEAT FROM CANADA & AUSTRALIA

ELECTRONIC EQUIPMENT FROM JAPAN

COTTON FROM USA

SHENYANG MiG-21
Delta wing interceptor equipped with air-to-air missiles. Manufactured and sold by China; copied from the Soviet design.

To cope with all this foreign trade the Chinese have made strenuous efforts to improve their port-handling facilities. Most of the old 'treaty ports' are now modern exponents of the 'quick turn-round' and can handle 50,000 ton tankers and the biggest freighters. Perhaps China's attitude to port improvement is best summed up by a big character poster erected in Shanghai during 1974: 'ARE WE MASTERS OF THE WHARF OR THE SLAVES OF TONNAGE?'
(Quoted in *THE TIMES* 30 September 1975)

SOVIET UNION

Turk-Sib Railway
Druzhba

KARAMAI

Urumchi

MONGOLIA

TACHING

Vladivostok

NORTH KOREA

JAPAN

YUMENSHIH

Peking
TAKAN

Tientsin

POKAI GULF

SOUTH KOREA

TSAIDAM BASIN

SHENGLI

YENCHANG

Lanchow

Hwang-ho

CHINA'S OIL EXPORTS

SZECHWAN

Wuhan

Yangtze-kiang

Shanghai

Chengtu

Nanchang

Changsha

Foochow

The Russians have built the Turk-Sib railway as far as Druzhba (Friendship) but the Chinese, though they have built the Chengtu-Kunming railway in some of the most difficult country in the world, have not extended their northern line beyond **Urumchi** and the spurs to the **Karamai** oilfields.

Kunming

TAIWAN

NANHAI COUNTY

Canton

China's new oilfields and railways

Nanning

VIETNAM

PARACEL ISLANDS
occupied by China, 1974

TAKAN Oilfield
Off-shore drilling area
Railways

55   China becomes a nuclear power

'Man is more important than the weapon'

In 1957 Mao Tse-tung had told a Yugoslav visitor that he was not afraid of atomic bombs. 'We have a very large territory and a big population. Bombs couldn't kill all of us. What if they killed even 300 million? We would still have plenty more.' As far as Mao was concerned, the atomic bomb had always been 'a paper tiger ... terrible to look at but not so strong as it seems'. This was precisely the attitude that had infuriated Khrushchev*— yet it was very similar to the view once taken by his predecessor, Josef Stalin. In 1946— before Russia had acquired the atomic bomb— Stalin had said that he didn't believe 'the atomic bomb to be so serious a force as politicians are inclined to think. Atomic bombs are intended for intimidating the weak-nerved, but they cannot decide the outcome of war since atomic bombs are by no means sufficient for this purpose.' Nevertheless, Josef Stalin was working hard to build an atomic bomb when he said this—just as Mao was in 1957.

China's atomic energy programme

China's interest in nuclear weapons pre-dated the Sino–Soviet split of 1960. It can be traced back to the Korean War when they had their first taste of 'nuclear blackmail' after the U.S.A. let it be known in 1953 that it was moving atomic bombs to its bases on Okinawa—presumably for use against China and North Korea. It is even possible that the Chinese had already started their own test reactors in Sinkiang; after all, the Russians had discovered uranium there in 1944. Certainly, China had an atomic energy programme in operation by 1955—because in that year Russia promised to send her particular items of equipment that she needed. By 1958 there were two heavy water reactors at work, one near Peking and the other in Manchuria, while the Chinese had opened up new uranium mines in eastern Tibet and Szechwan.

China builds the bomb

Understandably, the Americans took a keen interest in these activities. *General Electric Corporation* even published a report on the subject and it concluded that 'if the Chinese started their nuclear weapons at the beginning of 1958, they would explode their first bomb in 1963 ...' But Edgar Snow, one of the greatest experts on Communist China and a personal friend of Mao Tse-tung, thought the date would be 1964—and he was right.† On 16 October 1964 China exploded her first atomic device at the Lop Nor testing ground. Mao had his own 'paper tiger' and had broken the monopoly of the nuclear powers.

Air raid precautions

For most people in China, entry into the 'nuclear club' simply seemed to put their own lives at greater risk. This was certainly true in 1969 when border clashes with the Russians raised the spectre of nuclear attack. There were feverish air-raid precautions in most of China's northern cities. In Peking, for example, almost the entire workforce turned out to build shelters adjacent to courtyards, office blocks and factories. They were crude affairs—shallow and built in the main from stone taken from the Great Wall of China.‡ They offered more of a boost to morale than a chance of survival in a nuclear attack. But once they had taken these emergency measures, the revolutionary committees began the construction of much more elaborate shelters and linked them with the new underground subway being built in the city. These deep shelters had ample stocks of food, water, medical supplies, emergency power plants and special filtering systems for ventilation. They had been carefully designed to support a lengthy occupation by very large numbers of people.

China's strike capability

China sees her own nuclear weapons as essentially defensive. She has conducted over a score of tests—including her first hydrogen bomb in 1967—and according to American estimates now possesses several hundred nuclear warheads. However, her strike capability in no way matches that of the Soviet Union and any retaliatory attack upon Russia (for Mao stated quite categorically in 1964 that China would never be the first to use atomic bombs) must assume that some of the elderly *Tu-16* strategic bombers would manage to get through. So the Chinese were under no illusions. They accepted that they had invested perhaps an excessive amount of the country's resources in nuclear armaments. Perhaps the international respect they have won more than compensates for this. But they still think that their true strength lies in the *man* rather than in the *weapon* and anticipate that a substantial percentage of the population would survive a nuclear attack *and* be able to resist an invader by means of well-tried guerrilla tactics. It is significant that in 1977 the Russians chose to site their latest SS 20 intermediate range ballistic missiles in the east and point them directly at China.

*See Spread 53.

†For his analysis of China's nuclear policy see *The Other Side of the River* (Gollancz, 1963) pp. 642–5.

‡For details see Harrison Salisbury, *To Peking and Beyond* (Hutchinson, 1973) pp. 233–7.

CHINA'S STRIKE CAPABILITY

TU-16 jet bomber (code named 'Badger') China has 100 of these, some of which have test-dropped atom bombs at Lop Nor.

China's Earth satellites
China launched her first satellite in April 1970. Called China I, her 'man-made earth guiding star' effectively tested her medium range rocket. A second launch, China II, came in March 1971– after which China set up medium-range ballistic miss-iles along her frontier with Russia. Then in July 1975 she launched China III, which orbited Earth at heights between 111 and 283 miles. China III used a 'multi-stage' rocket which, if armed with a nuclear warhead, would reach targets such as Moscow and Leningrad. China III is capable of monitoring military sites in Russia, America and Western Europe.

China's 'limited range' ICBM is designed to carry a warhead 3,500 miles from the silos in Sinkiang. Most of Russia would therefore be within its range.

U.S.A.

SOVIET UNION

MONGOLIA— vital Soviet base

Leningrad

Moscow

UNITED KINGDOM

NORWAY

SWEDEN

FINLAND

WESTERN EUROPE

E. GERMANY

POLAND

CZECH.

HUNGARY

ROMANIA

BULGARIA

ALBANIA

TURKEY

SYRIA

IRAQ

JORDAN

ISRAEL

EGYPT

Suez Canal

SAUDI ARABIA

IRAN

AFGHANISTAN

PAKISTAN

INDIA
Exploded her own nuclear device underground in the Rajasthan Desert in May 1974.

MANCHURIA

Vladivostok

N. KOREA

S. KOREA

JAPAN

OKINAWA

Shanghai

Peking

C H I N A

Lop Nor

SZECHWAN

EASTERN TIBET

NEPAL

BHUTAN

BANGLADESH

BURMA

VIETNAM

LAOS

THAILAND

CAMBODIA

TAIWAN

Chinese missile site

Uranium deposits

ICBM Intercontinental ballistic missile

123

Sino–Soviet split widens

Nikita Khrushchev fell from power in October 1964—ironically, on the same day that the Chinese exploded their first atomic bomb. His successors were Leonid Brezhnev (Communist Party Secretary) and Alexei Kosygin (Soviet Premier). Neither seemed to make a favourable impression upon Mao Tse-tung and Chou En-lai so there was no improvement in Sino–Soviet relations. In fact, the Chinese tended to show an increasing contempt for Russian foreign policy. For example, Chinese students rioted in Moscow (1965) and Red Guards manhandled a Soviet merchant skipper in Dairen (1967). Then matters became serious in 1969 when several incidents on a remote island in the Ussuri River began a period of confrontation between the two Communist superpowers.

The Battles of Damansky Island, 1969

It is not often that details of events on the Sino–Soviet border become available in the West. However, both China and Russia have published detailed and conflicting accounts of the incidents on and around the island which the Russians call Damansky and the Chinese call Chenpao. According to the Chinese, a patrol commanded by Sun Yu-kuo came off worse in a fistfight when it met up with some Russian troops on the frozen Ussuri during February. On his next patrol (2 March), Sun was ready for trouble and he killed thirty-one Russians for the loss of twenty of his own men. After this, the Russians decided to drive the Chinese off Damansky Island and on 15 March shelled the Chinese side of the Ussuri for three hours before sending in assault troops supported by ten T-62 tanks. To cope with a Russian attack, the Chinese had hidden a variety of mortars and recoilless guns in their camouflaged bunkers and had also sprinkled the beaches with anti-tank mines. The battle lasted for ninety minutes, during which the Chinese managed to disable a T-62 which the Russians had to leave behind. Chinese propagandists seized on this as another marvellous example of Mao's assertion that 'the man is more important than the weapon'. But when the Chinese examined the tank in Peking they discovered that their projectiles had hardly damaged its interior. In fact, the tank had run over a mine. The crew had scrambled out—only to be shot down on the ice by Chinese machine-gunners.

Sino–Soviet summit, September 1969

Appalled by this fighting between Russia and China, the North Vietnamese President Ho Chi Minh made a deathbed appeal to the two countries to end their quarrel. He died on 3 September and for the next week Mao and Chou debated whether it would be worth while having a summit meeting with the Russians. On 11 September they sent Kosygin an invitation to come to Peking and the Russian leader received it at Dyushambe as he was flying back from Ho's funeral. He met Chou briefly in the V.I.P. lounge at Peking airport and agreed that the border issue should be examined round the conference table.

Increasing tension, 1974

However, the border disputes were not resolved. In their hearts, the Chinese believed that Russia was not really interested in discussing treaties signed over a hundred years ago. They knew that Russia's main concern was for the growing military power of the People's Republic. Soviet anxiety became obvious in 1974 when the Russians moved fifty divisions through Mongolia to take up positions along the Chinese frontier. With Russian tanks less than 600 miles from Peking, there were now three major flashpoints along this huge frontier zone: the Sinkiang flank in the west; the Mongolian centre; and the Khabarovsk flank in the east. Naturally, the Chinese felt bound to increase their defences in these areas, a move which led to 'the deadly paradox'.* Every time China improved her conventional and nuclear armouries she ran an even greater risk of provoking a Soviet attack.

*Neville Maxwell's phrase in his *Sunday Times* article 'On China's border: ready for a Soviet invasion', 30 September 1973.

The most popular poster in China during 1973—a 'combat hero' killed in the 1969 border clashes.

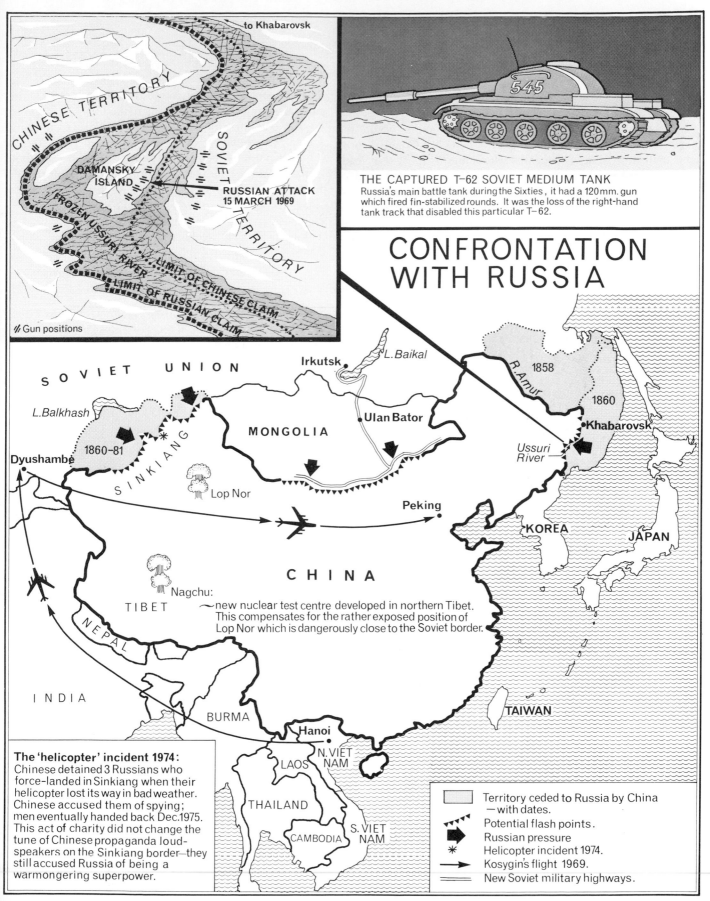

CHINESE TERRITORY

SOVIET TERRITORY

to Khabarovsk

DAMANSKY ISLAND

RUSSIAN ATTACK
15 MARCH 1969

FROZEN USSURI RIVER

LIMIT OF CHINESE CLAIM

LIMIT OF RUSSIAN CLAIM

Gun positions

THE CAPTURED T–62 SOVIET MEDIUM TANK

Russia's main battle tank during the Sixties, it had a 120mm. gun which fired fin-stabilized rounds. It was the loss of the right-hand tank track that disabled this particular T–62.

CONFRONTATION WITH RUSSIA

SOVIET UNION

L.Balkhash

Dyushambé

1860–81

SINKIANG

Irkutsk

L.Baikal

MONGOLIA

Ulan Bator

R.Amur

1858

1860

Khabarovsk

Ussuri River

Lop Nor

Peking

KOREA

JAPAN

CHINA

Nagchu:

new nuclear test centre developed in northern Tibet. This compensates for the rather exposed position of Lop Nor which is dangerously close to the Soviet border.

TIBET

NEPAL

INDIA

BURMA

Hanoi

LAOS

N.VIET NAM

THAILAND

CAMBODIA

S.VIET NAM

TAIWAN

The 'helicopter' incident 1974:
Chinese detained 3 Russians who force-landed in Sinkiang when their helicopter lost its way in bad weather. Chinese accused them of spying; men eventually handed back Dec.1975. This act of charity did not change the tune of Chinese propaganda loudspeakers on the Sinkiang border—they still accused Russia of being a warmongering superpower.

Territory ceded to Russia by China —with dates.

Potential flash points.

Russian pressure

Helicopter incident 1974.

Kosygin's flight 1969.

New Soviet military highways.

57 China joins the Third World

American hostility to China

From the Korean War onwards the United States and her supporters had always resisted attempts to vote the People's Republic of China into the U.N.* Consequently, all the Chinese delegates who came to the U.N. headquarters in New York were from Taiwan—the 'rump' of Nationalist China. Taiwan was a member of the U.N. General Assembly and had a permanent seat on the Security Council—with the right of veto. This was a farcical situation: the unrepresented People's Republic was the most populous nation in the world with nearly 800 million people. So why couldn't America accept the principle of '*dual representation*' and have both Taiwan and the P.R.C. as members of the U.N.?

Nixon breaks the ice

Apart from the fact that no American President had shown much sympathy for the idea before Richard Nixon took office in 1968, Mao himself was far from enthusiastic about dual representation. He refused to sit next to Taiwan in the U.N. as this would lend substance to the idea that there were really *two Chinas* in existence. So Nixon tried to find a compromise—a difficult task in 1968–9 because of U.S. involvement in the Viet Nam war. Nixon tried his policy of *Vietnamization*—which simply meant that as he pulled U.S. troops out of the fray he replaced them with increasing numbers of South Vietnamese soldiers. Any popularity he may have gained from this idea evaporated when he invaded Cambodia (1970) and Laos (1971)† in the vain hope of smashing Viet Cong assembly areas. Nevertheless he persisted in his efforts to open up contacts with the Chinese and eventually, in July 1971, Dr. Henry Kissinger made a secret trip to Peking to meet Chou En-lai and Deputy Foreign Minister Chiao Kuan-hua. Kissinger returned triumphant and presented Nixon with an invitation to visit Mao Tse-tung. So, in August 1971, Nixon was able to astound the American people by announcing that he not only favoured Chinese entry into the U.N. but was also planning a trip to the P.R.C. in 1972. Belatedly, Nixon now adopted the principle of dual representation and hoped that Mao would smile on the idea.

China joins the U.N.

Nixon was unlucky. There were so many differing shades of political opinion in the U.N.—especially among the newly independent Afro–Asian countries—that Nixon could no longer count upon an automatic majority for an American vote. And when Albania (China's faithful East European ally) introduced in October 1971 her annual proposal to admit China to the U.N., Nixon failed to win support for dual representation. Communist China was voted in; Taiwan was voted out. As *The Listener* put it a week later. 'There was no doubt about it: a great company of small nations enjoyed a moment of hilarious satisfaction in seeing the mighty United States brought so low.' Despite this defeat, Nixon kept his promise about visiting China and in 1972 he spent a week in Peking, where he made a very good impression upon Mao and Chou.

China's role in the U.N.

China's regular representative in the U.N. was Chiao Kuan-hua, one of the architects of Sino-American friendship and now promoted to Foreign Minister. The U.N.'s staple diet of endless paper-work and time-consuming speeches appalled him; he wanted the Assembly to get down to serious matters such as solving the Middle East crises and reducing the risk of nuclear war. In 1973 he proposed fundamental changes: 'We believe that present conditions in the U.N. should be changed and the charter revised …'

Definition of the Third World

But it was Teng Hsiao-ping who made the biggest impact on the U.N. delegates when he visited the General Assembly in April 1974. In a remarkable speech, he defined international politics as he saw them and described the role that China would play in world affairs. Because of the Sino–Soviet split, Teng believed that 'the Socialist camp' no longer existed. There were now 'Three Worlds': the *First World* was the world of the two superpowers, Russia and America, who had cut themselves off from everybody else in their struggle for 'world hegemony'; the *Second World* was made up of all the developed nations, irrespective of whether they came from capitalist or Communist blocs; the *Third World* consisted of the developing nations of Latin America, Africa and Asia. China, said Teng, placed herself squarely in the Third World; and it was time for developing nations to band together and help one another to secure 'economic liberation'. That would be China's basic motive for giving aid to her friends in the Third World.

*Before the Korean War, the U.S.A. 'was willing to abide by a majority decision of the Security Council as to who shall represent China in the U.N.' New York Times, 31 May 1950.
†S.V.N. ground troops carried out the invasion of Laos, but under cover of U.S. air support.

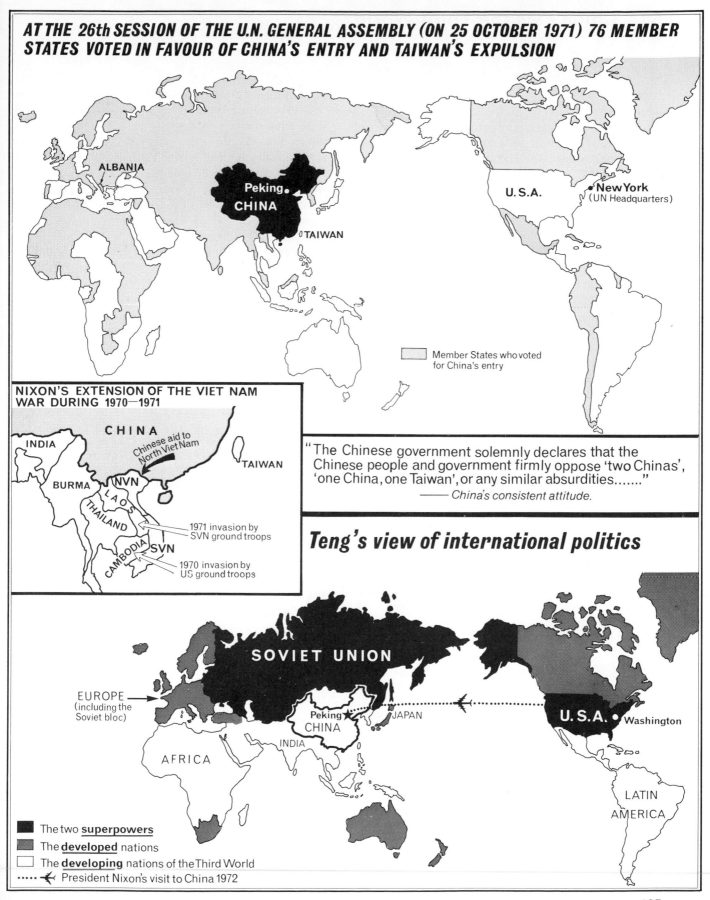

AT THE 26th SESSION OF THE U.N. GENERAL ASSEMBLY (ON 25 OCTOBER 1971) 76 MEMBER STATES VOTED IN FAVOUR OF CHINA'S ENTRY AND TAIWAN'S EXPULSION

ALBANIA

Peking·
CHINA

·TAIWAN

U.S.A.

·New York
(UN Headquarters)

Member States who voted
for China's entry

NIXON'S EXTENSION OF THE VIET NAM WAR DURING 1970—1971

CHINA

INDIA

Chinese aid to
North Viet Nam

TAIWAN

BURMA

NVN

LAOS

THAILAND

CAMBODIA   SVN

1971 invasion by
SVN ground troops

1970 invasion by
US ground troops

"The Chinese government solemnly declares that the
Chinese people and government firmly oppose 'two Chinas',
'one China, one Taiwan', or any similar absurdities......."
—— *China's consistent attitude.*

Teng's view of international politics

SOVIET UNION

EUROPE
(including the
Soviet bloc)

Peking★
CHINA

JAPAN

U.S.A. ·Washington

INDIA

AFRICA

LATIN
AMERICA

■ The two **superpowers**
▨ The **developed** nations
☐ The **developing** nations of the Third World
·····✈ President Nixon's visit to China 1972

58 China aids the Third World

China's objectives

According to China's definition, the Third World embraces a hundred developing countries in Latin America, Africa and Asia. Three thousand million people live in these three continents and make up more than 70 per cent of the world's population. Though China no longer accepts foreign aid for herself, she has sent aid to sixty of the developing nations. Her objective is quite simple. She seeks to foster abroad the same self-reliance characteristic of her own society. China believes that genuine national development requires every citizen to lend a helping hand. It is quite wrong to prop up a small country by foreign aid because this merely robs the people of their own self-confidence. China therefore helps with relatively small agricultural and industrial projects. However, there are one or two impressive exceptions to this policy such as the construction of the Tan–Zam railway in Africa.

China's aid to North Viet Nam

(i) *To 1973* Undoubtedly, China's most spectacular aid has been to North Viet Nam. Apart from the supplies of arms and equipment, Mao Tse-tung provided the North Vietnamese with advice and moral support. To preserve 'the integrity of North Viet Nam' Mao recommended President Ho Chi Minh to concentrate his main military effort on a guerrilla war south of the 17th Parallel. Of course, this meant that the Viet Cong guerrillas would have to fight the Americans who were still just as determined to block Communist expansion in South Viet Nam as they had been in Korea. But in South Viet Nam the Americans found themselves hamstrung by the fact that they were defending régimes led by men such as President Diem and President Thieu, neither of whom were capable of winning the hearts and minds of the Vietnamese people. They failed to provide a sympathetic government; they did not meet the needs of the people. It was this failure that strengthened Mao's advice. If the peasants had grievances against the government they would readily identify with the Communist guerrillas fighting on their behalf: 'The people are the water and the guerrillas are the fish; and without water the fish will die.' So for more than twelve years Chinese military aid came across the border to Hanoi, down the Ho Chi Minh trail and into the Viet Cong bases scattered across Cambodia and South Viet Nam. And though the Americans tried every device they could muster, they never succeeded in preventing the flow of arms or driving the Viet Cong out of the country. Eventually, in 1973, the Americans withdrew from the fray.

(ii) *To 1975* By the time of the American withdrawal regular units of the North Vietnamese army were in action south of the 17th Parallel. Soon they linked up with the Viet Cong and began a steady advance southwards. In October 1974 the Chinese and North Vietnamese signed the *Peking Protocol* which guaranteed free supplies of Chinese aid throughout 1975. It was this uninterrupted aid, supplemented by Russian weapons and captured U.S. material, that gave the Communists the edge. In April 1975 they forced President Thieu to flee from Saigon and the Communists triumphantly entered the South Vietnamese capital, renaming it Ho Chi Minh City. Over the years the Chinese had provided more aid to North Viet Nam than to any other developing country and had helped the Hanoi government to unite North and South under Communist rule.

The Tan–Zam Railway

One of the more remarkable sights in Dar-es-Salaam during 1970–75 was the regular arrival of Chinese freighters. They berthed at the quayside and disembarked hundreds of identically dressed Chinese workers who would clamber into waiting lorries and drive off to remote communes deep in the Tanzanian bush. They had come to build the Tan–Zam Railway and link Zambia's copper mines with Tanzania's ports and thus enable the two countries to by-pass the usual export routes through South Africa. The 20,000 Chinese worked side by side with 36,000 Africans and trained sufficient numbers to operate the railway when it opened ahead of its target date in 1975.

Other aid to Africa

China has sent aid to many African countries although not all of them have welcomed the Chinese presence. Her automatic weapons equipped the Frelimo and Angolan guerrilla movements during 1974–5. However, at the first sign of Soviet intervention in Angola's affairs (November 1975) the Chinese withdrew, indicating that they were not yet ready to become directly involved in African politics as a consequence of sending aid.

'PLENTY OF RED ON THE MAP'; CHINA AIDS THE COMMUNIST VICTORIES IN VIETNAM AND CAMBODIA

- ▨ COMMUNIST 1975
- ▪▪▶ HO CHI MINH TRAIL
- VC VIET CONG BASES
- ⇨ Final North Vietnamese advance 1973-75

CHINA

Rail spur to Hanoi

Hanoi

Haiphong

Russian freighters used South China ports during US attacks on Haiphong.

HAINAN

LAOS

THAILAND

17th Parallel

US bombardment of the North by air and sea.

VC
VC

Aid to Khmer Rouge guerrillas

CAMBODIA

VC

VC

America withdrew all combat troops in 1973 and evacuated the last of her personnel in 1975.

VC

Saigon — Ho Chi Minh City

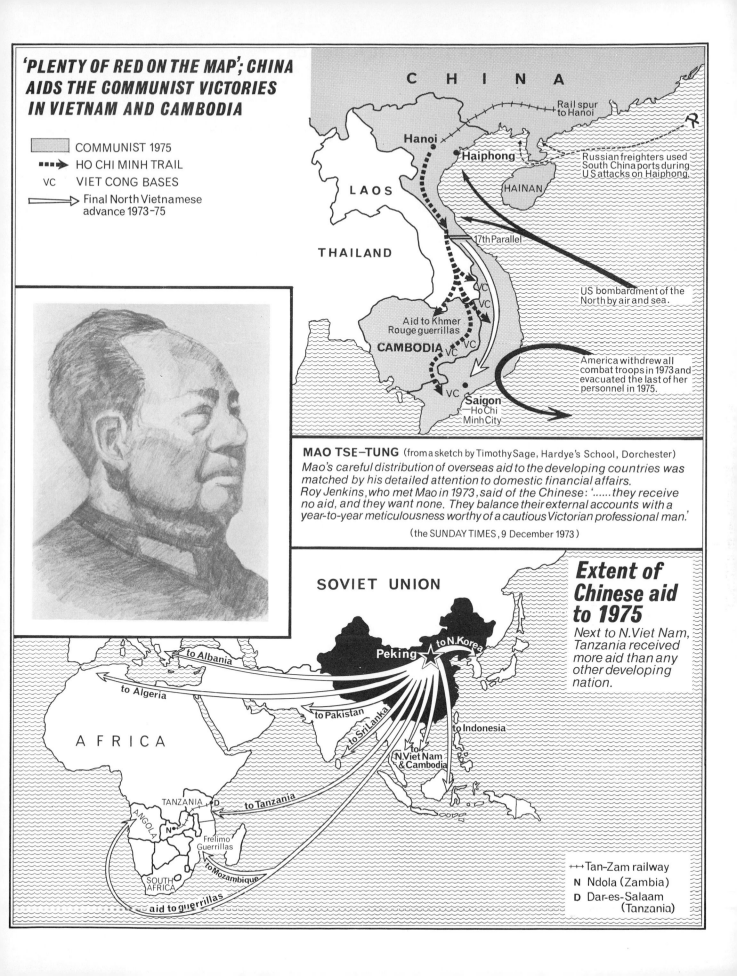

MAO TSE−TUNG (from a sketch by Timothy Sage, Hardye's School, Dorchester)

Mao's careful distribution of overseas aid to the developing countries was matched by his detailed attention to domestic financial affairs.
Roy Jenkins, who met Mao in 1973, said of the Chinese: '......they receive no aid, and they want none. They balance their external accounts with a year-to-year meticulousness worthy of a cautious Victorian professional man.'

(the SUNDAY TIMES, 9 December 1973)

SOVIET UNION

Peking to N.Korea

to Albania

to Algeria

to Pakistan

to Sri Lanka

to Indonesia

to N.Viet Nam & Cambodia

AFRICA

TANZANIA   D

to Tanzania

ANGOLA   N

Frelimo Guerrillas

to Mozambique

SOUTH AFRICA

aid to guerrillas

Extent of Chinese aid to 1975

Next to N.Viet Nam, Tanzania received more aid than any other developing nation.

- ┼┼┼ Tan-Zam railway
- **N** Ndola (Zambia)
- **D** Dar-es-Salaam (Tanzania)

59 The gradual détente with America

The original quarrel with America, 1950

One of the tragedies of the twentieth century was the love–hate relationship between the Chinese and American peoples. Traditionally, Americans had a warm affection for China; strong trade and missionary contacts had lasted well into the 1930s. And throughout the Second World War their support for Chiang Kai-shek and his Nationalist government had been entirely genuine. Yet when he fled to Taiwan in 1949 it seemed likely that the Americans were equally willing to accept the new Communist government in Peking. However, it was the Korean War that tipped the scales. By 1950, as far as the Americans were concerned, Communist China was 'a new Frankenstein monster' threatening the future of world peace; while the Chinese regarded the American people as the puppets of reactionary U.S. Presidents bent on extending their imperial powers. For China, the outcome of this was her entry into a period of prolonged isolation, as far as world affairs were concerned, while the Americans made up for their frustration in the Far East by giving aid to Japan. General MacArthur, their commander in Tokyo, had already tried to convert the Japanese to Christianity so that their islands might form 'a natural base from which … to advance the Cross throughout all Asia'. Now the Americans poured dollars into Japan in an effort to put her war-shattered industries back on their feet.*

The Dulles' view of China

One member of President Eisenhower's administration, Secretary of State John Foster Dulles, was the most forthright critic of the People's Republic of China. He accused Peking of representing an aggressive, expansionist force: 'It fought the U.N. in Korea; it supported the Communist War in Indo-China; it took Tibet by force. It fomented the Communist Huk rebellion in the Philippines and the Communist insurrection in Malaya. It does not disguise its expansionist ambitions. It is bitterly hateful of the United States, which it considers a principal obstacle in the way of its path of conquest …'† His was an extreme and inaccurate point of view, but it carried many Americans who were quite willing to believe that China was part of a world-wide Communist conspiracy to overthrow U.S. power and destroy all traces of Western-style democracy. Few of them objected to Dulles' refusal to grant China diplomatic recognition, to give it a seat on the U.N., to renew the broken commercial links.

Overcoming the hatred

It was not easy for Americans to change their views about China, to think of a détente—especially during the war in Viet Nam. While the Chinese said they were always ready to meet representatives of the American people, it would obviously take an American leader with considerable vision to break with the past. President Nixon had this vision—so Mao Tse-tung said he would be delighted to meet the President either in his official capacity or just as an ordinary tourist! With the help of Dr. Kissinger, Nixon made his first contact with the Chinese leader in February 1972.‡ That an American President should go to meet the leader of a country with which the U.S. had no diplomatic relations was remarkable enough but, as Nixon told Congress, 'Peace in Asia and peace in the world require that we exchange views, not so much *despite* our differences but *because* of them.' By 1973 Kissinger could assure the Chinese that 'friendship with the P.R.C. is one of the constant features of American foreign policy.' And to give substance to these words, the Americans sold China—and Russia—vast quantities of urgently needed wheat.

The Chinese welcome President Ford, 1975

When President Ford succeeded Nixon in 1974 he too felt that he should make a pilgrimage to Peking. However, his journey to the Great Hall of the People in Peking was not marked by a major improvement in Sino–American relations. It seemed that the Chinese were rather too anxious to score points against the Russians and Teng Hsiao-ping spent much of the time warning Ford that war between Russia and the West was 'inevitable'. Chou En-lai was not present at these meetings in December 1975. He was seriously ill and he died early in January 1976. America paid tribute to his statesmanship and to the role he had played in bringing about the partial détente between China and America—a sign of the 'normalization' that was developing between the two countries and something for which Chou had worked for over twenty-five years.

*See Richard Van Alstyne, *The United States and East Asia* (Thames and Hudson, 1973) p. 168.
†Quoted by Colin Brown, *The People's Republic of China* (Heinemann Educational Books, 1975) Broadsheet 21.
‡See Spread 57.

POINTS OF CONFLICT BETWEEN CHINA AND AMERICA AS SPECIFIED BY DULLES IN HIS STATEMENT, JULY 1953

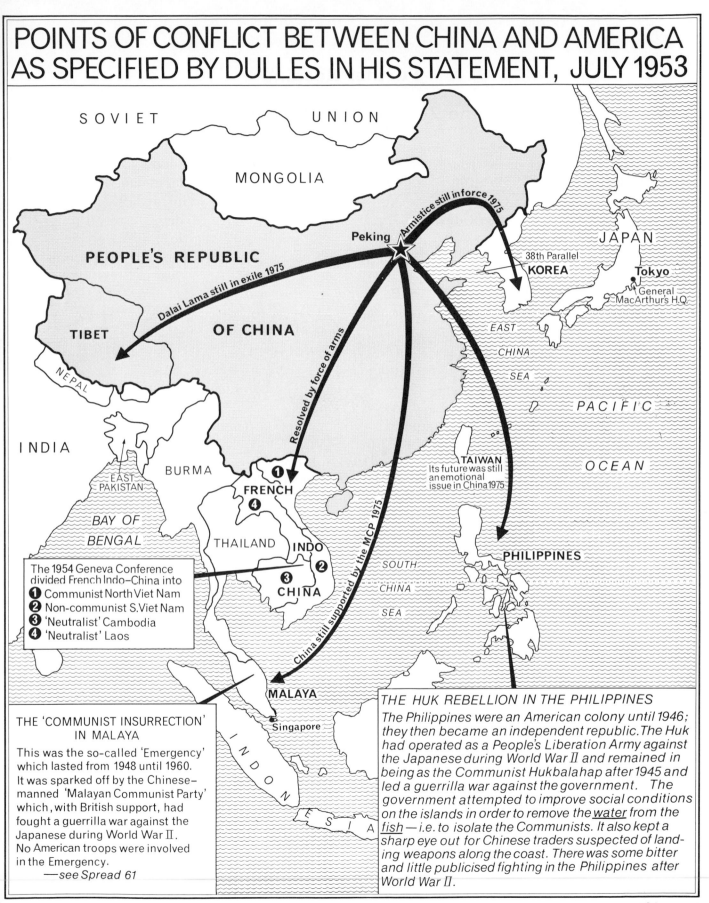

SOVIET   UNION

MONGOLIA

Peking

Armistice still in force 1975

JAPAN

38th Parallel
KOREA

Tokyo
General MacArthur's H.Q.

PEOPLE'S REPUBLIC

Dalai Lama still in exile 1975

TIBET   **OF CHINA**

EAST
CHINA
SEA

NEPAL

PACIFIC

INDIA

Resolved by force of arms

BURMA

EAST PAKISTAN

TAIWAN
Its future was still an emotional issue in China 1975

OCEAN

BAY OF BENGAL

❶
FRENCH
❹

THAILAND

INDO
❷

❸
CHINA

The 1954 Geneva Conference divided French Indo–China into
❶ Communist North Viet Nam
❷ Non-communist S. Viet Nam
❸ 'Neutralist' Cambodia
❹ 'Neutralist' Laos

PHILIPPINES

SOUTH
CHINA
SEA

China still supported by the MCP 1975

MALAYA

I N D O N E S I A

Singapore

THE 'COMMUNIST INSURRECTION' IN MALAYA

This was the so-called 'Emergency' which lasted from 1948 until 1960. It was sparked off by the Chinese-manned 'Malayan Communist Party' which, with British support, had fought a guerrilla war against the Japanese during World War Ⅱ. No American troops were involved in the Emergency.
—see Spread 61

THE HUK REBELLION IN THE PHILIPPINES
The Philippines were an American colony until 1946; they then became an independent republic. The Huk had operated as a People's Liberation Army against the Japanese during World War Ⅱ and remained in being as the Communist Hukbalahap after 1945 and led a guerrilla war against the government. The government attempted to improve social conditions on the islands in order to remove the <u>water</u> from the <u>fish</u> — i.e. to isolate the Communists. It also kept a sharp eye out for Chinese traders suspected of landing weapons along the coast. There was some bitter and little publicised fighting in the Philippines after World War Ⅱ.

Further Reading

Theme 7—'China shakes the world'

Spread

48.	Noel Barber	*From the Land of Lost Content*	Collins, 1969
49.	Allen S. Whiting	*China Crosses the Yalu*	Macmillan, 1960
	Robert O. Holles	*Now Thrive the Armourers*	Harrap, 1952
50.	Matthew B. Ridgway	*The War in Korea*	The Cresset Press, 1967
	Carl Berger	*The Korea Knot*	University of Pennsylvania Press, 1968
51.	G. Connell-Smith	*Pattern of the Post-war World*	Penguin, 1957
52.	Neville Maxwell	*India's China War*	Pelican, 1972
	Gerard Corr	*The Chinese Red Army* (pp. 92–111)	Osprey, 1974
53.	Edward Crankshaw	*The New Cold War: Moscow versus Peking*	Pelican, 1965
54.	A good up-to-date source is provided by *The Times* annual supplements on China		
55.	Edgar Snow	*The Other Side of the River— Red China today* (Part VII)	Gollancz, 1963
56.	Gerard Corr	*The Chinese Red Army* (for the Soviet viewpoint)	Osprey, 1974
	Colin Bown	*The People's Republic of China* (for the Chinese viewpoint)	Heinemann Educational Books, 1975
57.	See the Chinese periodical *Peking Review* and *Keesing's Contemporary Archives*		
58.	As for Spread 57		
59.	Colin Bown	*The People's Republic of China*	Heinemann Educational Books, 1975

THEME 8

The Overseas Chinese

It is tempting to see in the Overseas Chinese a 'fifth column' dedicated to the establishment of Communism in Malaysia, Singapore, Indonesia and the Philippines. Yet there is little evidence—apart from the activities of the Malayan Chinese during the Emergency, 1948–60—that they have sought to overthrow the legitimate governments of the countries in which they live.

Article 26 of the Constitution of the People's Republic claims that the state 'protects the just rights and interests of the Overseas Chinese'. But the People's Republic seems far more interested in its 'overseas compatriots' on Macao, Hong Kong and Taiwan than it is in the Chinese who live further afield.* Peking has instructed the U.N. Decolonization Committee to exclude Hong Kong from its considerations because Hong Kong 'is not a colony but a part of China'. This view led to some depressing side effects. For example, Peking always described the 'freedom swimmers' who escaped from China to Hong Kong not as refugees but as persons illegally visiting their relatives. So, in the 'seventies, the Hong Kong government studiously avoided using the expression 'colony' and reversed its policy of accepting refugees from the mainland by repatriating all 'illegal visitors'.

*For example, the 100,000 Chinese who live in Britain.

Britain and Portugal possess two tiny outposts of empire on the southern fringe of the People's Republic: the colonies of Hong Kong and Macao. Britain's Crown Colony of Hong Kong includes part of the mainland—the New Territories and Kowloon. Macao lies on a peninsula jutting out into Canton Bay.

The Japanese occupation of Hong Kong, 1941–5

When Captain Elliott acquired Hong Kong for the British in 1841, Lord Palmerston commented that he saw little point in acquiring a 'barren island with hardly a house upon it'. One hundred years later the colony had grown both in extent and population: more than one million Chinese were living side by side with a tiny handful of British administrators, traders and soldiers. These British residents frequently asked for self-government but the Colonial Office always refused on the grounds that it would be politically unwise—and unjust—for a tiny white minority to rule so many Chinese settlers. So Hong Kong was still a Crown Colony when the Japanese attacked on 8 December 1941, one day after Pearl Harbor. They soon pushed the British out of the New Territories and Kowloon and then invaded the main island. On Christmas Day 1941 the island's defence forces surrendered and Hong Kong fell under Japanese rule for the next three and a half years. Some civilians managed to flee to Macao where, because Portugal was neutral, life went on as before. The unlucky ones who stayed behind endured a harsh life in the Stanley internment camp, although their misery was not as great as that of the troops penned up in various prisoner-of-war camps.

Liberation—and the fear of a Communist invasion

Conditions were pretty grim on the island when units of the British Pacific Fleet arrived at the end of August 1945. Thousands of Chinese squatters had taken over abandoned Japanese airfields and built their shanty towns on the runways. In Aberdeen, families crowded aboard the lines of boats in search of a floating home. When the British administrators began to evict squatters—in an effort to minimize the risk of fire and epidemics—the plight of the Chinese aroused a series of sympathetic demonstrations on the mainland. There were anti-British riots in Canton and Shanghai—and in 1948 these cities were still in the hands of Chiang Kai-shek. Then came news of the Communist advance south and the British began frantic preparations to counter another invasion. Warships, fighter planes and infantry battalions arrived in Hong Kong during 1948–9. The spearhead of the Communist armies appeared at the border in 1949 and there were a few scuffles between British and P.L.A. patrols. But it was soon apparent that the P.L.A. had no intention of occupying either Hong Kong or Macao. However, they did point out to the Europeans that they could stay only as long as the Communists were prepared to tolerate them. Yet even when the British sent troops from Hong Kong to fight the Communists in Korea (1950) the Chinese made no move to occupy the colony.

The role of the two colonies since 1950

Over four million people—most of them Chinese—have crowded into the Crown Colony of Hong Kong. They have come in successive waves of refugees, most of them since the Communist victory on the mainland during 1949–50. Hong Kong has managed to absorb them because of its quite extraordinary commercial vigour; it is 'a brilliantly efficient money machine with thriving industry, banking and gambling'.* Since 1953 Hong Kong has become one of the busiest centres of world trade, partly because the P.R.C. uses both it and Macao as agencies for the re-export of Chinese goods to other countries. It is possible that Hong Kong will gradually lose its pre-eminence as China's most important source of foreign exchange; and it is also likely that Britain will lose Kowloon (centre of a huge textile industry) when the lease expires in 1997. However, during the period 1950–75 both the Chinese and British governments seemed to approve the arrangements as far as international trade was concerned. Whether the 4 million Chinese felt equally satisfied was another matter. Hong Kong has a high *per capita* income—higher than in Spain or Greece. But because of the overcrowded residential conditions, the standard of living is often low. In 1976 the British Fabian Society exposed certain deplorable social conditions on the island and stated that Hong Kong's social problems 'should shame a Labour Government'.†

*Michael Pye, writing in the *Sunday Times*, 25 January 1976.
†*Hong Kong: Britain's Responsibility* (Fabian Society, 1976). The writer, Joe England, was of course referring to the Labour Government in Britain.

U.S.S.R.

Chinese intervention _after_ British troops saw action in Korea

★ Peking

KOREA JAPAN

Pusan

C H I N A

Shanghai

1950
BRITISH TROOPS (1st Argyll & Sutherland Highlanders; 1st Middlesex Regt.) IN HONG KONG WERE KNOWN AS THE 'FIRE BRIGADE'—the British 'Strategic Reserve' ready to go anywhere in the world at 10 days' notice.

Canton
Macao
Hong Kong
TAIWAN

GURKHA BATTALIONS 1949

MALAYA

Singapore

HONG KONG AND ITS ROLE IN INTERNATIONAL AFFAIRS 1949–50

HONG KONG and MACAO

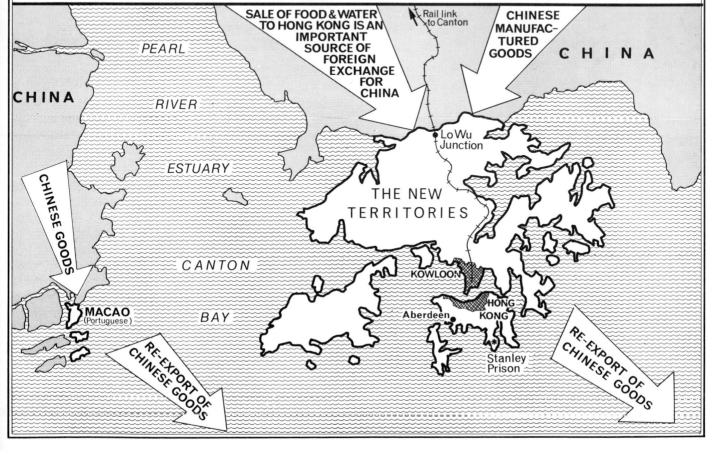

PEARL

RIVER

ESTUARY

CHINA

SALE OF FOOD & WATER TO HONG KONG IS AN IMPORTANT SOURCE OF FOREIGN EXCHANGE FOR CHINA

Rail link to Canton

CHINESE MANUFAC-TURED GOODS

C H I N A

Lo Wu Junction

THE NEW TERRITORIES

CHINESE GOODS

CANTON

BAY

KOWLOON

HONG KONG

Aberdeen

MACAO (Portuguese)

Stanley Prison

RE-EXPORT OF CHINESE GOODS

RE-EXPORT OF CHINESE GOODS

61 The Chinese in Malaya

The Chinese settlers

Chinese settlers had been arriving in Malaya since the fourteenth century, though it was not until the British acquired Penang (1786) and Singapore (1819) that their numbers became significant. Thousands travelled in 'coolie ships' from Hong Kong to seek work on the timber estates, in the tin mines* and, later on, in the rubber plantations. One constant problem for the British administrators was how to maintain harmony between the native Malays and the immigrant Chinese. Their early enmities persisted, partly because the Chinese educated their children in their own schools where a great deal of anti-British and anti-Malay was taught.

The Japanese occupation, 1941–5

This division worsened after the Japanese invasion (8 December 1941). Japanese soldiers never disguised the fact that they hated the Chinese settlers, especially those who had joined the Malayan Communist Party (M.C.P.) during the 'thirties. In 1942 they murdered over 5,000 Chinese; then they abolished the Chinese schools, replacing them with *Nippon Go* (Japanese language) courses. Many Chinese reacted by joining the M.C.P. resistance movement and received weapons and instructors from the British. Yet this resistance movement intensified the dislike existing between Malay and Chinese as the latter believed that the native population was meekly collaborating with the invader. In fact, when the war ended in 1945 and the British returned, the M.C.P. genuinely considered that it had been responsible for the liberation of Malaya—a feeling which the British reinforced when they invited Chin Peng, the M.C.P. leader, to take part in the 1946 Victory Parade in London.

The Emergency—the War of the Running Dogs

In the hope of creating a unified Malaya, the British now offered the Chinese 'common citizenship' as Malays. But the Chinese were far more interested in their own national aspirations. Chin Peng was already promising them a 'People's Republic of Malaya': all they had to do, he said, was to strike terror into the hearts of the British rubber planters and mine managers and then drive them out of the country, just as the Japanese had done during the war. Any Malay or Chinese who obstructed the M.C.P. would be considered a 'running dog'—and would die like a dog. Chin Peng was sure his plan would work in a matter of weeks and in June 1948 his 4,000 C.Ts. (Communist Terrorists) began their campaign of bombings and assassinations. Three days after the first attack the British declared a state of emergency and the fight was on. When Mao Tse-tung came to power in China the following year he made a modest military contribution to Chin's 'war of liberation'. But his claim that the War of the Running Dogs was a *Malay People's War* was quite untrue; 99 per cent of the C.Ts. were Chinese Communists.

The jungle war

The C.Ts. chose their own battlefield—the tropical rain forest that covered 80 per cent of Malaya. The C.Ts. actually outnumbered the British troops at the start of the Emergency. Apart from the Gurkha battalions from Hong Kong, most of the soldiers were young National Servicemen who had to learn jungle fighting the hard way. So the initiative was with the C.Ts. However, the British had the very sound *Briggs' Plan*: they deprived the C.Ts. of their source of food and shelter by shifting thousands of Chinese farming families into brand-new villages. They then surrounded the new villages with barbed wire and forced the Chinese to use communal kitchens for all their meals. This was Britain's way of removing the 'water' from the 'fish'. But its immediate effect was to escalate the war. The C.Ts. began a new wave of murders and killed Sir Henry Gurney, British High Commissioner, in 1951. In his place came General Templer with 50,000 troops and the promise that Malaya would soon have its independence. Templer completed the job of resettling the Chinese farmers. He then cleared the jungle at the northern frontier to stop Chinese infiltrators from slipping across from Thailand. By 1954 he had the C.Ts. on the run, though the true turning point came when Chinese and Malay civilians formed the new *Alliance Party* and won the 1955 General Election. In 1957 they created the independent Federation of Malaya—and thus cut the ground from under the C.Ts. who claimed to be fighting for the same thing.

The end of the Emergency, 1960

A few hard-line C.Ts. stayed in the jungle but the British sent in squadrons of *Lincoln* bombers and teams of paratroopers to winkle them out of their isolated hide-outs. By 1960 Chin knew he was beaten and advised his surviving C.Ts. to return to civilian life. Most of the original 4,000 were dead, and of the other 8,000 recruits who had joined him in the jungle nearly half had been killed or wounded. The War of the Running Dogs ended officially on 31 July 1960—one of the few examples of the failure of a Chinese Communist guerrilla operation.

*For centuries China had been importing tin from Malaya—for making joss sticks.

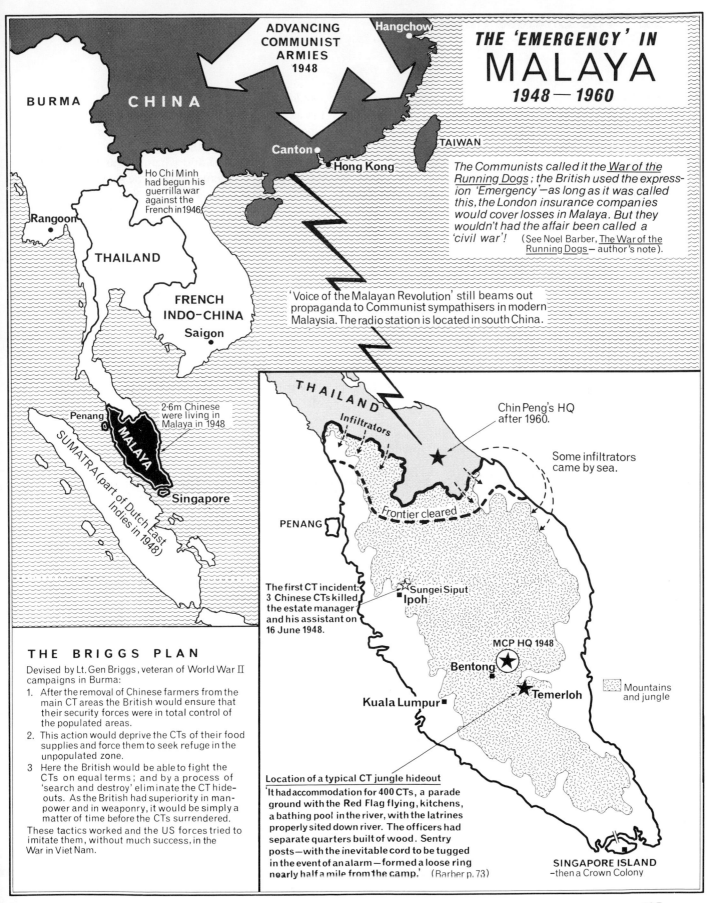

ADVANCING COMMUNIST ARMIES 1948

BURMA

CHINA

Hangchow

Rangoon

THAILAND

Canton

Hong Kong

TAIWAN

Ho Chi Minh had begun his guerrilla war against the French in 1946.

FRENCH INDO-CHINA

Saigon

Penang

2·6m Chinese were living in Malaya in 1948

SUMATRA (part of Dutch East Indies in 1948)

MALAYA

Singapore

THE 'EMERGENCY' IN
MALAYA
1948 — 1960

The Communists called it the War of the Running Dogs; the British used the expression 'Emergency'—as long as it was called this, the London insurance companies would cover losses in Malaya. But they wouldn't had the affair been called a 'civil war'! (See Noel Barber, The War of the Running Dogs— author's note).

'Voice of the Malayan Revolution' still beams out propaganda to Communist sympathisers in modern Malaysia. The radio station is located in south China.

THAILAND

Infiltrators

Chin Peng's HQ after 1960.

Some infiltrators came by sea.

Frontier cleared

PENANG

The first CT incident: 3 Chinese CTs killed the estate manager and his assistant on 16 June 1948.

Sungei Siput
Ipoh

MCP HQ 1948

Bentong

Kuala Lumpur

Temerloh

Mountains and jungle

Location of a typical CT jungle hideout

'It had accommodation for 400 CTs, a parade ground with the Red Flag flying, kitchens, a bathing pool in the river, with the latrines properly sited down river. The officers had separate quarters built of wood. Sentry posts—with the inevitable cord to be tugged in the event of an alarm—formed a loose ring nearly half a mile from the camp.' (Barber p. 73)

SINGAPORE ISLAND
–then a Crown Colony

THE BRIGGS PLAN

Devised by Lt. Gen Briggs, veteran of World War II campaigns in Burma:

1. After the removal of Chinese farmers from the main CT areas the British would ensure that their security forces were in total control of the populated areas.

2. This action would deprive the CTs of their food supplies and force them to seek refuge in the unpopulated zone.

3   Here the British would be able to fight the CTs on equal terms; and by a process of 'search and destroy' eliminate the CT hide-outs. As the British had superiority in man-power and in weaponry, it would be simply a matter of time before the CTs surrendered.

These tactics worked and the US forces tried to imitate them, without much success, in the War in Viet Nam.

62 The Chinese in Indonesia

The Chinese settlers

The history of the Chinese in Indonesia (formerly the Dutch East Indies) has been even more tragic than that of their fellow-countrymen in Malaya. After 1800, thousands of Chinese immigrants arrived every year to play an important role in the community. They came as merchants, farmers or as transient workers who would spend a year or two on the tobacco estates before returning to their families in China. Yet though they never became popular with the native Indonesians, they did develop a reasonable relationship with the Dutch administrators who ran the islands as part of the highly profitable empire of the Netherlands. Admittedly, the Chinese who lived in the towns tended to congregate in ghettoes; and up to 1910 they did not have the right of free movement between the various islands. But despite these restrictions, many Chinese became wealthy residents—particularly those who set up trading companies or who went in for opium dens, pawnshops and money-lending.

The Second World War and its aftermath

When the Japanese invaders arrived in December 1941 they were primarily interested in exploiting Indonesia's rich reserves of oil and rubber. In exchange for peaceful co-operation, they promised the Indonesians a measure of self-government and appointed nationalist leaders such as Dr. Sukarno to important posts in the Japanese administration. But they imposed a harsh discipline on the Chinese—by then about 2 million strong—and there was no resistance movement in Indonesia comparable with the one organized by the M.C.P. in Malaya. During the closing stages of the Second World War the Indonesian army (trained and equipped by the Japanese) turned on their masters and the Chinese population became entangled in a confused 'war of national liberation'. Sukarno proclaimed himself President of the 'Republic of Indonesia' (August 1945) but the Dutch soon returned to challenge him. British and Indian units arrived from Malaya to lend the Dutch a hand and the Chinese merchants began supplying the soldiers and administrators with their needs—just as they had done before the war. This infuriated the Indonesians and in 1946 their guerrillas murdered 600 Chinese at the Tangerang River massacre. Over the next three years the Chinese suffered increasing losses as the Dutch and Indonesian armed forces fought a bitter war. Finally, the Dutch gave up the struggle in 1949 and the Indonesian people had at last won their *merdeka*—freedom.

The fate of the Chinese, 1949–64

It was less certain whether the Chinese had won theirs. Once the world acknowledged Sukarno, the Chinese became fearful about the future. In Peking, Chou En-lai was equally worried and when he was in Indonesia for the Bandung Conference (1955) he signed the *Dual Citizenship Treaty* with President Sukarno. This was intended to give the Chinese a chance to choose their own nationality—an unusual step as Peking normally regarded all Overseas Chinese as citizens of the People's Republic. But the treaty didn't seem to be of much value. Sukarno began to discriminate against the Chinese. He closed their schools and newspaper offices; he levied very heavy taxes; he forbade Chinese residents to send money to the P.R.C.; and in 1959 he ordered all Chinese traders in the rural areas to abandon their premises and return to the cities. Naturally, these displaced Chinese found it hard to begin a new life in unfamiliar surroundings and during 1960–64 several thousand managed to return to China. But as Victor Purcell commented, '... the problem of disposing of the excess nationals in Indonesia was still a long way from solution.'*

The Communist massacres, 1965–6

For some of the Chinese, at least, Sukarno found a horrific solution. There was an unsuccessful plot in 1965 to overthrow the President and Sukarno accused the P.K.I. (Indonesian Communist Party) of being behind the conspiracy. He immediately ordered the massacre of all suspected Communists. He actually admitted to 87,000 killings and, as many Chinese had joined the P.K.I., it was obvious that some had fallen victim to the bloodthirsty Indonesian killer squads armed with their deadly *kris*. The worst incidents were in Bali and on Lombok Island and by the beginning of 1966 the Indonesians were specifically blaming the Chinese for the P.K.I. 'conspiracy'. Demonstrators marched through Djakarta shouting 'Down with the People's Republic of China!' and 'Hang the Chinamen!'† Serious riots in 1967 wrecked the Chinese embassy and injured several diplomats. Eventually, China and Indonesia broke off diplomatic relations and the Chinese residents were left to an uncertain fate.

---

*Victor Purcell, *The Chinese in South-East Asia* (O.U.P., 1966) p. 491.
†See *Keesing's Contemporary Archives*, 5–12 February 1966.

THE MISERY OF THE CHINESE
There were rather less than two million Chinese living in Indonesia in 1945.
They suffered
(a) from the distrust of the Dutch who believed they secretly supported the Indonesians and
(b) the hatred of the Indonesians who thought they were pro–Dutch !
Therefore the Chinese did their best to stay at peace with both sides—a task that became very difficult in the confused fighting of 1945–46.

Some Chinese suffered at the hands of the British when the RAF burnt down a village near Djakarta in December 1945 as a reprisal against Indonesian atrocities.

TANGERANG 1946
The most terrible atrocity was at Tangerang, a Chinese settlement 20 miles outside Djakarta. At least 600 died: '.....the suburbs of Tangerang have been turned into a hell for the Chinese who had lived for so many years amicably with the Indonesians'.

Quoted by Victor Purcell, 'The Chinese in South East Asia', p.555

Limited Chinese Repatriation

The Chinese in Sarawak ran an intelligence service for the British 1942–5.

Chinese settlers aided British paratroopers who dropped in Borneo 1945.

Palembang Massacre January 1947—(250 Chinese died)

The Tangerang River Massacre June 1946

JAVA the main centre of Chinese settlement in Indonesia.

Modern Indonesia

BURMA

CHINA

FRENCH INDO-CHINA

THAILAND

HAINAN ISLAND

TAIWAN

PHILIPPINES

SOUTH CHINA SEA

MALAYA

.Kuala Lumpur

SUMATRA

SINGAPORE

BRUNEI

SARAWAK

BORNEO

CELEBES

MOLUCCAS

NEW GUINEA (West Irian)

Palembang

Djakarta
Bandung
Surabaya
BALI
LOMBOK
JAVA

TIMOR

AUSTRALIA

BRITAIN SENDS MILITARY AID TO THE DUTCH
Britain had expected to fight a bitter war against the Japanese in Malaya during 1945. So when the Japanese suddenly surrendered in August (after the atomic bomb attacks on Hiroshima and Nagasaki) the British had some spare combat units available to go to the help of the Dutch. For example, the Indian 49th Infantry Brigade was soon in action; so was the 26th Australian Brigade. No. 60 Squadron of the RAF flew into Djakarta and Surabaya to lend air support - and used up all their surplus Thunderbolt fighter planes in the process !

THE CHINESE AND THE INDONESIAN WAR OF INDEPENDENCE

63 Taiwan—the last stronghold of the Nationalists (to 1977)

Although there are millions of Overseas Chinese scattered across the world, there are only two territories over which they exercise total political control—Singapore and the fortress of Taiwan.

Taiwan: a Japanese colony

Most of the 14 million Taiwanese are of Chinese descent, although about 200,000 aborigines originate from the islands of Indonesia. From 1895 to 1945 they were all* ruled by the Japanese who arrived with very specific plans for the island's future. They wanted to develop agriculture and industry so that Taiwan could provide a cheap source of food for the expanding Japanese population, a home for migrant Japanese farmers and a consumer market for Japan's industrial products. So they harnessed the rivers that flow in torrents down the steep mountain sides (Taiwan's annual rainfall ranges between 40 and 200 inches in different parts of the island), built hydro-electric plants and undertook some major irrigation projects. They wiped out smallpox and cholera. But they had no time for talk about a 'Taiwan Independence Movement' and ruthlessly crushed the many attempts at rebellion. During the 1937 Sino–Japanese 'Incident' Taiwan became a target for Chinese Nationalist bombers; and during the Second World War American *Superfortresses* flattened the Japanese-built air and harbour installations.

Under Nationalist rule

Taiwan's next drama was the influx of over 2 million Nationalist refugees during 1946–9. From their arrogant behaviour, it appeared that the Kuomintang war-lords were no better than the Japanese soldiers had been and so the Taiwanese rebelled in 1947—with their usual lack of success. However, once they were caught up in the various Cold War crises after 1950 the Taiwanese discovered the enormous importance the Americans attached to their islands. U.S. dollar aid soon managed to make Nationalist rule more bearable and the Taiwanese grew to accept the 'Gimo'—Generalissimo Chiang Kai-shek. Thousands of tons of fertilizer from America helped to revitalize Taiwan's worn-out farmlands. Rice and sugar crops doubled. Geologists discovered rich reserves of natural gas in 1959 and by 1966 had piped it the length of the island. These were all signs that Taiwan was beginning to enjoy her own private 'economic miracle' and inevitably this attracted a lot of interest from Japanese and Western businessmen. After all, Taiwan was exceptionally well placed. She had a huge work force; wage levels

were low; energy costs were cheap. So by the 1970s the TV sets, scooters and textile products were streaming out of Taiwan. One effect of this was to raise living standards, though wages stayed relatively low. A girl working in a Taipeh textile factory would take home around 65 dollars a month in 1975. But it was enough to convince the Taiwanese that their way of life, in a material sense, was far more attractive than anything the People's Republic of China could offer. Their economy boomed throughout 1976–7. Wages shot up by 16%; but inflation stayed at 3%.

Fortress Taiwan

This was just as well, for the Taiwanese had to contribute a great deal of money to their defence budget and their young men had to serve up to three years in the armed forces. Taiwan's 600,000 troops are some of the best-trained and equipped soldiers in all Asia. The Nationalist Air Force has the latest jet interceptors; the Navy has a variety of warships to patrol the seas east of Quemoy and Matsu. All the islands have elaborate underground defence systems though, since 1962, the main activity has been the propaganda war between the P.R.C. and the battered little island of Quemoy. Nationalist gunners fire over pop records and photos of well-stocked stores in Taipeh's shopping centre; the Chinese Communists retaliate—on alternate days—with leaflets and cheap transistor sets. Both sides blast one another with loudspeakers and after Gavin Young visited Quemoy in 1972 he recalled that 'Across the narrow strait, over the fishing boats, a tremendous voice, metallic, echoing, like an angry god in a cave, boomed out towards us harsh, throaty Chinese sounds.'†

The Death of Chiang

Generalissimo Chiang Kai-shek, President of the Nationalist Government of Taiwan, died in April 1975 at the age of eighty-seven. Re-elected to office in 1972, he had handed over affairs of state to his son, Prime Minister Chiang Ching-kuo. The 'Gimo' had always dreamed that one day he would return to the mainland, crush the 'Communist bandits' and restore Nationalist rule. It seemed that this unrealistic ambition would not disappear overnight. The day after the Generalissimo's death President Yen took the oath of office. He wanted, he said, '... to recover the mainland and restore the national culture ...'

*There were 3 million Taiwanese in 1895; 5·5 million in 1939; 0·5 million Japanese were repatriated between 1949 and 1954.
†Gavin Young, 'The China no one wants to know', *Sunday Times* Supplement, 14 May 1972, pp. 6–14.

SOME OF TAIWAN'S UNSUCCESSFUL REBELLIONS DURING THE PERIOD 1895—1947

1895 Rebellion: *the Japanese shot over 500 Taiwanese as a reprisal.*

1896 Rebellion: *this was widespread and for a time Japanese troops had to evacuate the mountainous interior.*

1907–1928: *there were eight major rebellions during these years and they were led, in the main, by the aborigines.*

1930 Uprising: *the Japanese were reputed to have dropped gas bombs in a drastic attempt to wipe out the mountain villages.*

1934 'Friends of the Masses' Rebellion: *A total failure and many Taiwanese arrested by Japanese security police.*

1940 Resistance movement: *marked increase in sabotage attacks on Japanese military installations.*

1947 Rebellion: *the unsuccessful uprising against the Kuomintang supporters who had begun to arrive from the mainland.*

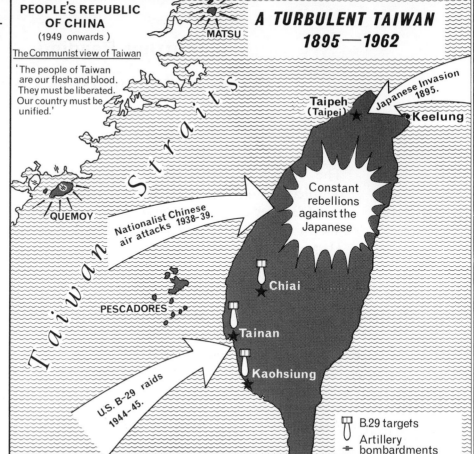

PEOPLE'S REPUBLIC OF CHINA
(1949 onwards)

The Communist view of Taiwan

'The people of Taiwan are our flesh and blood. They must be liberated. Our country must be unified.'

A TURBULENT TAIWAN 1895—1962

MATSU

QUEMOY

Taiwan Straits

PESCADORES

Japanese Invasion 1895.

Taipeh (Taipei)

Keelung

Nationalist Chinese air attacks 1938–39.

Constant rebellions against the Japanese

Chiai

Tainan

Kaohsiung

U.S. B-29 raids 1944–45.

B.29 targets

Artillery bombardments

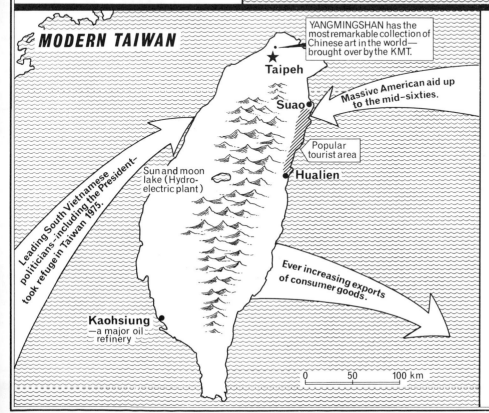

MODERN TAIWAN

YANGMINGSHAN has the most remarkable collection of Chinese art in the world—brought over by the KMT.

Taipeh

Massive American aid up to the mid-sixties.

Suao

Popular tourist area

Leading South Vietnamese politicians—including the President—took refuge in Taiwan 1975.

Sun and moon lake (Hydroelectric plant)

Hualien

Ever increasing exports of consumer goods.

Kaohsiung —a major oil refinery

0   50   100 km

1. Until 1972 Taiwan was, for most Americans, 'a living symbol for every Chinese in the world..... the testing ground for the American policy towards the Asian people....... a focus for democratic society.....'
   (Hsieh Chiao-min: China–ageless land and countless people, Van Nostrand, 1966 p.104.)

2. Then Nixon cold-shouldered Taiwan and began a policy of détente with the PRC. It was a policy that retained Mao's admiration for Nixon even after the President's disgrace— witness Mao's invitation to Nixon to visit Peking in 1976. Britain too, has grown lukewarm towards Taiwan and did not maintain a consulate there.

3. Many PRC sympathizers considered that Chiang Kai-shek's death in 1975 marked the end of an era and stated that it foreshadowed 'defeat for all the conservative forces of East Asia'.
   (Derek Bryan: China now June 1975.)

4. There is still a Taiwanese Independence Movement on the island but it exerts very little political force. It believes that Taiwan should cede Quemoy and Matsu to the PRC and then apply for independent status in the United Nations.

Further Reading

Theme 8—The overseas Chinese

Spread

60.	Gene Gleason	*Hong Kong*	Robert Hale Ltd., 1964

The *Hong Kong Government Press* publishes a detailed annual report.

61.	Noel Barber	*The War of the Running Dogs*	Fontana, 1972
62.	Victor Purcell	*Chinese in South-East Asia*	O.U.P., 1965
63.	H. Maclear Bate	*Report from Formosa*	Eyre and Spottiswoode, 1952

———————

Some collections of source materials:

Meyer and Allen	*Source Materials in Chinese History*	Warne and Co., 1969
Myra Roper	*China in Revolution*	Edward Arnold, 1971
Franz Schurmann and Orville Schell (eds.)	*China Readings* (3 vols.)	Penguin, 1967
Roger Pelissier	*Awakening of China 1793–1949*	Secker and Warburg, 1966
John Gittings	*A Chinese View of China*	B.B.C., 1973

———————

A useful current publication:

Modern China (an international quarterly)	Saga Publications

———————

Chinese publications:

Contact Guozi Shudian (China Publications Centre), Peking, China.

Peking Review (weekly—dealing with political affairs)

China Pictorial (monthly—very good colour pictures)

China Reconstructs (monthly—a general survey of Chinese economic developments with good illustrations)

———————

The *Society for Anglo-Chinese Understanding* (S.A.C.U.) publishes a monthly magazine entitled *China Now*

INDEX

Index